Marriage Proposals

Marriage Proposals

Questioning a Legal Status

EDITED BY

Anita Bernstein

New York University Press

NEW YORK AND LONDON

NEW YORK UNIVERSITY PRESS
New York and London
www.nyupress.org

Library of Congress Cataloging-in-Publication Data
Marriage proposals : questioning a legal status / edited by Anita Bernstein.
p.   cm.
Includes bibliographical references and index.
ISBN–13: 978–0–8147–9110–3 (pbk. : alk. paper)
ISBN–10: 0–8147–9110–7 (pbk. : alk. paper)
ISBN–13: 978–0–8147–9929–1 (cloth : alk. paper)
ISBN–10: 0–8147–9929–9 (cloth : alk. paper)
1. Marriage law—United States—Philosophy.
2. Marriage law—Philosophy.   I. Bernstein, Anita.
KF510.M37 2005
306.81'01—dc22   2005019500

New York University Press books are printed on acid-free paper,
and their binding materials are chosen for strength and durability.
We strive to use environmentally responsible suppliers and materials
to the greatest extent possible in publishing our books.

Manufactured in the United States of America
c 10 9 8 7 6 5 4 3 2 1
p 10 9 8 7 6 5 4 3 2 1

For John Witte Jr.

Contents

Acknowledgments

The Center for the Interdisciplinary Study of Religion at Emory University provided myriad supports for this project that went beyond advice, collegial exchange, administrative attention, professional contacts both inside and outside Emory, and financing. Inside Emory School of Law, colleagues Michael Broyde, Eliza Ellison, Anita Mann, Marc Miller, John Witte, and the dean, Thomas C. Arthur, were both inspiring and stalwart. Luke Johnson, of Emory's school of theology, and Steven Tipton, of its religion department, added nuances to the abolish-marriage notion. Deborah Gershenowitz and Salwa Jabado at NYU Press gave the *Marriage Proposals* project generous helpings of patience and ingenuity. *Marriage Proposals* would never have happened without the ministrations of John Witte.

Introduction

Questioning Marriage

Anita Bernstein

The same query kept recurring: Why marriage? Historian George Chauncey raised the question in his 2004 book title. Evan Wolfson chose a declarative version, *Why Marriage Matters,* for the title of his own book, also published in 2004. Launched five years earlier, when E. J. Graff named her book *What Is Marriage For?,* the marriage-interrogation genre settled into place in 2004 and began to grow.

The year 2004 was a big marriage-policy year away from the bookshelves, too. Consider the political and legal landscape. In July 2004, the U.S. House of Representatives overwhelmingly passed the Marriage Protection Act, a law written to take from federal courts their power to review a portion of the Defense of Marriage Act, the first federal statute that had ever prescribed a definition of marriage. A month later, in August, the California Supreme Court issued its first judicial decision nullifying thousands of putative marriages—3,995, to be precise—that had been solemnized during February and March 2004 after the San Francisco city government had issued licenses to couples. In the late summer of 2004, the Republican National Convention proclaimed support for a measure called the Federal Marriage Amendment to the U.S. Constitution. A nonprofit group called American Center for Law and Justice announced in August 2004 that it had gathered more than half a million signatures on a petition in support of this marriage amendment, introduced in Congress about a year earlier. On November 2, 2004, voters in eleven states were asked to consider amendments to their constitutions concerning the definition of marriage: all eleven proposed amendments won majority approval, as had a similar amendment put on the ballot in Missouri three months earlier, in August 2004.

All these 2004 developments—Chauncey's question, Wolfson's answer, the Republican platform, the strengthening of a constitutional amendment cause, the court-stripping Marriage Protection Act, the California court decision, the dozen state constitutional amendments—focused on one fraction of the marriage debate: whether American laws and governments should recognize, via the fully fraught term "marriage," the conjunction of a man and a man or a woman and a woman. While this topic was taking root in American law and policy, opposite-sex marriage—or what some wistfully call "traditional marriage"—receded from discussion.

The same-sex controversy used to have to compete for space in the marriage debates. By 2004 all its rivals were in retreat. Reformers used to tout covenant marriage, for instance, where couples would pledge in advance to have a tougher time should they later choose to divorce. In 2004 it was a fad, stalled. Pledges like "True Love Waits" by adolescents to retain their virginity until they marry, as a measure against teen pregnancy and sexually transmitted diseases? Ditto. Marriage promotion by the federal government? It is under way (and this volume does not neglect it), heartily funded, and yet . . . so 2003. Divorce reform? Ongoing but less compelling. *Marriage Proposals* joins a discussion where the word "marriage" as a policy topic has come to be shorthand, almost, for same-sex marriage.

Furor over same-sex marriage does pay heed to a vital topic, one that has been too long neglected. Partisans on both sides may occasionally exaggerate the stakes pro and con, and cynics on the outside may urge the public to care less (saying, for instance, that same-sex marriage is just a ploy to "mobilize the Republican base").[1] Yet if state-recognized marriage were made available to same-sex couples—beyond small Massachusetts, which has gone this route alone—the lives of all Americans would change. Parallels between the same-sex marriage cause and the race-focused American civil rights movement, though contested, reveal similarities between this struggle and the most profound conflict in American history.

Same-sex marriage affects Americans who will never seek legal recognition for themselves and partners of their own gender. It is an important issue for feminists: feminism has struggled to move marriage away from oppressive antecedents, especially coverture, the British legal doctrine that submerged a married woman's identity under that of her husband and prevented her from bringing lawsuits or holding personal property.[2] Same-sex marriage matters to sexual minorities beyond those who identify themselves as homosexual: those who scorn conventional notions about the proper way to order one's sex life, or who do not see themselves as branded with one of two immutable genders or sexual orientations. Same-sex marriage is even more important for the increasing number of children now growing up in two-mother or two-father households; their lives change in response to which recognition (or lack thereof) their parents' unions can have. Religious establishments like churches, most of which have been compelled to take a position on the question (sometimes with painful consequences to their flocks), have experienced the importance of this subject. In making decisions about same-sex marriage, they speak in part for the large majority of Americans who consider themselves as faithful to, or members of, a particular religious group.

Because of these extensive stakes in the same-sex marriage question, contemporary marriage debates reach beyond the question of which new rights a minority ought to attain. This wide-scale strife implies the possibility of resolution or synthesis: whenever big, divisive social challenges like this one arise in the United States, compromises tend to emerge. American marriage, we all might agree after 2004, experienced big, divisive social challenges and now has embarked on transition. Marriage policy cannot return to an idyll. Even the most potent "defense of marriage" effort will not revive the day when nobody dared ask out loud why, why not, what for, and for whom.

Marriage Proposals starts with a provisional answer to these newly broached questions: one way to see marriage, our contributors agree here (before they start diverging), is as a legal status that meets societal needs. Legal statuses—identities that apply to individuals and get acknowledged by societies—emerge from negotiation rather than fiat; collectives build something like a consensus to say what marriage now must be. American governments can change legal statuses, of which marriage is no exception. Governments have always altered the boundaries around marriage, accepted new kinds of couples, and reassigned power.

This lens used in *Marriage Proposals* replaces more romantic or familiar alternatives. One might prefer to see marriage as a spiritual venture or a religious condition, for instance, or maybe a metaphor. *Marriage Proposals* instead looks at marriage as a legal artifice with consequences for adults regarding their property, their individual freedom, and the enforceable duties they owe to other adults.

For readers willing to think of marriage as an artifice, this perspective delivers a fresh take on the rise of marriage-like new statuses, of which civil unions and domestic partnerships are the best known. The pattern of challenge followed by compromise starts with individuals' needs and questions. Civil unions and domestic partnerships originated in an activism that wondered, in public, why couples seeking to marry required an opposite-sex admissions ticket to get into the institution. The cause declared that marriage was malleable. Indeed it is: the statuses that emerged may be new, but meeting one's opponents partway on marriage policy is not. In past centuries, the term "marriage" used to recognize the power of other entities—among them family alliances, religious establishments, and even couples themselves—to declare a new marriage formed. Lord Hardwick's Act, enacted in England in 1753 to centralize state power over marriage, declared marital status a legal bright line: you were or you weren't. While retaining this heritage, American law has also been more open-minded on the question of whether persons are married.

A handful of American states, for example, consider certain unsolemnized pairings to be "common-law marriages" that entitle participants to all the marital accouterments—inheritance, property division, statutory preferences, and even divorce. Common-law marriage can exist even if one party later swears sincerely that he or she was never married. The Uniform Marriage and Divorce Act, a model statute available for adoption by the states, expresses no disapproval of common-law marriage. One neologism from the 1970s, "palimony," refers to court-ordered financial obligations owed to spouselike former partners that resemble the duty of postmarital support: to win palimony, the less wealthy partner must depict the relationship as close to a marriage. In the name of equity—or sometimes invoking the need to protect vulnerable innocents—state courts have recognized an array of anomalous unions: foreign polygamous marriages, bigamous marriages entered into in good faith, marriages that violate a state's consanguinity prohibitions, and even what appear to be same-sex marriages.[3] The august American Law Institute identifies as one of its "principles of the law of family dissolution" the notion that for many couples, the end of a long-term nonmarital relationship should be treated the same as the end of a long marriage with respect to property dissolution and child support.

Against this backdrop, "domestic partnerships" in California and New Jersey, "reciprocal beneficiaries" in Hawaii, and civil unions in Vermont and Connecticut, along with the numerous variations on state legislatures' drawing boards around the country, join a tradition that explores compromise about what it means to be married. They offer a set of hitherto-excluded persons—mostly gay couples but also, in the Hawaii experiment, partners unconnected by a sexual or conjugal affiliation—many of the privileges that had been monopolized by formal state-sponsored marriage. Of these innovations, Vermont's experiment is of particular interest to *Marriage Proposals* for its venturesome jurisprudence into the meaning of marital status.

The Vermont Supreme Court in its 1999 landmark decision *Baker v. State* announced that the state constitution's common benefits clause, which resembles on its surface the equal protection clause of the U.S. Constitution, compelled the state to make civil unions available to same-sex couples. Writing for the court, Chief Justice Jeffrey Amestoy explained that although the equal protection clause originated in racial subordination and was written to remove state-enforced oppression of African Americans, the common benefits clause is a device to share good things equally with all citizens:

> [T]he Common Benefits Clause mirrors the confidence of a homogeneous, eighteenth-century group of men aggressively laying claim to the same rights as their peers in Great Britain or, for that matter, New York, New Hampshire, or the Upper Connecticut River Valley. The same assumption that all the people should be afforded all the benefits and protections bestowed by government is also reflected in the . . . [wording that] prohibits not the denial of rights to the oppressed, but rather the conferral of advantages or emoluments upon the privileged.[4]

When it said "everything," *Baker* meant *every*thing: "[T]he benefits and protections incident to a marriage license in Vermont have never been greater," as the court continued. The Vermont Supreme Court was not the first state supreme court to go this far—the supreme courts of Alaska and Hawaii had both held that the opposite-sex ticket to marriage implicated state-level versions of equal protection rights—but the Vermont legislature was the nation's first to accede. In legislation that followed *Baker v. State,* Vermont extended all the privileges of marriage to persons conjoined by a civil union. Same-sex couples in Vermont may even file a joint state income tax return—not all that radical a step, perhaps, but one to date not taken in the states that recognize domestic partnerships.

Four years later, in *Goodridge v. Department of Public Health,* the Supreme Judicial Court of Massachusetts made marriage available to same-sex couples. It insisted, when formally asked, that nothing short of marriage would do. No civil unions here, even if civil unions in Vermont really do share officially in all the "common benefits" of marriage accessible to same-sex couples. With this decision, the Massachusetts court inverted David B. Cruz's phrase, "just don't call it marriage," to command that the state had damn well better call it marriage and nothing but marriage.

The Massachusetts choice pulled the marriage spectrum sharply in a novel direction. Until Massachusetts took its fateful step, the civil unions of Vermont had marked the outermost acceptance of man-man and woman-woman couples ever enacted in the United States. Back in 1999, the judicial ruling in *Baker v. State* had made Vermont politicians tremble. Town clerks filed a lawsuit alleging that the new obligation to issue licenses for civil unions infringed on their religious liberty. Howard Dean, the governor, became nationally famous for having signed enabling legislation. Legal commentators speculated endlessly about recognition of Vermont civil unions in the other forty-nine states, on whether a Vermont-united couple could get a divorce or quasi divorce from another state court; they chatted about how far Vermont's winds would blow to influence the nation. Then came *Goodridge,* shoving Vermont perforce nearer to the center. Vermont was now furnishing a compromise between the "real" marriage available in Massachusetts and the slammed-door "defense of marriage" laws in place in a majority of the states. Accordingly, in April 2005, when Connecticut became the first state to enact civil unions without preceding judicial pressure, two opposing camps of activists denounced the legislation: it went too far, said one, and did not go far enough, said the other.

Contributors will say more, later in this volume, about the same-sex marriage endeavor, and I return to it later. Here we can identify it as one of two late twentieth-century events that necessitate a book like this one. The other of these two developments is a rise of prescriptive social science that received its most prominent expression in a book published in 2000: *The Case for Marriage: Why Married People Are Happier, Healthier, and Better Off Financially.*

Like most coauthors, Linda J. Waite, an academic demographer, and Maggie Gallagher, an activist committed to keeping same-sex couples excluded from the status of marriage, had to put aside some disagreement (Waite would have preferred to stay out of the same-sex marriage controversy) in order to write a monograph. But they did reach agreement on marriage as a goal for American law and policy. Lining up married Americans on one side opposite unmarried Americans on the other, *The Case for Marriage* deemed the former category significantly advantaged. Waite and Gallagher, joined by other writers, gathered evidence to show that married persons enjoy longer life and better health than the unmarried. In addition, the contemporary "case for marriage" holds that married persons also possess more wealth, have sex more often and with more satisfaction, report more happiness, and rear better-adjusted children. Without denying that many individuals suffer detriment in their marriages and would be better off single, this "case" finds no aggregate drawbacks to marriage. As many see the data, there is no significant demographic variable where single persons as a group enjoy more well-being than married persons.

There is more to the "case." It turns out that marriage is good for bystanders—"society"—as well as for individuals. Streets get safer, because the pool of violent offenders shrinks: women of all marital statuses constitute a small minority of street criminals, and married men confine almost all their criminal activity to white-collar frolics. Married fathers living with their children bestow more support (both financial and nonpecuniary) than do divorced or never-married fathers. Going beyond children, marriage provides a structure to promote live-in caregiving, which eases burdens that taxpayers would otherwise have to shoulder. Clear policy implications emerge, or so advocates who identify with "the marriage movement" have said. At a minimum, the United States needs more marriages—simply because every marriage, all other things being equal, flips two persons from the disadvantaged into the advantaged category. The government, then, should encourage individuals to choose marriage over singleness.

Here, as political scientist Mary Lyndon Shanley observes (Shanley, this volume), the two developments in contemporary marriage debates, same-sex marriage and "the case for marriage," come together: the case-for-marriage claim that marriage is useful—good for an individual who wishes to become part of a couple, good for that individual's partner, and good for us bystanders and everyone else—receives similar expression from proponents of same-sex marriage. Jonathan Rauch subtitles his book *Why [same-sex marriage] Is Good for Gays, Good for Straights, and Good for America.* According to Rauch, the state fosters marriage mainly because it needs one-on-one caregiving for dependent adults; it could furnish millions more Americans with a devoted law-linked partner if it were willing to drop the same-sex restriction on marriage. Evan Wolfson prefers a noninstrumental human rights argument, analogizing his cause to American struggles against the kinds of race discrimination that law used to enforce, especially state-level bans on interracial marriage that did not end until 1967. His nonprofit organization, Freedom to Marry, sees marriage as a locus of privileges and responsibilities from which no person should be excluded on the basis of sex or gender. Yet even Wolfson the noninstrumentalist devotes a chapter in his book to the social consequences of legalizing same-sex marriage, and he calls other chapters "What About the Children?" and "Discrimination: Protections Denied to Same-Sex Couples *and Their Kids*" (emphasis added)—a reference to third-party stakes in same-sex marriage. Other activists have argued that children will be made better off when the couple that is rearing them can marry, while yet another writer roots his argument for same-sex marriage in law and economics, linking same-sex marriage to numerous financial savings for both couples and the state.[5]

Two social movements, then, have been offering the United States divergent—and occasionally parallel—claims and demands regarding marriage. The same-sex marriage movement seeks to make marriage available to two adults regardless of their gender. The marriage movement, unmodified, uses data to contend that the government ought to encourage people to marry.

Implicit in both movements is an expansionist gospel, a sense of good news that needs to be spread. "Let marriage bloom!" This gospel, now familiar, reflects a fast-paced change in American marriage. Only a couple of decades ago marriage as an American legal status was rooted firmly in religion, layered with a vague semisecular "tradition."[6] Law-based consequences would follow, but they drew little attention at a national level. Each state had its own criteria to withhold this legal badge from some, make it available to many, and nullify it after one or both parties applied for exit. For its part, federal law, though riddled with more than a thousand recognitions of individuals' marital status, seemed to consider certain basic questions about marriage—What is a marriage? Who may marry? Which rules govern the recognition of marriages formed in another state or another country?—to be none of its business. A less likely subject for constitutional amendment could hardly have been imagined. In this near past—recent enough for marriage-policy activists to remember well—few doubted that this status belonged only to opposite-sex couples. "I did not understand and acknowledge my homosexuality until well into adulthood," as Jonathan Rauch wrote in his *New York Times* editorial, "but I somehow understood even as a young boy that I would probably never marry." Marriage was "private" terrain, not to be manipulated or intruded on. Since the late 1990s, however, these two sets of activists have called out *More!* "Let us in," says the same-sex marriage movement.

"Extend it," says the marriage movement. Both would enlist the law to advance their agendas.

And so it makes sense that around the time of the Vermont and Massachusetts changes, a same-sex marriage activist like E. J. Graff or George Chauncey would ask, "Why marriage?" or "What is marriage for?" to broach book-length arguments, joining the "case for marriage" books that urge the government to spend money on promoting the choice of marriage as a voluntarily assumed status. Confident in their advocacy, these queries nevertheless express anxiety about the social role of marriage; and bold as they were, the Vermont and Massachusetts judicial decisions exposed uncertainty and ambiguity in state-sponsored marriage.

The landscape lacks consensus. Siding with the gay couples who had challenged the opposite-sex criterion as a condition for marital privileges, the *Baker* and *Goodridge* decisions also highlight what these couples do not have. Vermont's legislation declined to bestow the word "marriage," giving same-sex couples something else. Something less. Massachusetts purported to go all the way, and it did, but its decision provoked a backlash that undid gains. Counteractivists revived an old favorite term of opprobrium, "activist judges." Other states kick-started their old defense-of-marriage lawmaking machinery by adopting constitutional amendments to deny recognition to same-sex marriages. The governor of Massachusetts declared that while out-of-state opposite-sex couples were welcome to go on eloping to the Berkshires for weddings, their counterparts in Provincetown, so to speak—same-sex couples domiciled out of the state—would be turned away at the town hall door. Family-values congresswoman Marilyn Musgrove of Colorado reacted to *Goodridge* by introducing the constitutional amendment with which we began.

No matter what views one holds of same-sex marriage, the *Baker* and *Goodridge* results look mixed. "Judicial victories" like the wins in these New England states portray state-sponsored marriage as quotidian yet transformative—"just a piece of paper," but out of reach. A simple question of justice, or rights, or family law (type the phrase "a civil right" into Nexis and see which of many possible candidates was called a civil right most often in 2004!) but also a skein of tangled compromises and incomplete measures. Published answers to Why Marriage? and What Is Marriage For? recite lists of ideals: companionship, commitment, haven in a heartless world, a venue for relatively secure rearing of a new generation. Putting aside the high risk of failure to reach these ideals when new marriages are formed—or the complementary question, What is divorce for?

—this volume asks, Are the answers correct? Might the goods that marriage partisans cite instead result from couples' doing something other than registering with the state as half of a marital unit?

Try an easier query: Can two people bond themselves into coupledom without the imprimatur of government? No, say many. Or at least not adequately, if only because third parties will get in their way. Immigration officials exclude non–blood relatives at the border; hospitals keep all but officially sanctioned family away from sickbeds; a host of unseen default rules like the law of intestacy give a range of boons to couples beyond what they can plan. All right, then; couples need some kind of status that outsiders must acknowledge, let us suppose. Will the civil union or domestic partner label do, or must they have access to the M word first bestowed by Massachusetts?

What, in other words, does it mean to be married, in contrast to the statuses that the two marriage movements have implicitly portrayed as lesser—not only the civil unions and domestic partnerships that some would give gay activists instead of what they demand, but also every other way to be a not-married person? The chapters that follow here in *Marriage Proposals* explore a government-recognized institution, a category that determines whether a person will receive favored or disfavored treatment from the state, and a powerful source of coercion.

Though incomplete, this vantage point has the virtue of covering much ground. Chief Justice Amestoy of the Vermont Supreme Court undoubtedly was on to something in 1999 when he counted a recent increase in the number and scope of government-mandated consequences that derive from marital status. Moreover, the status is not entirely binary: in this juridical model, as we have noted, yes and no are not the only possible answers to the question of whether a person is part of a two-person sexual affiliation. Marriage is complemented by other statuses beyond civil unions and domestic partnerships and reciprocal beneficiaries: contemporary law recognizes the status of being "single" as sometimes distinct from "divorced," and also gives legal weight to being "engaged."[7]

Married, single, divorced, engaged—all legal terms, signifying privileges and detriments that the government will carry out. Their persistence —joined with, as we have seen, two sectors of activism that want to paste these labels on more people—is odd in light of a truism long in place within American legal anthropology: legal development is said to be moving away from all-encompassing roles that define legal duties and entitlements. When anthropologist Henry Sumner Maine issued his famous proclamation that modern legal development evolved "from Status to Contract," he used juridical categories to make a statement about progress. Voluntary relations now build the law, Maine declared. The alternative to voluntary relations—identity-based legal labels to decree what people may and may not do—must relocate to the dustbin of history. Only a backwater society would keep them.

American legal change in the century and a half since Maine's death in 1888 has given support to the claim that status inexorably yields to contract. At one level, newer developments refute the Maine thesis. "Stalkers," "telemarketers," "date rapists," "reciprocal beneficiaries," "surrogate mothers," and other noun phrases have joined the roster of what the law recognizes as shorthand for duties, entitlements, and liability. Labels continue to emerge; rights and obligations attached to them flourish. Older status roles like "tenant," "landlord," and "employer" have acquired more legal force, rather than less, in the last dozen decades.

Good reasons support the use of status as an instrument for lawmaking and law enforcement: whether ancient or newly coined, status labels today tell individuals what the law permits and forbids. They pack meanings into a word or two. The phrase "dependent child," for instance, makes it clear that somebody—at least one person—can be prosecuted for not coming up with food and shelter. Designations like "owner," "felon," "attorney of record," or "residual legatee" are worth fighting over in court. Law would be verbose if not incoherent without the swift, compact punch of a legal label. If status is holding strong in the law, one need not wonder why any label category is still with us. All statuses might be burgeoning.

"From Status to Contract," however, challenges the existence of state-sponsored marriage. Maine's contention that status is primitive and contract modern reminds us that marital status is critically different from other legal statuses that have been thriving. Becoming a "stalker" or a "surrogate mother" fits the Maine progression: it looks like contract rather than status. The terms connote episodes or parcels of individual lives rather than a comprehensive social identity. A person can put on the label and take it off with little formality.

The status of marriage, by contrast—that is, becoming, or ceasing to be, a wife or a husband—spreads into the far corners of one's life. Marriage is different also from the other key status category of family law—parenthood—in that the relation between parent and child addresses a relatively clear and uncontroverted need. Infants cannot survive without resources from adults. A husband or wife can provide care to a dependent spouse, but care for dependents is not a defining condition of the marital relation, as it is of parenthood. Marriage, in short, is a peculiar status. Most other legal statuses relate directly either to episodes or transactions, on the one hand ("agent," "mortgagee," "harasser"), or to dependency, on the other ("parent," "guardian," perhaps "fiduciary").

Law does have a history of recognizing a couple of personal, or comprehensive, statuses that do not fall into these two broad categories of transaction and dependency. Such statuses partake of tautology. They are what they are; they must be because they have been. Legal consequences follow to status-bearers without consent; only a rare person who acquires a comprehensive status understands what it means before the label is bestowed. These labels are hard to shed. Principal examples of this kind of status are race—a legal category still not extinguished—and coverture, which used to shackle most women. And then there are the categories that come from binary gender, where each person is assigned one (and only one) of two (and only two) legal statuses. The anti-individualistic, choice-denying nature of these comprehensive statuses has clashed with progressive legal development.

It is in the law of marriage that the legal categories of "man" and "woman" retain their power. During the years when the government's distinguishing a woman from a man accreted disapproval in numerous legal realms—employment, military service, prisons, higher education—the defense-of-marriage movement insisted on this distinction and engraved it into federal and state statutory law. Marriage, in federal law and in most states, must consist of a dimorphous pair, "one man and one woman." These new laws are not the last word on this subject: as we have seen, insistence on gender dimorphousness in each legally recognized marriage just might reach the U.S. Constitution.

In this picture, marriage joins a lineup of statuses for human beings in contemporary American law. On one side are the comprehensive labels: race and the successor to coverture, gender. On the other side are noun phrases tailored to respond either to dependency or to something resembling free choice in one's encounters. Where does marriage land? *Marriage Proposals* notes that marriage imbues individuals with a comprehensive legal identity. This status is not transactional, the way signing a contract can turn a person temporarily into a lessee or a mortgagor. Nor is it targeted to address dependency, although it may aid a dependent person incidentally. Like race and coverture, the social category of marriage occupies space in the law, and not only in society. Also like race and coverture, marital status functions to elevate some individuals and to subordinate others, based on their membership in groups that they did not choose to join.[8]

The condition of marriage in American law is noteworthy. Although Maine-like reports of their death might be greatly exaggerated, most comprehensive legal statuses are on their way to oblivion in the United States. Race, once a category that signified either enslavement or the privilege to enslave others, and later a marker of privileges either withheld or bestowed, such as where one could gather in public, or which schools one could attend, now exists almost nowhere in American law beyond "affirmative action," itself on the wane. American law used to speak of lunatics and idiots; the status label now assigned to cover this ground, "disability," sees human variation in briskly functional and specific terms. According to the Supreme Court, the government may not classify homosexually inclined persons as categorically less entitled to benefits that they obtain by democratic means. And "men" and "women" are rapidly exiting most of the law; "persons" take their place. Except in the law of marriage.

Marriage Proposals now asks: Should marriage make an explicit transition away from status, toward either contract or no-contract as individuals choose? If it opted to maximize the prerogatives of contract, this change would encourage the law to abandon its recognition of the sexual, gender-dimorphous dyad. All domestic relations between adult individuals would be formed by issue-specific agreements. Family law would survive to regulate the care of children, but two would no longer become one in any legal sense. The law would intervene in a couple's life just as it now uses the law of contracts, torts, crimes, and property to moderate relations between any other adults.

Recall the cry of *More!* that we have heard from both the same-sex marriage movement and the marriage movement. Some American data suggest a tacit *Less!*—repudiation whereby individuals vote against marriage with their feet. Most Americans give marriage a try sometime during their lives, but they have also been withdrawing from marriage. They express this withdrawal in a relatively high divorce rate and a rising average age of first marriage. One survey, sponsored by marriage-movement partisans, found in 2001 that 45 percent of young adults agreed that the government should not be involved in licensing marriage.[9] Demographic changes like these suggest a reduction in the percentage of Americans who want to register with the state as half of a couple.

Along with these changes, legislatures and courts have been reflecting and fostering a newer individualism in the law of marriage that has undermined the old two-into-one status. Current divorce law, liberalized in the last few decades, has made unions easier and cheaper to escape. In less than thirty years, state governments swerved from almost unanimously rejecting antenuptial contracts that purported to allocate marital property; they now almost unanimously enforce these "prenups." Even traditionalist reforms that have appeared in recent years (such as the harder-to-exit "covenant marriage" noted earlier, premarital counseling imposed on applicants for marriage licenses, and tightening the grounds for divorce), all designed to strengthen marriage, focus more on the marrying individual as party to a contract and less on the oneness of a marital union.[10] As noted, a number of state governments in the United States have decided to allow pairs of individuals to sign up for some of the benefits of legal marriage without imposing on these pairs any demand to be gender-dimorphous or have a sexual bond. This innovation understands law-based coupling as a choice that two adults can make, beyond mere compliance with an old imperative to build child-producing households. In other words, marrying—and its important correlatives, repudiating marriage and being foreclosed from it—now yields much less homogeneity. Back in 1861 Henry Maine wrote that, starting "from a condition of society in which all the relations of Persons are summed up in the relations of Family, we seem to have steadily moved towards a phase of social order in which all of these relations arise from the free agreement of individuals."[11] A century and a half later, his statement has become more true.

The prospect of abolishing the state-sponsored status of marriage, then, comes after at least portents, if not out-and-out precedents, elsewhere in American legal change. More support for the proposal comes generally from a focus on the individual as the locus reached, regulated, and tutored by law. What happens to individuals is the measure of law's ambition and legitimacy. And more than ever, married people are individuals. In contrast to the common law of centuries past, American husbands do not sue in tort for their wives' injuries. When a wife commits the crime, she, not her husband, does the time. Marriages now contain separate personal property and permit contracting between the spouses. The persistence of a comprehensive legal status that conjoins individuals into pairs —when in so many respects each person is a solitary creature in the law— calls for reexamination. Continuing in the same direction past advocacy for *More!* and *Less!* state-licensed and state-sponsored marriage, *Marriage Proposals* wonders: How about *None?*

The *None* alternative fills in a corner of the contemporary marriage debate. At the current center stage of this debate, the same-sex and the marriage-movement endeavors both rest on the same unchallenged truism: that marriage offers favorable contrasts to the alternatives to being married, that is, singleness and nonmarital cohabitation. Activists—the same-sex and the marriage-movement types alike—endorse and pursue marriage because it is a good thing to have. In addition, the human rights strand of the same-sex marriage movement regards marriage as similar to religious liberty or freedom from state-supported race discrimination. Because marriage is available to opposite-sex couples, there is no human rights strand within the "traditional" marriage movement; nevertheless, marriage-movement activists claim that married people are "happier," as well as less of a drag on the public fisc.

What this consensus misses is that welfare disparities between the married and unmarried, as well as the human rights gap identified by Wolfson and others, could be eliminated not only by extending marriage, as activists have demanded, but also by eliminating it. After the hypothetical abolition of marriage, "singleness," "cohabitation," and "marriage" would lose their legal status, and indeed some of their meaning. Most of "the case for marriage" would evaporate at this point, because the "case" has contrasted being married only to being divorced and to never marrying; it has never confronted state-sponsored marriage as an option that right-thinking people might reject on the same quasi-utilitarian basis that now commends getting married over not getting married. For the same-sex marriage cause, abolition would offer another way for same-sex couples to gain parity—they would hold the same status that opposite-sex couples now enjoy in their relationships.

In considering this question, contributors to *Marriage Proposals* bring a range of distinguished voices to a discussion that necessarily demands pluralism. Because "a status" in this conversation means "a legal status," the volume features lawyers and legal scholars. Half the contributors come from the law professoriat, while the other half (Miller, Rosen, Shanley, Solot) devote a significant portion of their work time to collaborations with legal scholars or legislators. Each contributor does multiple duties in response to the abolish-marriage proposal identified most prominently with contributor Martha Fineman: Peggy Cooper Davis brings in history and African American studies; Lawrence Rosen is not only a scholar of family law but a prominent anthropologist; Dorian Solot and Marshall Miller, founders of a successful nonprofit, combine activism with social science; Linda McClain adds expertise in federal marriage policy and welfare reform; Mary Lyndon Shanley studies marriage from her scholarly base in political science and political theory.

A word on the contributions not present in this volume. The design of *Marriage Proposals* stands a short distance from, while commenting on, the same-sex marriage movement and the marriage movement described earlier, and so these two activist groups are not represented here. Other anthologies give these groups the voice that a chapter or two here could not have provided. The reference to "proposals," connoting invitation rather than resolution, postpones for the moment the firm-sounding answers that social science could give, and so this volume presents no new empirical work about the success or failure of marriage as a status, although contributors do relate some of these findings while advancing their own views.

The book proceeds in two parts. Part I, "Challenges to the Status of Marriage," begins with a chapter from the legal scholar most associated with questioning marriage as a status. When Martha Fineman wonders, What is marriage for? in her chapter, "The Meaning of Marriage," she joins, as we have seen, a cohort of writers who have been posing the same question when they press for same-sex marriage. Rooted deeply in the field of family law, Fineman when she asks this question focuses on what she sees as family law's central domain, the care and nurturing of dependents. In earlier work Fineman has argued that family law can and should evolve to deny marriage—that is, move away from what is none of its business, freely chosen and fleeting affiliations between adults—while acknowledging relation-based dependency. Fineman's stance is especially antagonistic to marriage promotion by the state (detailed in McClain, this volume)—the stance that, among other pursuits, encourages economically disadvantaged women to gain material security through marital unions with men. Fineman sees the dependency of healthy adult women as made worse, not better, by marriage. Whereas children come into the world inherently needy and helpless, those who do caregiving work within the family have their dependency—economic vulnerability, conflicts between paid and unpaid work, unequal bargaining power vis-à-vis their partners—imposed upon them. Thus state-sponsored marriage, to Fineman, is not a cure for the plight of dependent mothers. Marriage *creates* their plight.

The Fineman thesis can be broken into increments. First Fineman calls dependency the center of, and the reason for, legal regulation of the family. She next calls women's familial dependency on men a contingent and reparable condition and a problem that marriage makes worse. Finally, while opposed to the injustice done to caregiving same-sex partners in particular and same-sex partners in general in the name of marriage, Fineman sees no a priori reason to prefer extending marriage over abolishing it. Abolishing state-sponsored marriage would not ignore, eliminate, or increase dependency: on the contrary, it would force the law to recognize that dependents need care.

Whereas Fineman writes about abolishing marriage from the academy, activists Dorian Solot and Marshall Miller address the same proposal as founders of the Alternatives to Marriage Project (ATMP). Solot and Miller started the ATMP in Boston in 1998 and soon expanded it into visible national-scale advocacy. Their chapter, "Taking Government Out of the Marriage Business: Families Would Benefit," adds detail to Fineman's broader strokes. Solot and Miller call on American governments to recognize the "diversity of family types" (Solot and Miller) that increasingly fill the landscape.

The Solot and Miller stance on the very fraught word "family" differs slightly from Fineman's. Fineman sees the dependent-caregiver relation as the only family that the law should regulate; she would steer the law away from ascribing family status to adults who are not related to each other by blood. Solot and Miller prefer a broader vision of "family" that would unite people in a variety of patterns that feature "emotional and financial interdependence," a looser bond than Fineman's "dependency."

Whether characterized by "dependency," as Fineman sees it, or the "emotional and financial interdependence" that forms a unit for Solot and Miller, "the family" is at the center of marriage. Marriage as a legal status forms a family. Questioning marriage as a legal status entails questioning what a family—including one crucial type of family, the multigenerational kind into which children are born or arrive at a young age—is for. Here Linda McClain offers salient expertise, not only in family law and policy but in political theory and philosophy. In "What Place for Marriage (E)quality in Marriage Promotion?" McClain uses marriage-promotion initiatives started in the late 1990s—which continue—to ask what the government ought to promote when it promotes "marriage." She finds two legitimate ends: government ought, first, to help with "orderly social reproduction," which means not only feeding and clothing young children but rearing them to be conscientious and democratic citizens; and, second, to help make intimate association between two adults safer, more conducive to individual flourishing, and a better venue for the nurturing of other people, should the two adults choose to undertake that work.

Income-tax favoritism, advantageous ways to hold real and personal property, Social Security payments to wives of retired workers, a range of privileges and immunities, and other law-based preferences for marriage already constituted "marriage promotion" well before the twenty-first-century congressional appropriations to encourage lower-income persons to marry. As long as there is state-sponsored marriage, McClain points out, there will be "marriage promotion." If the existence of state-sponsored marriage necessarily means the existence of marriage promotion, then questioning marriage as a legal status means asking our old favorite question: What is marriage for? but in a different form: What are we trying to promote here?

Like Fineman before her, McClain identifies a range of possible answers. Like Solot and Miller, McClain finds "family" central to this question. But McClain's chapter draws harder lines than the previous chapters. McClain has a less pluralistic or eclectic view of "marriage," a word she uses as shorthand for what governments press onto families. Call it ideology if you must, but McClain insists that the government in its approach to marriage must take a stand for democracy, and also equality along many axes: foremost, perhaps, the equality of men and women, but also equality among types of couples (i.e., privileging opposite-sex pairs no more and no less than same-sex pairs), and a sense of equality as something to be instilled in children of the household.

Fineman, Solot and Miller, and McClain thus offer readers a variety of answers to the question of whether marriage ought to be retained, or alternatively abolished, as a legal status. One answer might be summed up as, Yes and here's why, and here's how. Another answer: Yes, but protect and nurture families—and start by reenvisioning what it means to be a family. A third: Don't overrely on one flickering word whose meanings shift. Interpret "marriage," in this law and policy context, to mean the government's interest in the domestic lives of couples and their children. Once we agree on that interest, it will become relatively straightforward to retain some state interventions and abolish others. Different answers, and yet each is committed to changing, even radically changing, this legal status.

The second set of responses to *Marriage Proposals* take a different tack; one might call it questioning questioning marriage as a status. Coming, respectively, from the (multi)disciplines of anthropology, law and African

American history, and political theory, authors Lawrence Rosen, Peggy Cooper Davis, and Mary Lyndon Shanley—none of them "conservative" or otherwise devoted to the marriage status quo—doubt that rejecting or revising the legal category of marriage will advance the goals that every author in this volume shares. Every writer contributing to this volume endorses gender equity, finds the history of race discrimination pertinent to the question of discriminations within the law of marriage, applauds toleration and pluralism, and (in particular) approves of the U.S. Supreme Court decriminalization of same-sex sexual intimacy as a step toward the abolition of de jure oppression of homosexual persons. Rosen, Davis, and Shanley identify what part II calls "some perils of attempting abolition."

If marriage is "a cultural universal"—that is, a phenomenon found in all societies, one of the items to be named in response to Martha Nussbaum's query, "What activities characteristically performed by human beings are so central that they seem definitive of a life that is truly human?"[12]—then an attempt to "abolish" marriage in the United States must fail; even the lesser project of withdrawing state sponsorship from it will collide with deep-rooted imperatives. Accordingly, questioning marriage as a legal status calls for the counsel of anthropology, the social science that studies cultures and human origins; *Marriage Proposals* profits from the counsel of Lawrence Rosen, a legal scholar as well as a professor of this discipline.

Without arguing, on anthropological evidence, that marriage is a social fixture incapable of abolition, Rosen expounds on the conceptual and methodological difficulties that must accompany any proposal to abandon this institution. Anthropology deepens the abolition questions. Even Fineman's bare-bones version of "family," which rejects adult dyads as an entity of interest to the state and strips the unit down to caregiver-parent and dependent-child, could also be dispensed with, Rosen argues, citing the Na of southern China as a culture that does not see the family in that light. While many begin with Why marriage? or What is marriage for?, as noted at the beginning of this volume, Rosen rejects this starting point, reminding readers that "functionalism," though probably ineradicable in social science, has long been exposed as incapable of rendering solid answers.

For Rosen, questioning marriage as a legal status is much more than an inquiry into preferred family forms. Throughout Western history, he argues, challenges to the authority of religion and the state have used the regulation of marriage as one of several "vehicles for protest" against pre-existing assertions of legitimacy. It may be impossible to separate the challenge to state-sponsored marriage from a larger challenge to the state, and even to the very notion of legitimacy. Consequences do not stop there. If anthropology is right to presuppose that "every domain of a sociocultural system has some bearing on the other," it becomes reasonable to predict the unpredictable following the abandonment of marriage as a legal category: American society will change, as institutions and practices that are much closer to marriage than abolitionists might think respond to this shift. Rosen identifies American nationalism, "concepts of time and space," "images of the self," and other disparate fixtures as tangent to the abolition of marriage as a legal status.

In this analysis, anthropology—which Rosen hastens to remind readers is not a predictive science—imagines the future, looking ahead to a day when the state reverses itself on the question of recognizing marriage as a status with legal effects. Peggy Cooper Davis's chapter, "Marriage as a 'Badge and Incident' of Democratic Freedom," complements Rosen by looking to the American past. Davis turns this way not for any direct precedent on point: there is none; the United States has not yet experimented with formal abandonment of this legal category. Instead, Davis considers a group of Americans who had their marriage abolished on them, as it were.

Slavery could not have existed, Davis argues, if enslaved persons had enjoyed the state support for their marriages that contemporary Americans enjoy for theirs. Withholding marriage was a necessary constituent of withholding human identity. In civic life marriage signifies recognition of people as "progeny and progenitors," in contrast to the notion that they are property. Extending the work of sociologist Orlando Patterson, who has found in American slavery "a critical absence of democracy" that made democracy and freedom look more vivid to unenslaved Americans who bore witness to slavery in the nineteenth century, Davis revives a connection between state-sponsored marriage and individual freedom. A belief that matrimony makes people free may seem perverse after decades of misogynous imagery about marriage as oppressor: Which people engage in nagging and henpecking? Think of mothers-in-law, the old ball and chain, fishwife, trouble-and-strife, Stepford wife. Yet abolitionists and lawmakers argued fluently in the nineteenth century that lack of marriage revealed the nonhumanity, or the inhumanity, of the American slave's life. Moreover, the question of marriage, Davis shows us, informed the framing of the Thirteenth and Fourteenth Amendments to the U.S. Constitution. As to whether this American experience before and after slavery means that American governments should not withdraw from recognizing marriage, Davis will say only that "this history suggests that the right to choose to participate in the culture through marriage should be protected."

Davis's enlightened uncertainty about marriage carries over into the next chapter, "The State of Marriage and the State in Marriage: What Must Be Done," by political scientist Mary Lyndon Shanley. Unlike Davis, who retreats from prescription, Shanley is willing to recommend one specific new policy: universal civil unions of the kind now available to same-sex couples in Vermont and Connecticut. Comfortable with neither abolishing marriage nor the state-sponsored status quo, Shanley argues for universal civil unions as a means to salvage the best of marriage while shedding some of its oppressions. Universal civil unions, as Shanley sees them, would replace state-sponsored marriage for opposite-sex couples— as far as the government is concerned, these people would no longer "marry" each other—and be extended in the mode that Vermont pioneered to same-sex couples. While Shanley is not the first writer to commend civil unions for all couples,[13] her crucial contribution to this new literature about universal civil unions is to situate it in political theory.

Any theorist who endorses universal civil unions has a twofold task. The advocate must say, on one hand, why these unions are better than making the current version of marriage more available to categories of couples and why, on the other, they are better than simply getting rid of the oppressive status. To undertake this defense, Shanley needs a working notion of marriage. Like Fineman, she begins with a history of marriage that scrupulously records its roots in religious and civic authoritarianism. Like many other statuses in American law, marriage has told Americans what they may and may not do without reference to either any voluntary agreement they have made (the way the law tells parties to contracts that they must perform or else pay damages) or antecedent behavior that warrants limiting their freedom (the way criminal law punishes, and tort law orders some defendants to pay compensatory damages). Under the regime of state-sponsored marriage, both married and unmarried persons, in different ways, are bossed around, burdened, and deprived of liberties. If they have any inclination to freedom, they would want both the chance to change their marital status and room to negotiate what that status gives them. Shanley conceives the history of American marriage-law reform, especially the liberalization of divorce, as an attempt to cast off shackles.

Yet for Shanley, individual freedom demands more than ready exit from commitments and oppressive relations. Persons also need public recognition of the bonds they choose. Shanley quotes with approval the Canadian government report urging recognition of relational interests to go "beyond conjugality"; the Canadian proposal would give formal status to partnerships without demanding that they display sexual affiliation or romantic love. For Shanley, state recognition of this kind of much-cherished partnership makes intimate connection both more attainable and more likely to endure. She suggests that the future of this recognition is too important to be left to the fraught institution of "marriage," with its record of oppression and exclusion. More satisfactorily than marriage, universal civil unions can fulfill something like a universal human craving.

The volume concludes with an afterword, written after I had reflected on the contributors' chapters to this volume. These concluding thoughts are informed by the prior chapters but also stand separate, and instead of restating what the chapters have expressed so well on their own, I advert to writers not yet heard from in this book: John Stuart Mill, Jeremy Bentham, and Oliver Wendell Holmes on the coercion inherent in all law, including the status-category corner of law we are addressing here, and Milton Regan Jr. and George Gilder, as defenders of marriage. The afterword finishes off *Marriage Proposals* with my cautious vote for retention rather than abolition.

NOTES

1. Dao 2004.

2. "By marriage, the husband and wife are one person in law: that is, the very being or legal existence of the woman is suspended during the marriage, or at least is incorporated and consolidated into that of the husband; under whose wing, protection, and *cover,* she performs every thing; and is therefore called in our law-French a *feme-covert,* foemina viro co-operta; is said to be *covert-baron,* or under the protection and influence of her husband, her *baron,* or lord; and her condition during her marriage is called her *coverture*" (Blackstone 1979 [1765], 442–43).

3. See *In re Dalip Singh Bir's Estate,* 188 P.2d 499 (Cal. App. 1948) (allowing two widows to inherit from one husband); Weisberg and Appleton 2002, 242–44 (discussing "putative spouse doctrine and other curative devices" that occasionally recognize marriages otherwise invalid). Recognition of same-sex marriages outside Massachusetts to date has been limited to cases of transsexuality, where one

party to the marriage was born into one gender assignment and then relocated to the other, before or after a marriage ceremony. See *M.T. v. J.T.*, 355 A.2d 204 (N.J. Super. Ct. App. Div. 1976).

4. *Baker v. State*, 744 A.2d 864, 874 (Vt. 1999).

5. Chamblerlain 2004, 495; Eskridge 1996, 112; Nishimoto 2003.

6. This vagueness is manifest in a leading treatise, which declared in 1987 that marriage is "some sort of relationship between two individuals, of indeterminate duration, involving some kind of sexual conduct, entailing vague mutual property and support obligations, a relationship which may be formed by consent of both parties and dissolved at the will of either" (Clark 1987, 81)—a curious (and oddly gender-neutral) legal definition.

7. For example, a ring might be a gift "made in contemplation of marriage" and hence returnable on demand to the donor under certain conditions, even though usually a donee need not return a gift on a donor's demand (Brinig 1990; Tushnet 1998).

8. Popular phrases like "single by choice" advert to prerogative in determining one's marital status. Many people choose to be married or unmarried; others, however, experience the status they hold as imposed on them against their will. Unwanted singleness can result from widowhood, abandonment, rejection by prospective partners, and incarceration, among other conditions; meanwhile, some unhappily married persons feel, and perhaps are, "trapped." The law extends this theme of nonchoice by treating some children worse than other children based on their parents' marital statuses (e.g., states may limit their right to inherit through intestacy from an unwed father), which the children did not choose.

9. National Marriage Project, "The State of Our Unions" (Rutgers, N.J., 2001), available at http://marriage.rutgers.edu/Publications/SOOU/TEXTSOOU2001.htm.

10. Reforms of this late 1990s vintage did not focus on increasing state-bestowed rewards for long marital duration—stay married twenty years, say, and enjoy lower property taxes. Nor did they advocate new legal-financial privileges for the married, although Congress soon took up this kind of "marriage promotion" funding (see McClain, this volume). Rewards to couples for getting or staying married would have provided a less individualistic buttress to marriage than divorce reforms like covenant marriage, which address individuals' choices to leave a marriage rather than the marriage itself as an entity.

11. Maine 1861, 163.

12. Nussbaum 1999, 39.

13. Alisa Solomon called this law reform not only fair to same-sex couples but a good way to reopen now-stalled debates over the allocation of benefits like health insurance to individuals based on their marital status: "Once queer folks' emotional need to see their love recognized is separated from the practical need for various economic and legal benefits (especially revolving around children), the

community can look more clearly at what the state proffers to those civilly united —and why" (Solomon 2004). Following the onset of civil unions in Vermont, Mary Anne Case (2003) argued that women like herself—those inclined to choose men as their partners but who recoil from marriage because of its history—are now in a sense worse off than the Vermont lesbian who can join a legally recognized union with the partner of her choice without the yoke of "marriage."

REFERENCES

American Law Institute. 2002. *Principles of the Law of Family Dissolution*. Philadelphia: American Law Institute.

Anderson, K., D. Browning, and B. Boyer. 2002. *Marriage: Just a Piece of Paper?* Grand Rapids, Mich.: Eerdmans.

Baker v. State. 744 A.2d 864 (Vt. 1999).

Bernstein, A. 2003. "For and Against Marriage: A Revision." *Michigan Law Review* 102:129.

Blackstone, W. 1979 [1756]. *Commentaries on the Laws of England*. Chicago: University of Chicago Press.

Brinig, M. 1990. "Rings and Promises." *Journal of Law, Economics, and Organization* 6:203.

Case, M. 2003. "What Stake Do Heterosexual Women Have in the Same-Sex Marriage/Domestic Partnership/Civil Union Debates?" Unpublished manuscript.

Chamblerlain, G. 2004. "A Religious Argument for Same-Sex Marriage." *Seattle Journal for Social Justice* 2:495.

Chauncey, G. 2004. *Why Marriage? The History Shaping Today's Debate over Gay Equality*. New York: Basic Books.

Clark, H. 1987. *The Law of Domestic Relations in the United States*. 2nd ed. St. Paul, Minn.: West.

Coontz, S. 1992. *The Way We Never Were: American Families and the Nostalgia Trap*. New York: Basic Books.

Cossman, B., and B. Ryder. 2001. "What Is Marriage-Like Like? The Irrelevance of Conjugality." *Canadian Journal of Family Law* 18:269.

Cott, N. 2000. *Public Vows: A History of Marriage and the Nation*. Cambridge, Mass.: Harvard University Press.

Cruz, D. 2001. "'Just Don't Call It Marriage': The First Amendment and Marriage as an Expressive Resource." *Southern California Law Review* 74:925.

Dao. J. 2004. "State Action Is Pursued on Same-Sex Marriage." *New York Times*, February 27.

Eskridge, W. 1996. *The Case for Same-Sex Marriage: From Sexual Liberty to Civilized Commitment*. New York: Free Press.

General Accounting Office. Defense of Marriage Act. Rep. OGC 97-16 (1997).

Goodridge v. Department of Public Health. 798 N.E. 2d 941 (Mass. 2003).

Graff, E. J. 1999. *What Is Marriage For?* Boston: Beacon Press.

Maine, H. 1861. *Ancient Law: Its Connection with the Early History of Society and Its Relation to Modern Ideas.* London: John Murray.

McClain, L. 2005. *The Place of Families.* Cambridge, Mass.: Harvard University Press.

National Marriage Project. 2001. "The State of Our Unions." Rutgers, N.J. Available at http://marriage.rutgers.edu/Publications/SOOU/TEXTSOOU2001.htm

Nishimoto, R. 2003. "Marriage Makes Cents: How Law and Economics Justifies Same-Sex Marriage." *Boston College Third World Law Review* 23:379.

Nussbaum, M. 1999. *Sex and Social Justice.* New York: Oxford University Press.

Patterson, O. 1991. *Freedom.* New York: Basic Books.

Popenoe, D. 1998. "Life without Father." In *Lost Fathers: The Politics of Fatherhood in America,* ed. C. Daniels, 33–49. New York: St. Martin's Press.

Post, D. 1997. "Why Marriage Should Be Abolished." *Women's Rights Law Reporter,* 18:283.

Rauch, J. 2004a. *Gay Marriage: Why It Is Good for Gays, Good for Straights, and Good for America.* New York: Times Books/Henry Holt.

Rauch, J. 2004b. "Imperfect Unions." *New York Times,* August 15.

Romer v. Evans. 517 U.S. 620 (1996).

Solomon, A. 2004. "State to Church: I Want a Divorce." *Village Voice,* March 3.

Stell, B. n.d. "18th Century Weddings." Available at http://www.delareine.free-online.co.uk/NFOE-WEBSITE/articles/18th-c-weddings.htm.

Sullivan, A., ed. 2004. *Same-Sex Marriage, Pro and Con: A Reader.* New York: Vintage Books.

Tushnet, R. 1998. "Rules of Engagement." *Yale Law Journal* 107:2583.

Waite, L. J., and M. Gallagher. 2000. *The Case for Marriage: Why Married People Are Happier, Healthier, and Better Off Financially.* New York: Doubleday.

Wall, J., ed. 2002. *Marriage, Health, and the Professions: If Marriage Is Good for You, What Does This Mean for Law, Medicine, Ministry, Therapy, and Business?* Grand Rapids, Mich.: Eerdmans.

Weisberg, D., and S. Appleton. 2002. *Modern Family Law.* 2nd ed. New York: Aspen Law and Business.

Wolfson, E. 2004. *Why Marriage Matters: America, Equality, and Gay People's Right to Marry.* New York: Simon and Schuster. See also www.freedomtomarry.org.

Part I

Challenges to the Status of Marriage

Chapter 1

The Meaning of Marriage

Martha Albertson Fineman

The Future of Marriage

This chapter asks the question, Given changes in the legal regulation of marriage, coupled with changing patterns of intimate behavior, why should marriage continue to be the exclusive, preferred core or basic family connection? It is marriage that is asserted to be the tie that defines which families are legitimate.

For some critics of the status quo, the issue is the inclusion of alternatives to the husband-wife dyad within the category of marriage. For others, the question is marriage itself as a legal construct that carries with it significant societal benefits. Why should marriage be so privileged? Some proponents of abolishing marriage as a legal category argue that marriage should be replaced by contract in the first instance, allowing couples to structure their own relationships in the ways they want. According to this position, there is no reason for the state to be involved in the articulation and imposition of those terms any more than it would be involved in the enforcement of contracts in general.

Feminists might also point out that one of the state's historic interests in the institution was to use regulation of marriage and divorce to mediate relations of dependency between husbands and wives. Since wives are no longer dependent persons, confined to home and hearth, there is no longer any appropriate rationale for the state's involvement in marriage. Given aspirations of gender equality, which posits that couples are capable of making their own marital terms and freely deciding when and for what reasons to dissolve their relationships, it should be they, not the state, who make determinations about their relationship. What is, what should be, left of marriage as a status in modern American society? What societal purposes could state intervention and regulation of marriage serve in a no-fault, prenuptial, gender-egalitarian world? Shouldn't private lives be left to private ordering—to contract?

Further indicating to many that it is time for a serious reassessment of marriage and its role in society is the fact that marriage drags along with it certain historic assumptions about the institution and its members that limit the coherent development of family policy. Marriage also impedes other policy formation; it is offered as the social policy resolution for poverty in welfare debates. Marriage may in fact be the only clear and consistent family policy idea developed in the United States. The existence of the institution and assumptions surrounding it distort our policy and politics. The theoretical availability of marriage interferes with the development of other solutions to social problems involving children and poverty.

As the various (and by no means exhaustive) meanings of marriage listed in this chapter indicate, marriage is expected to do a lot of work in our society. It is not to quibble that much of this work must be done. Children must be cared for and nurtured, dependency must be addressed, and individual happiness is of general concern. However, we should be asking ourselves as we consider each of these tasks: What does marriage have to do with it? Is the existence of the institution of marriage, in and of itself, essential to accomplishing any of the societal goals or objectives we seek to bring about?

In this chapter I argue that for all relevant and appropriate societal purposes, we do not need marriage and we should abolish it as a legal category, transferring the social and economic subsidies and privilege it now receives to a new family core connection—that of the caretaker-dependent. In making this proposal I want to be very clear about two things. First, to state that we do not need legal marriage to accomplish many societal objectives is not the same things as saying that we do not need a family to do so for some. However, family as a social and legal category should not be dependent on having marriage as its core relationship. Nor is family synonymous with marriage.

Family affiliations are expressed in different kinds of acts, only some of which are legal. Some affiliations are sexually based, as with marriage. Some are forged biologically, as with parenthood, although this tie can be created legally through adoption also. Other affiliations are more relational in nature, such as those based on nurturing or caretaking or those developed through affection and acceptance of interdependence.

Second, even if we conclude we do not need marriage as a legal category, this does not mean that marriage as a societal institution would disappear. The symbolic dimension of marriage—the coming together of two individuals with vows of love and commitment—would most likely continue to exist as a social, cultural, and/or religious construct. Without legal status, however, marriage would no longer be the privileged mechanism whereby the state distributes certain social goods.

Why Marriage?

The marital family has designated functions within a society. It is also a significant status to many individuals. But what exactly is that marital family? What does it mean to society and to individuals as a practice as well as a politics?

In thinking about this question, it is important to remember that marriage is an institution susceptible to societal pressure and change. This means that marriage has a history of transformation and reconstitution that may be relevant to contemporary consideration of the relationship. Certainly marriage as both practice and aspiration is not the same institution today as it was for young people in the mid-twentieth century.

Consider how we as a contemporary, modern, and secular society might imagine the legal institution of marriage if we were able to work upon a clean slate, freed from the religious and common-law history of the institution. What would be our sense of the appropriate content, purpose, and function of this legal institution of modern marriage? One way to begin to answer that question is to look at what marriage does mean today on a cultural and social level, looking to see how people are "living marriage" in their everyday lives.

This line of inquiry might be pursued along two separate paths. First, what does the word "marriage" convey to us as individuals? In addressing this question, we look at marriage from a personal perspective—as a cultural and social practice in which we engage. Second, what does marriage convey to us collectively, as a society? From this perspective, we look at the functions that marriage performs on political, ideological, and structural levels—its construction as an institution in law and policy.

Related questions that might also be asked in making these inquiries include: How is it possible to have only one legal definition of marriage in a diverse, pluralistic, and secular society such as ours? Further, is marriage about behavior and functioning, or is it about legality and form? What does the legal designation of marriage foster, reform, facilitate, support, preserve, or protect?

Individual Meanings

Of course today to both individuals and society, marriage constitutes a legal relationship. The law defines some meanings of marriage for individuals. It is an exclusive and excluding institution—not everyone can enter. Through law the state establishes uniform standards for marriage, specifying who may marry whom and what formalities must be observed. In addition, law establishes the consequences of marriage at the dissolution of the relationship, be it by death or divorce. These consequences increasingly tend to be both relatively clear and susceptible to prediction by lawyers and others administering the system.

However, making predictions about the ultimate content and conduct of any given ongoing marriage—how a functioning marriage would look on a day-to-day basis from the perspectives of the individuals in the relationship—is far from a clear-cut task. Within the boundaries establishing entry into and exit from the institution, individuals are free to create a variety of meanings of marriage for themselves. This is because society through its laws has historically covered existing marriage relationships in a shroud of "privacy," shielding them from direct state micromanaging and supervision, which allows the conduct of marriages to vary widely. This concept of privacy still affects the way we think about the relationship between the state and the marital family.

For ongoing marriages, the norms for state-family relations are those of nonintervention and minimal regulation. There are exceptions to this norm of privacy, but most of them are fairly recent innovations, such as increased legal recognition and response to domestic abuse and neglect and removal of the common-law interspousal tort immunity that precluded one spouse from recovering from the other for negligently inflicted injuries. Other regulatory interventions into ongoing family relationships, such as the rules in *Trammel v. United States* that preclude spousal testimony in criminal cases, are trivial from the perspective of concern with institutional dynamics (Olson 1983).

In other ongoing formal and legal relationships—the relationship between shareholders and corporations, for example—there is no expectation of privacy. Rights and obligations are defined, limited, and structured so that the range and nature of interactions are predictable and potentially publicly enforceable even without dissolution. By contrast, the issuance of a marriage certificate does not determine the legally mandated conduct of the partners to any specific marriage. Modern marriage does not come with a charter of incorporation, bylaws, and an oversight body such as the Securities and Exchange Commission to interpret what the union means to its participants and to monitor how those participants fulfill their designated responsibilities and duties within the relationship.

The law governing marriage leaves the day-to-day implementation of marriage to the individual spouses. It is the conduct of the parties that defines their marriage, giving it content and meaning. Ongoing marriages are individualized, idiosyncratic arrangements. Even if external articulations in cultural institutions, such as the media, or religious imagery, might influence how some understand what constitutes an ideal marital relationship, these norms are not mandated and coercively imposed on individuals by law.

The doctrine of "marital privacy" facilitates and reinforces the individualized nature of ongoing marriage. For purposes of the discussion here it is only necessary to know that the doctrine provides that, except in extreme situations, there are no mechanisms of legal enforcement available to resolve disputes over the terms of an ongoing marital relationship. This is true even when the terms sought to be enforced are those that are established by the state—imposed in its "marital contract." So, while a wife might have a "right" to support under family law, she cannot enforce that right against her husband in a court of law (Weisberg and Appleton 2002). She may be able to use the doctrine of "necessaries" if she is able to persuade a third person, such as a merchant, to provide her with essential goods or services without her husband's consent and knowledge. In those instances, however, the action is the merchant's, not the spouse's. The doctrine of marital privacy mandates that the marital relationship be ruptured through some form of dissolution proceeding such as the divorce process before the right can be enforced in court (Fineman 1999, discussing *McGuire v. McGuire*).

I argue that in practice and in form marriage is as diverse as the inhabitants of our contemporary, secular state. Our legal doctrine and structures create a vacuum—an absence of legally mandated-meaning—leaving open for negotiation the content of every individual marriage. Couples fill this vacuum with various nonlegal and sometimes conflicting aspirations, expectations, fears, and longings. Reflection on the prospect of varied possibilities for the meaning of marriage suggests the institution's individualized and malleable nature.

Marriage, to those involved in one, can mean a legal tie, a symbol of commitment, a privileged sexual affiliation, a relationship of hierarchy and subordination, a means of self-fulfillment, a social construct, a cultural phenomenon, a religious mandate, an economic relationship, the preferred unit for reproduction, a way to ensure against poverty and dependence on the state, a way out of the birth family, the realization of a romantic ideal, a natural or divine connection, a commitment to traditional notions of morality, a desired status that communicates one's sexual desirability to the world, or a purely contractual relationship in which each term is based on bargaining. Of course, this is not an exhaustive list —there are many additional potential meanings for marriage, perhaps as many meanings as there are individuals entering, or not entering, the relationship.

Societal Meanings

The contemporary meaning of marriage is no easier to pin down and ascertain if we look at it from a societal, rather than an individual or legal, perspective. It is true that there are more public justifications for marriage from society, but marriage also has multiple potential meanings to the society that constructs and contains it. In fact, the express, explicit reasons for marriage from society's perspective have not changed all that much over time. Some are mundane, such as the need for a certain formal record keeping and for the assignment of responsibilities and rights among persons (e.g., to facilitate property transfers at death or identify persons responsible for payment of household debts).

There are some benefits for society expressed through its interest in marriage in regard to public health. The application for a marriage license can also be the occasion for mandatory health screening or counseling on genetics. It can be used for social engineering purposes, such as to supply information on the importance of marriage or to educate couples about the purported negative impact on their children, should they have any, from any future decision to separate and divorce.

Other societal justifications for marriage are more sweeping and abstract and, thus, perhaps also more questionable. Marriage, it has been argued, is an effective method of containing and harnessing (male) sexuality in the interests of the larger society (Cohen 1995). Sociobiologists (and some legal and policy analysts) view men as naturally polygamous and aggressive when it comes to sexual conquest. The expression of such "innate" qualities would result in violence toward other males and ultimate abandonment of women and their children by a mate in pursuit of new conquests (Thornhill and Palmer 2000). In assigning responsibility for a woman and her children to one man, marriage channels his socially acceptable sexual expression and frees the energy he might otherwise expend in sexual activity for socially productive work.

Such assertions present complex theoretical and empirical issues. Do men in *this* society at *this* time in history, given our *existing* sets of cultural, economic, and social relationships desire and need intimate connections with women and children? If so, is their need for such connection with women different from and more complicated than mere sexual desire? Can men care about children independent of those children's role as carriers of genes into the next generation? If the answer to such questions is yes, then the male need and desire for intimate connections may not require the loose and tenuous bonds modern marriage supplies. In addition, it may be noted that even if men do not need intimate connection and the sociobiologists are right, it is not the end of the matter. The so-called male problematic—men abandoning women and children—need not be problematic if there is social and economic support for those women and children from other sources. If women and children do not need physical protection from predators in modern American society and have access to material and other goods, it may not matter if men leave them, at least not to their ultimate survival.

This mention of the needs of children brings to the fore an important and historic state interest in marriage. The institution of the marital family has been the traditional site for the socially essential reproductive process. Reproduction clearly entails important societal interests—society must reproduce itself and often creates policies that encourage women to have children. Society is also rightly concerned with the ways in which those children are educated and disciplined into productive workers, voters, and citizens, tasks traditionally undertaken by the marital family. In fact, the state interest in children continues to be used to justify state regulatory interest in the marital family.[1] As more and more nonmarital families perform this important task, however, it becomes increasingly difficult to use marital status as a basis for distinction in the allocation of social goods to children and parents.

Of course, if there is some demonstrable harm to children or others—clear links between cause and effect—associated with the absence of marriage or its replacement with an alternative relationship, then that fact might provide an argument for some state-provided incentives for marriage. However, the harm alleged should be something more concrete than an affront to an abstract sense of morality or to the symbolic order preferred by some officials. In any case, even if there was some harm, that would not necessarily support negative regulation and prohibition of alternatives. Quite the contrary. If our concern is really with the well-being of children, then we should have policies in place that seek to put alternatives to marriage on an equal footing with that relationship in regard to social subsidy and support. We should strive to see that children are not disadvantaged merely by the form of the family in which they find themselves.

One reason increasingly offered for maintaining marriage in its privileged position is that the weakening of that institution is potentially harmful to society itself. Marriage is argued to be an essential institution for democracy. This argument, based in political theory, is supported by "evidence" largely historical in nature. Proponents of the position that marriage provides the "seedbed" of democracy bolster their arguments with ringing declarations about its position as the "most important relation in life," traceable back to nineteenth-century Supreme Court decisions like *Maynard v. Hill*[2] and *Reynolds v. United States*.[3] They also, not surprisingly, resort to statements by various Founding Fathers about the need for a "moral" nation in order to have democracy flourish (Wardle 2003, 3).

It seems however, that the coup de grâce of nineteenth-century sentiments about marriage is the assessment of Alexis de Tocqueville. He wrote in 1835 that there was "no other country in the world where the tie of marriage is more highly or worthily appreciated," and that "the American derives from his own home that love or order which he afterwards carries with him into public affairs." To some, Tocqueville on American matrimony bolsters the connection between marriage and freedom (Wardle 2003).

These arguments conflate marriage and family (and also virtue and marriage). Having done so, they fail to recognize that even if marriage was central in the nineteenth century, it may not be so today—this is the very move that the current debate about marriage and family seeks to interrogate. Perhaps the institution of marriage was assumed central in discussions about the necessity of "domestic habits" as "necessary 'preconditions' for maintaining the constitutional Republic" (Wardle 2003, 3) in the nineteenth century, but merely reiterating ancient platitudes does not adequately respond to today's critics.

Those who urge that marriage is essential to democracy are using nineteenth-century arguments based on nineteenth-century institutions—historic notions of what constitutes democracy, virtue, marriage, and family. Our democracy in the nineteenth century denied all women and a good number of men the right to vote and otherwise participate in political life. Our virtuous nation and its Constitution legitimated slavery. So, too, the marriage invoked was the common-law version reflecting a very different sort of sensibilities—lifelong, patriarchal, and hierarchical. Even if called by the same name, the institution of the nineteenth century is certainly not the vision of marriage we have today. Neither marriage nor democracy has remained constant in definition over time and across changes in our political and legal culture.

Finally (and I believe this is the real issue for many advocating its centrality), marriage can have important expressive meaning for a society, reflecting its moral or religious conventions. This role, however, seems the most problematic for a diverse and secular state such as the United States, which considers policy issues under a constitutional system mandating separation of church and state. This separation between religion and the state is particularly significant and important when marriage is the means whereby the state distributes significant economic benefits. And it is not only the economic relationship between husband and wife that the state shapes through marriage. It also structures the relationship between state and its citizens (as husbands or wives). For example, in considering the legal significance of marriage, the Supreme Court of Vermont listed a variety of interests or relations affected by marriage:

> the right to receive a portion of the estate of a spouse who dies in testate and protection against disinheritance through elective share provisions; preference in being appointed as the personal representative of a spouse who dies intestate; the right to bring a lawsuit for the wrongful death of a spouse; the right to bring an action for loss of consortium; the right to workers' compensation survivor benefits; the right to spousal benefits statutorily guaranteed to public employees, including health, life, disability, and accident insurance; the opportunity to be covered as a spouse under group life insurance policies issued to an employee; the opportunity to be covered as the insured's spouse under an individual health insurance policy; the

right to claim an evidentiary privilege for marital communications; home-stead rights and protections; the presumption of joint ownership of prop-erty and the concomitant right of survivorship; hospital visitation and other rights incident to the medical treatment of a family member; and the right to receive, and the obligation to provide, spousal support, mainte-nance, and property division in the event of separation or divorce. (*Baker v. State,* 744 A.2d 864 (Vt. 1999))

The list encompasses not only the reciprocal economic relationship be-tween spouses but also the significance of the couple's relationship in regard to claims they can make on third parties, such as landlords and tortfeasors. It demonstrates the premise that marriage also conveys access to benefits and subsidies from the state for a spouse.

Considering the role of the institution of the family in the allocation of these and other economic goods,[4] it becomes particularly important to ask why one religious group's sense of what is moral or divinely ordained should act to limit the options and possibilities for us all. Why should marriage be the price of entry into state support and subsidy? Why define the family through this connection?

Arguing Meanings

People are not always clear about which of the many ways of thinking about marriage inform the arguments that they make. It is legitimate to demand that our policymakers and politicians be specific about the roles or functions they ascribe to marriage as they tinker with the institution. How do they understand marriage from a societal perspective, and how are they filling the marriage-meaning void as the institution relates to in-dividuals?

It may be the case that some advocates of privileging marriage are sub-stituting an individualized meaning for a societal rationale in their sup-port for the institution. I argue that only societal rationales should be considered legitimate in fashioning society-wide regulations and rules associated with the institution of marriage. So long as we leave the infu-sion of meaning into marriage to the individuals engaged in the institu-tion one couple at a time, the state should maintain a neutral stance. State privileging is justified only when there is a corresponding legitimate state interest in the institution. Therefore, society must justify the expression of its interest in marriage through regulation and subsidy. What exactly is the state interest? should be the first question; the second is, Why is this particular intervention necessary to preserve or manifest it?

In regard to the historic societal-based rationales for state involvement with marriage, some, perhaps most, may no longer seem appropriate in our changing world. For example, a couple may want to marry because marriage means access to state subsidy in the form of economic and social benefits not available to other forms of sexual affiliation. The same couple may also want to marry because of the institution's meaning to them as individuals: a symbolic, cultural, or religious manifestation of their relationship that will affirm their commitment to each other.

If they are a same-sex couple, however, some religious leaders and politicians will oppose such a marriage. On the one hand, they may do so because they regard marriage as a natural, divinely ordained relationship (an individualized, religious meaning). On the other hand, they may do so because they view the subsidies of marriage as appropriately confined to heterosexual couples who form reproductive units (a moral or tradition-based societal meaning).[5] It is at this point that the debate should begin. Individual meaning should not remove the need for the state to articulate a societal reason for exclusion of same-sex couples from the economic benefits the state confers through the institution of marriage. I would argue that if we are to keep marriage as a legal and privileged tie in a secular state such as ours, the state may appropriately allow religious leaders to deny the ceremonial blessings to a union of which they disapprove, but it may not correspondingly deny the secular legal and economic consequences of that status. It is illegitimate for the state to thus discriminate against same-sex couples merely because they fail to fit within the traditional, religious definition of marriage.

Given the recognition and openness of same-sex relationships, as well as the rise of other alternatives, and the general decline of the traditional family, the issue is whether the historic role of marriage as the exclusive mechanism to provide certain economic benefits and protections can be appropriately maintained. This was the question that set off the line of reasoning used in *Baehr v. Lewin* and *Baker v. State,* the Hawaii and Vermont cases in which the supreme courts of those states mandated that same-sex couples be entitled to all the privileges and benefits conferred on marital couples. Looking at the current state of both marriage and patterns of intimate behavior, the majorities in those cases concluded that the state must either open up that institution to same-sex couples or create a nonmarriage category that confers all the economic benefits of that status.

The allocation of state economic benefits was not to be limited by the moral or historical and traditional meanings of marriage.

The questions faced by the courts in those cases—the questions the rest of us have been avoiding thus far—included a consideration of when history and tradition should give way to new patterns of behavior (such as nonmarital and same-sex cohabitation), as well as a reflection on the broader issue of when laws should mirror a purely moral condemnation. This consideration is particularly compelling when there is no societal consensus as to whether the conduct in question is immoral. As the Hawaii majority in *Baehr* noted, "[C]onstitutional law may mandate, like it or not, that customs change with an evolving social order."

As illustrated in this example, the questions associated with a modern consideration of marriage might become more complicated and difficult to answer if we must first reveal the meaning (or meanings) we assign to the institution of marriage. This type of consideration forces our focus away from the historic, symbolic nature or form of the marital relationship to the role or function we want the institution of the family to serve in our society. It also reveals that we are making certain assumptions about the capabilities and capacities of marriage as distinguished from other types of family relationships in society—assumptions that may no longer be warranted about its unique ability to accomplish certain societal functions.

Further, if we are clear about our expectations for and assumptions about marriage, it may become apparent that marriage is not the tie that warrants our concern. If we are concerned with dependency and want to ensure caretaking through social and economic subsidy of family, then why not focus on the relationship of caretaker and dependent? It is not necessary to support this unit indirectly through marriage when we can do so directly with policies that address the caretaker-dependent relationship.

The Law of Marriage

Of course, as the Hawaii and Vermont experiences indicate, when it comes to marriage, we do not have a clean slate. Nor do we have an institution consistent in nature and form over time. There is a lot of writing on the wall, much of it in legalese in the form of the special rules of "family law." Not surprisingly, given the way we have historically divided up the world into public and private, the law also reflects the notion of separate spheres.

This legal division complements the political and theoretical tendencies to distinguish the rules that apply to the family from those that structure the state and the market. Law has conformed to the assumption that each of these distinct spheres demands specialized rules focused on the unique issues and institutional arrangements contained within. While the market and state are concerned with the law of contract and property, mediated by notions of due process and equity, the law of the family is rooted in the status of marriage.

The special laws that apply to the family are consistent with the idea that it is an autonomous, separate, and self-sufficient entity. The unique nature of these rules has been justified by reference to the family's relational aspects and its intimate nature. In fact, "family law" can be thought of as a system of exemptions from the everyday rules that would apply to legal interactions among people in a nonfamily context, such as the law of contract and tort, as well as criminal law, property law, and rules of equity. These exemptions are complemented by the imposition of a set of special family obligations. Law defines the responsibilities of family members toward one another and the claims or rights they have, placing more duties on them vis-à-vis each other than would apply were they strangers.[6] It is not surprising, therefore, that one typical subject of family law literature has been how to use law to redefine, reform, or regulate intrafamily dynamics.

But family law does more than confer rights, duties and obligations within the family. It also assumes and reflects a certain type of relationship between family and state. As noted earlier in this section, during the nineteenth century this relationship was typically cast as one of "separate spheres." Family (the private sphere) and state (the public sphere) were perceived as largely independent of one another. This metaphor of separation reflected an ethic or ideology of family privacy in which state intervention was the exception.

The characterization of the family as autonomous—distinct and separate from the state—still resonates in our rhetoric about families. The family is designated the quintessentially "private" institution. Family is distinguished from both the market and the state (the quintessentially public institution) by its privateness. In a sense, privacy is what defines the family, sets it apart from other societal entities, and gives it coherence as a concept. For the modern private family, protection from public interference remains the articulated norm—in cases like *Griswold v. Connecticut* and *McGuire v. McGuire*, state intervention continues to be cast as exceptional, requiring some justification. However, privacy has not been awarded to just any group considering itself a family. The contour of the family entitled to protection through privacy was historically defined as the reproductive unit of husband and wife, giving primacy to the marital tie. It was anticipated that this basic pairing would eventually be complemented by the addition of children. In earlier times others, such as apprentices or servants, might "join" the family (Demos 1979, 43–60). Extended family members, such as elderly parents or unmarried siblings, also may have been incorporated into the family once its basic tie was forged. The legitimate family, however—the one entitled to privacy and protection—was defined in the first instance through marriage.

Defining the Family

While there might have been some consensus about the superiority of the marital family over other forms at some point in our nation's history (at least among political and economic elites), today there is much disagreement about just who should be considered "family." The traditional core of husband and wife (with or without children) seems to qualify under all definitions of family. In fact this reproductive unit is considered by many people to represent the "natural" and essential form of the family. Some people argue that it should also be considered an exclusive vision of family in terms of policy and law (Wardle 1996; Pham 1996; Nielsen 1990). In spite of the tendency of traditionalists to continue to equate *the* family with the marital family, family-like intimate entities, on an empirical level, come in many different forms.

The most recent census data for the United States reveal that for the first time in our nation's history less than a quarter of households are made up of married couples with their children (Fields and Casper 2001).[7] This is the form of family labeled by the census bureau as "traditional." Commentators point out that this can be the result of a number of factors, such as couples living longer after their adult children have "left the nest," many men and women delaying marriage and children until they are older than in previous generations, and the relatively more rapid growth of single-parent families over those of married parents. The number of married-couple families with children grew by just under 6 percent in the 1990s. By contrast, families with children headed by single mothers increased by 25 percent during the same period, accounting for nearly 7 percent of all households. Single-mother families increased from 3 million in 1970 to 10 million in 2000 (Fields and Casper 2001). These families are not centered around sexual affiliations. They are caretaking units and reflect increases in nonmarital births and the continued relatively high divorce rate in the United States.

Empirically, it also seems that marriage is a less dominant form of intimate connection for heterosexual couples than in the past. The number of heterosexual unmarried couples has increased geometrically over the past few decades. Census figures indicate that in 2000, 3.8 million households were classified as unmarried-partner households. In 1970 there were only 523,000 such households identified (Fields and Casper 2001). Many of these cohabiting couples are also caretaking units and have children. In fact, according to the census data, about half of the children living with cohabiting parents are living with both their biological parents (Fields 1996). Others live with one biological parent and his or her cohabitant, resembling a stepfamily situation.

Also growing at a rapid rate are those units designated as "nonfamily households," which consist of people living alone or with people to whom they are not affiliated or related in terms the Census Bureau recognizes. Growing at twice the rate of family households, these nonfamily households now make up about one-third of the total units (Fields and Casper 2001). Some of these households undoubtedly consist of same-sex partners who would obviously resent the label "nonfamily" being applied to their relationship. Since my objective is to replace the marital family and its sexual and reproductive affiliation as the core tie, with the caretaking family and its relationship of care and dependency as central to the objective of social policy, the sexual orientation of the adults within the entity is irrelevant. This chapter focuses on heterosexual marital relationships simply because family law and our political sense of family have been organized around that particular intimate configuration. Same-sex couples are organizing around demands for access to marriage, and this is increasingly a topic of scholarship.

Of course, other "nonfamily" units may have forms of intimate connection other than the sexual one—they may be families of choice forged through bonds of platonic affection. Such groupings may be constituted by nonsexual affiliates who are merely "friends" or household units composed of siblings or adult children and their elderly parents. These units may also be desirous of family status and the material and symbolic rewards it confers.

The census figures show us changed and changing forms of intimate connection, but understanding family is about more than awareness of the current demographics. The family has an institutional and cultural history, and for many, the term "family" represents a constellation of values and norms with far-reaching emotional and psychological significance.

It is the *marital* family that has historically been viewed as the foundation of society, as the "healthy" form of family essential for the well-being of the nation, as well as for individuals. Many in our society would not even count some of the units described in the census report under that category of families. Others might concede the designation but modify "family" with terms such as "broken" or "nonmarital," even "illegitimate," signifying that those units deviate from the ideal marital norm. For them, it is the traditional unit alone—based on the marriage of one man and one woman—that is indisputably entitled to the label "family."

This notion of the marital family as foundational to society has resonated across centuries in our legal rhetoric. It is reflected in the very organization of our laws and the nature of legal subjects constructed under them. Compare Justice Field's 1888 opinion in *Maynard v. Hill* that marriage "is an institution, in the maintenance of which in its purity the public is deeply interested, for it is the foundation of the family and of society, without which there would be neither civilization nor progress," with the language of a more recent court case. In *Feliciano v. Rosemar Silver Co.*, the court held that "[m]arriage is not merely a contract between the parties. It is the foundation of the family. It is a social institution of the highest importance. The Commonwealth has a deep interest that its integrity is not jeopardized."

We can also look to the privileged positioning of marriage in the welfare reform bill that came into effect in 1996 (the Personal Responsibility and Work Opportunity Act):

> Congress makes the following findings: (1) Marriage is the foundation of a successful society. (2) Marriage is an essential institution of a successful society, which promotes the interests of children. (Personal Responsibility and Work Opportunity Act of 1996 §101, 1996 HR 3734 (1996))

In the twenty-first century, our president echoes this ancient mantra, linking it to more focused concerns about the relationship between marriage and child well-being. The presidential initiatives have resulted in the passage of new, marriage-oriented legislation: bringing the issue of marriage onto the national stage, George W. Bush in March 2002 opined that too many families were fragile and broken. The president proposed spending $300 million to promote marriage as part of the reconsideration of the 1996 welfare reform that was scheduled (Sealey 2002). Bush called for funding programs that help couples work out their problems before and during marriage. His analysis was based on the following assertion: "You see, strong marriages and stable families are incredibly good for children, and stable families should be the central goal of American welfare policy." Promoting marriage was also part of the 1996 law that ended welfare as an entitlement, but only five states actually ended up using federal dollars for this purpose. As Congress prepares to hash out the reauthorization of the welfare law, marriage is more central, and a debate looms over what role government-sanctioned marriage promotion should play in fighting poverty.

Some commentators argued we would do much better to fight poverty more directly. According to the 2000 census figures, 6 percent of families with two parents lived in poverty, compared with 33 percent of families headed by single mothers. Responding to such figures and asserting that marriage is not the answer to relieve the poverty of women and children, feminist groups such as the National Organization for Women point out that poor women would benefit more from higher-wage jobs with good benefits than from premarital counseling.

Stephanie Coontz, national cochair of the Center for Contemporary Families, was also interviewed when the Bush proposals first surfaced. While not arguing against providing counseling for fragile families who cannot afford it, Coontz worried that marriage promotion would be stressed at the expense of what she considered "true anti-poverty programs."

Often, Coontz said, not being married is a symptom, not a root cause, of poverty. Her own research shows that men who become unwed fathers are more than twice as likely as married fathers to be unemployed and to have physical or psychological problems that interfere with their ability to hold jobs. In addition, unemployed men are far less likely than employed men to form and sustain stable relationships, while men who have stable jobs tend to seek mates who also have higher educational levels and earnings potential.

Coontz and other researchers point out that pushing marriage while failing to give parents long-term support systems may do more harm than good. "Job education and training are what people need," Coontz said. "It makes them more marriageable and makes marriages more likely to be stable but doesn't penalize children in those families if the marriage breaks up or they don't get married" (Sealey 2002). While good marriages may be positive, endorsing marriage at all costs could put children at risk of living in unhappy two-parent homes. Another potentially destructive consequence is setting children up for instability and disappointment when their parents' relationships fail. Statistics show that marriages and long-term relationships among poor adults are more at risk of breaking than those of financially stable citizens.

Marriage in Context

The American marital entity has an interesting lineage as a legal category. It is directly tied to one religious set of concepts and beliefs. Looking back into its legal history, we see that marriage was not created de novo as an American institution. As a legal relationship, its content and terms were drawn from British institutions that had evolved rules exemplifying rigid relationships (Krause et al. 1998, 47).

In England there was a direct historic connection between the state religion and the legal treatment of intimate relationships. Marriage was a sacrament administered by the church and subject to its rules. Under the common-law system in effect in England until fairly recently (as legal institutions go), issues concerning the creation and dissolution of marriage and other aspects of family formation were left to the ecclesiastical courts. It was not until the passage of the Matrimonial Causes Act of 1857 that jurisdiction over marriage and divorce was transferred to civil courts (Krause et al. 1998, 47).

Consistent with the precepts of their religious approach, these courts viewed marriage as a lifelong commitment. An annulment or, failing that, desertion, was virtually the only route out of an unhappy union (Krause et al. 1998, 533, on annulment; Friedman 1988, 204–8, 498–504, on desertion). The Church of England's ecclesiastical courts could grant a divorce "from bed and board," which allowed couples to live apart but not remarry (Krause et al. 1998, 534). Divorce was theoretically available, but only through a special act of Parliament, and between 1800 and 1836, an average of three such bills of divorce were granted each year (Weisberg and Appleton 2002, 533). Generally, access to divorce was limited until the late twentieth century.

This view of the presumed permanence of marriage was also evident in colonial America, where divorce could be granted by a secular judiciary, but this rarely happened (Weisberg and Appleton 2002, 533–34). In fact, prior to the mid-twentieth century in the United States, judicial divorce, although increasingly more common over time than in the colonial period, was available only for "cause." "Cause" could include adultery (in New York this was the only cause that justified divorce in 1787), as well as "impotence, adultery, intolerable severity, three years' willful desertion, and long absence with presumption of death" (Vermont in 1798) and "gross misbehavior and wickedness in either of the parties, repugnant to and in violation of the marriage covenant" (Rhode Island; Weisberg and Appleton 2002, 534).

An "innocent" spouse could ask the state to sever the marital tie when she or he was successful in demonstrating the "fault" of her or his mate. Fault grounds indicated there had been some egregious offense to the very marital union. States such as New York at that time permitted divorce only for very serious offenses that were considered to undermine the nature of the marital connection, such as adultery (Krause et al. 1998, 534). Other states considered the amorphous category of "cruelty" to be a sufficient basis for dissolution.[8] Colonial divorce laws varied considerably by region, with the northeastern states tending to be slightly more liberal than their southern neighbors (Krause et al. 1998, 534; Riley 1991, 8–29).

In the United States there was no established state religion, but the relationship between religious perceptions and beliefs about marriage and the construction of state principles regarding that connection were still evident, if attenuated. The individual states incorporated common-law concepts and definitions from the religiously shaped English rules into their laws governing family. American judges tracked the religious rhetoric of their English counterparts when considering issues involving the family.

Divine laws governed family relationships, setting out the natural order for the individuals who entered them.[9] The content of the marital relationship was also divinely structured. In what has become one of the most famous concurrences in the American legal tradition, in the 1873 Supreme Court case of *Bradwell v. Illinois,* Justice Bradley made what is still considered the classic statement regarding the common-law perception of the divinely determined distinct roles of husbands and wives:

[T]he civil law, as well as nature herself, has always recognized a wide difference in the respective spheres and destinies of men and woman. Man is, or

should be, woman's protector and defender. The natural and proper timid-
ity and delicacy which belongs to the female sex evidently unfits it for many
of the occupations of civil life. The constitution of the family organization,
which is founded in the divine ordinance, as well as in the nature of things,
indicates the domestic sphere as that which properly belongs to the domain
and functions of womanhood. The harmony, not to say the identity, of
interest and views, which belong, or should belong to the family institution
is repugnant to the idea of a woman adopting a distinct and independent
career from that of her husband. So firmly fixed was the sentiment in the
founders of the common law that it became a maxim of that system of
jurisprudence that a woman had no legal existence separate from her husband, who was regarded as her head and representative in the social state.[10]

As this passage so clearly illustrates, the marital family—the "traditional
family" of the common law and the Church of England—was defined by
distinct and hierarchical roles across gender.

The organization of the traditional family in the British and American
legal tradition was also patriarchal, with the husband—"head" of the family—owed obedience and domestic and sexual services from his wife. In
return, he was obligated to support her and their children. The husband's
role conferred rights as well as responsibilities, including the right to punish family members. Because he bore responsibility for their actions, a
husband had the right to reasonably chastise both wife and children. His
support obligations also gave him a corresponding right to the earnings
of his wife and children, and to control over their property (Blackstone,
442–45).

Further, the view of marriage expressed by Justice Bradley and the divinely ordained respective positions of the spouses also limited the expectations and opportunities for married women in the larger society. The
marital family's hierarchically organized and well-defined gender roles
placed the spouses in different spheres. Women, excluded from many of
the public aspects of life, were perceived as appropriately dependent. As
the Bradley concurrence in *Bradwell* expressed, their true calling was considered to be the home and family.[11]

This ordering of domestic life was intuitive—a response to the natural
dependency of women. Common law imposed disabilities on women that
supported this ordering of the world. Married women were not able to
own property or make contracts (Gottlieb 1993, 90–92). In some instances
they could not even be held responsible for their own torts or crimes.

Their husbands, perceived as controlling them absolutely, were charged instead (Krause et al. 1998, 152).

The common law expressed a structure in which the distinct specializations of the spouses complemented each other: the wage earner and the housewife; the protector and the protected; the independent and the dependent. Each spouse needed his or her complement in order to attain and maintain a whole, complete family entity, one that provided for all its members' needs. This specialization, bringing together the head and the heart of the family in the form of husband and wife, allowed the marital family to function in a self-sufficient manner, providing both economic and domestic resources to the unit.

This unequal, if complementary, positioning of men and women within the common-law family became problematic for women when divorce became more prevalent under no-fault statutes (Carbone and Brinig 1991). These statutes changed a fundamental aspect of marriage. Marriage in its common-law manifestation was considered a lifelong commitment, but no-fault divorces ushered in a revolution in our way of thinking about the permanence of the relationship of marriage. No-fault meant much easier access to divorce. In many states divorce became available on unilateral demand of one spouse even over the objection of the other that the relationship could be salvaged. Men who wanted to be free of their "faultless" wives (as determined under the previous fault divorce statutes) no longer had to bargain with those wives and buy their complicity in the divorce process through concession of property or other economic incentives.

Initiated by both wives and husbands, no-fault opened the divorce floodgate and exposed the economic vulnerability of the common-law assignment of ownership of all wages and property to the wage earner. Wives were not considered entitled to a share of property accumulated during the marriage, since they did not earn the money to buy it and typically title was in the husband's name. As a result, women found themselves and their children destitute at divorce (Weitzman 1985; *Wirth v. Wirth* (1971)).

The discouragement of married women from participation in the workplace and investment in a career under the *Bradwell* system also had more general negative economic implications. After a divorce, women found that they had to work in the marketplace as well as in the home, yet the old vision of marriage had discouraged them from honing the skills they needed to do so.

All this has changed, of course. The no-fault revolution coincided with another revolution in the way we understand the world—the gender equality movement, which ushered in massive changes in all phases of life, including marriage.

"Man and Wife": From Protected to Partnered

The move to no-fault divorce might have altered our view of marriage, but the gender equality revolution altered the way women perceive their societal, nonfamilial roles. It seems hard to believe that it was less than a century ago that women won important political and civil rights, such as the vote, which was achieved in 1920 with the passage of the Nineteenth Amendment. Even after women achieved the right to vote, they were still excluded from service on juries. Although the first women were summoned to jury service in 1870, as a rule, women were systematically denied or exempted from jury service for the next century, usually for reasons that were considered "benign" and "practical" (Hebard 1913; Grossman 1994). It was not until 1994, in *J.E.B. v. T.B.*, that the Supreme Court declared that peremptory challenges based on sex violate the equal protection clause of the Fourteenth Amendment.

Until recently, the common-law rule was that a woman's domicile (essentially her legal place of residence) was always the same as her husband's. This caused difficulty for many married women, as a person's domicile is used in determining numerous legal entitlements, categories, and qualifications. Because a woman's legal identity had traditionally been merged with that of her husband, her domicile was assigned based on her husband's place of residence, and a woman had no control over this determination. As divorce laws changed and women's destinies were less tied to the institution of marriage, the inappropriateness of this situation became more obvious. The common-law rule began to change in the 1970s, and the American Law Institute finally ratified this change in 1988.[12]

An important part of the move to gender equality involved women seeking to (or being forced to) forge an attachment to the workplace independent of marriage and husband. Many younger and well-educated women began to think of self-fulfillment and careers as their due, but certainly the instability of marriage after the introduction of no-fault divorce also helped to build momentum, pushing and pulling women out of the private family sphere and into the world of wage work. But in addition to altering expectations for women about work and career, the gender equality revolution had profound implications for the way we as a society view marriage and divorce.

Further, other rules beyond those governing divorce reflect the idea that women and men are equal. Massive changes have occurred in the workplace and other aspects of public life, which have had a profound impact on how women are perceived as actors both in the family and in the larger society. Women are no longer seen as incapable of bargaining and conducting business. Women have effectively undermined the idea that they are "unfit for the many occupations of civil life," in Justice Bradley's terms.

The view that women are competent in regard to business transactions has had an impact within, as well as without, the family. This has been particularly evident in the courts' changing approach to the validity of prenuptial agreements. Historically, in cases like *Stratton v. Wilson,* courts refused to recognize such agreements, asserting that they violated public policy by altering the essential aspects of marriage, specifically the support obligation. Judges were also concerned with the unequal bargaining position of women relative to men. As women gained the presumption of equality in the work world, "paternalistic" notions in the context of family law were eroded. Today such agreements are routinely enforced providing there is disclosure of financial information and meaningful consent to the terms.[13]

When applying these ideas in the context of real divorces, judges have explicitly recognized that women are equally capable of making valid contracts that alter the otherwise default legal rights and responsibilities of a marriage. In *Simeone v. Simeone* (1990) the court set aside the presumption that prenuptial agreements were invalid, acknowledging that society had changed in ways that required corresponding changes in the law:

There is no longer validity in the implicit presumption that supplied the basis for . . . earlier decisions. Such decisions rested upon a belief that spouses are of unequal status and that women are not knowledgeable enough to understand the nature of contracts that they enter. Society has advanced, however, to the point where women are no longer regarded as the "weaker" party in marriage, or in society generally. . . . Nor is there viability in the presumption that women are uninformed, uneducated, and readily subjected to unfair advantage in marital agreements. Indeed, women nowadays quite often have substantial education, financial awareness, income, and assets. . . . Accordingly, the law has advanced to recognize the equal status of men and women in our society . . . further, [earlier decisions]

embodied substantial departures from traditional rules of contract law. . . .
Prenuptial agreements are contracts, and, as such, should be evaluated
under the same criteria as are applicable to other types of contracts. Absent
fraud, misrepresentation, or duress, spouses should be bound by the terms
of their agreements.[14]

Prenuptial agreements came to enjoy a presumption of validity, as long as
they were made voluntarily and with full disclosure of financial information. Some courts still maintain the additional requirement that an agreement be substantively "fair" to both parties. Even while they do so, recognition is typically given to the changes in gender expectations. For
example, while the Supreme Court of Kentucky in *Edwardson v. Edwardson* maintained that the terms of prenuptial agreements must still be "fair,
reasonable, just, equitable, and adequate in view of the conditions and circumstances of the parties,"[15] it also observed that "the legal status of marriage partners is vastly different today,"[16] and that earlier cases had been
decided at a time when "the status of women in this society was decidedly
second class."[17]

The more modern approach is exemplified by the case of *In Re Marriage of Greenwald,* in which the Wisconsin Court of Appeals upheld a
prenuptial agreement that resulted in a highly unequal division of property between the parties, despite the fact that Wisconsin law in *Button v.
Button* had previously required that the division of the property at divorce
must be fair to each spouse. The *Greenwald* court based its decision on
the fact that at the time of contracting, both parties were fully aware of
each other's financial situation, and that they had intentionally created an
agreement that would keep their property separate and allow it to pass to
their respective lineal heirs rather than to each other. The court stated that
if a person would have entered into the marriage anyway, and if the agreement was freely and voluntarily made, then "we see no sound reason why
the law should later intervene and undo the parties' contract." Rather than
uphold the (newly) traditional presumption of equal property division, the
court recognized that as equals, the parties had the right to make an agreement that was intended to have an unequal result in the event of a divorce.

Several uniform laws also explicitly recognize the ascendancy of a contractual view of marriage, based on the parties' equal status. The Uniform
Premarital Agreement Act of 1983 states that premarital agreements should
be enforced as long as they are voluntary, the terms are not unconscionable, there was fair and reasonable disclosure of the parties' property and

financial obligations, and the agreement does not cause either party to become eligible for public assistance or support. Note the limited possibility of a fairness review in this model legislation. A court would retain the right to modify such agreements, even if otherwise valid, to the extent necessary to require a party to financially support a former spouse to the extent necessary to prevent that person from transferring his or her economic dependency onto the state.

A key recent statement on this issue from a national body is found in the Principles of the Law of Family Dissolution, drafted by the American Law Institute (ALI), which is composed of lawyers, judges, and policymakers. The ALI recommends that married couples, as well as those in domestic partnerships, be allowed to "accommodate their particular needs and circumstances by contractually altering or confirming the legal rights and obligations that would otherwise arise."[18] This ability would be "subject to constraints that recognize competing policy concerns and limitations in the capacity of parties to appreciate adequately, at the time of the agreement, the impact of its terms under different life circumstances."[19] Like the Uniform Premarital Agreement Act and the majority of case law, the ALI recognizes that married couples, like unmarried domestic partners, are qualified to make agreements that modify the traditional obligations that attend such relationship. It also recognizes, however, that the state might want to reserve the right to oversee and amend these agreements in conformance with public policy to a much greater degree than is permitted with commercial contracts that arise in the public sphere of the market.

As the evolution in the rules governing the acceptance of premarital contracts indicates, marriage is becoming more and more like other legal relationships in regard to the individual's ability to create or limit responsibilities and risks through contract. With the recognition of equality between women and men, we assume parity in bargaining capacity on the part of individuals entering these relationships and no longer see a need for the protective intervention of the state.

A further twist on the changing significance of the formal marriage tie to define relationships, and consistent with the trend blurring the historic lines for family-like connections, we now see nonmarital relationships between sexual affiliates being given marriage-like consequences. Equitable or implied contractual principles result in allocation of property or other economic adjustments at the termination of a nonmarital cohabitation relationship in ways similar to the rules that apply upon divorce in many states, as illustrated by the California case *Marvin v. Marvin*. In its

Principles, the ALI recommends that when domestic partners terminate their partnership, their property be defined and divided by the same body of rules by which this process would occur if the parties were legally married.[20] Domestic partners are defined as "two persons of the same or opposite sex, not married to one another, who for a significant period of time share a primary residence and a life together as a couple."[21]

Unlike the Vermont statute following *Baker v. State,* which recognizes civil unions for same-sex couples and grants them the "common benefits and protections that flow from marriage under Vermont law," the ALI's Principles include all domestic partnerships, whether the parties are same-sex or opposite-sex nonmarital couples. The rules also do not require registration or any kind of formal affiliational act, which further distinguishes the ALI Principles from the Vermont statutory scheme.

In fact, the ALI Principles create a presumption based on certain behavior that people who are living together are domestic partners:

> Persons not related by blood or adoption are presumed to be domestic partners when they have maintained a common household . . . for a continuous period [of specified duration]. The presumptive is rebuttable by evidence that the parties did not share life together as a couple."[22]

Sharing life as a couple is determined by reference to such things as representations to others, intermingling finances, a relationship that fostered economic interdependence or dependence, the assumption of specialized or collaborative roles in furtherance of their life together, emotional or physical intimacy, and other factors indicating commitment even without a formal declaration of such.

The point is that it is not the formal status of marriage, or even a certificate or registration process that is being used to assess rights and responsibilities, but the nature and quality of the relationship that the partners have crafted. There is, at least on a theoretical level, less and less need for a well-established system of default rules imposed by the state.

Backlash

The move to a more liberal divorce process has generated a backlash that extends beyond the transformations in the institution of marriage to the whole concept of gender equality that undergirds many of those changes. Religious pockets of resistance are particularly visible; they seek to restore not only the lifelong aspect of marriage but also its patriarchal organization.

One of the most extreme expressions of this backlash is the growth of the Promise Keepers movement, a Christian men's group that claims to be "committed to building strong marriages and families through love, protection and biblical values."[23] The Promise Keepers believe that these changes will be accomplished by a return to the traditional family structure in which the husband is the head of the household and the wife is subservient and obedient to him in all ways.[24]

The Southern Baptist religion has also demonstrated a growing commitment to the return to traditional marital roles. At the Southern Baptist Convention in Salt Lake City in 1998, a majority of the attendees declared their adherence to Paul's words to husbands and wives. The first word was to wives, who are instructed to "[s]ubmit yourselves to your own husbands, as to the Lord." This was interpreted by the delegates to the convention as calling for a *voluntary yielding in love* on the part of the wife. Husbands are not directed to subjugate wives; rather, wives are directed "to take submission into their own hands." This state of affairs is viewed not as benefiting the husband, at least not primarily, but as consistent with God's natural order of things—"a mirror of the relationship between Christ and church" (Brand 1998).

Feminist criticism of such a positioning was noted during discussions of this position but was dismissed because even though such objections may raise "sensitive and important issues . . . none of them is substantial enough to move Bible-believing Christians away from affirming the truths [Paul teaches]" (Brand 1998, 3). Feminist theologians and others who favor a more egalitarian approach to marriage have been accused of taking a position that

> assumes the egalitarian worldview and then "hijacks" the Bible to make it fit. Texts are either accepted, rejected, ignored, revised according to the way they fit in with that motif . . . a mistake of the greatest gravity [because] it is plain that while the Bible teaches equality, it does *not* affirm egalitarianism or interchangeability in all things, but rather calls for distinguishable roles between men and women. (Brand 1998, 4; emphasis in the original)

The Promise Keepers treat feminists even more harshly. A prominent Promise Keepers leader has said: "I believe that feminists of the more aggressive persuasion are frustrated women unable to find the proper male leadership. If a woman were receiving the right kind of love and attention and leadership, she would not want to be liberated from that."[25] In this view, women, like children, are not equals, but dependents who must be guided and controlled.

Even if pro-traditional-marriage and antidivorce sentiments are not based in religion, as they are with the Promise Keepers, assertions about the significance of marriage abound. These ideas do not exist in isolation but are also an integral part of systems of belief about the appropriate ordering of the world. Some members of society believe that the no-fault divorce laws have gone too far in that people can now marry without serious consideration of the consequences (since they know they can leave the relationship more easily than before) and can divorce too quickly without trying to address solvable problems in their marriage.

Part of the political backlash against no-fault divorce has resulted in the introduction in Louisiana and a few other states of something called "covenant marriage," which has been described as "part of a larger effort to redefine and bolster traditional marriage in order to reduce divorce, unwed mothering and single parenthood" (Sanchez 2001, 194). Covenant marriage is an attempt to create a situation that is described as supporting the more "traditional" vision of marriage, in that it is more than just a return to the former fault-based requirements for divorce.

Couples who wish to enter a covenant marriage must attend premarital counseling, after which they must produce a notarized affidavit signed by them and their counselor indicating that they have discussed topics relating to the seriousness of marriage. They also must sign a "Declaration of Intent" that affirms the following principles:

> [A] marriage is an agreement to live together as husband and wife forever; the partners chose each other carefully and disclosed to each other everything about their personal histories that might hurt the marriage; the couple received premarital counseling from a priest, minister, rabbi, or state-recognized marriage counselor; and that the partners agree to take all reasonable efforts to preserve their marriage if they experience marital difficulties. (La. Rev. Stat. Ann. § 9:273(A))

Although the name evokes religious imagery, covenant marriage, proposed and passed by the legislature, is a legal entity rather than a religious construction. It is an alternative to the marriage in operation under the no-fault divorce system, presumably more difficult to dissolve. Despite the fact that it is available to all Louisianans who apply for a marriage license, it appears that covenant marriage has not become widespread since its introduction in 1997. One survey, done in 1998, showed that only 1.5 percent of new marriages were covenant marriages, and some people believed the entire idea was just "a cynical attempt by legislators to cater to pro-family constituencies without having a real effect" (Sanchez 2001, 221).

In spite of the backlash trends, the liberalization of divorce rules is likely to persist. As statistics reveal, Americans freely take advantage of access to no-fault divorce, and census figures show that nonmarital cohabitation continues to grow in popularity as an alternative to marriage (Fields and Casper 2001). It seems clear that marriage no longer represents the lifelong commitment it reflected in the common law, nor do many women now expect that entering into marriage will be, for them, a relationship of domination and subordination.

Rethinking the Relationship of State to Marriage

The shift to a more individual and egalitarian form of marriage raises the question of whether the institution should continue to be given a preferred status by the state vis-à-vis other affiliative relationships. Marriage certainly does not have the same relevance as a societal institution that it did even fifty years ago, when it was the primary means of protecting and providing for the legal and structurally devised dependency of wives and children.

How should these changes affect our perceptions of marriage? Covenant marriage offers an instance where the state establishes two legal forms of marriage from which couples can choose. Why stop with two? We could open up the category of marriage to the alternative arrangements that people are now practicing. On the other hand, we might take seriously the idea that adults should be free to fashion the terms of their own relationships and rely on contract as the means of so doing, effectively replacing the marital status with actual negotiation and bargaining building on the increased acceptance of premarital agreements.

What are the advantages of abolishing marriage as a legal category? For one thing, it would make policy conform to our modern aspirations. On an individual level, abolishing legal marriage and the special rules associated with it would mean that we are taking gender equality seriously. If people want their relationships to have consequences, they should bargain for them, and this is as true with sexual affiliates as with others who interact in complex ongoing interrelationships, such as employers and employees. This would mean that sexual affiliates (formerly labeled husband and wife) would be regulated by the terms of their individualized agreements, with no special rules governing fairness and no unique review or monitoring of the negotiation process. This is common with prenuptial agreements and is doctrinally required (even if not typically practiced) with settlement agreements.

It is possible to view this call for the abolition of marriage as a demand for private ordering. But a proposal for the abolition of marriage as a legal category involves much more than just a simple preference for privatization of potential economic consequences. It is a step necessary for gender equality. Abolishing marriage as a legal category would not mean there would remain no protection for the economically weaker party.

For example, the interests of a cohabitant who contributed to the accumulation of wealth for the other even if she did not have a contract would be protected to some extent by default and equity rules. General regulatory rules, such as those found in equity (such as unjust enrichment or constructive trust), partnership, and labor law could provide rules for decisions in disputes involving sexual affiliates. Constitutional and civil rights law offer some suggestive possible parameters for exploration of potential economic consequences of joint endeavors undertaken by those who formerly would have been exempt as family members. I am uncommitted to any particular set of principles for these default rules at this time. The only requirement would be that they apply to all types of transactions between legally competent adults and that specific categories of affiliation not be segregated for different treatment.

In other words, in addition to contract rules, I anticipate that ameliorating doctrines would fill the void left by the abolition of this aspect of family law. In fact, it seems apparent that a lot more regulation (protection) would occur once interactions between individuals within families were removed from behind the veil of privacy that now shields them. For example, without the defense of marriage, there would be no justification for not applying the regular rules of tort and criminal law to sexual affiliates.

Feminists have been pointing out for more than a century that the institution of marriage is the location of much abuse and violence. This is not surprising in an institution that is based on an unequal and hierarchical social arrangement in which men are considered the heads of households, with power and authority over wives and children. Once the institutional protection is removed, behavior would be judged by standards established to regulate interactions among all members of society.

What would be the practical implications of abolishing marriage from this perspective? Marriage, since it would be no longer available as a legal status, would no longer be considered a defense to rape. It would also be more problematic to conceptually bracket off some assaults as "domestic" violence, rendering them somehow less serious than the nondomestic variety. In the past, certain types of domestic violence were not even considered criminal behavior. Husbands had not only a right but also a duty to chastise and punish wives and children. Physical chastisement was considered appropriate as long as it did not exceed certain limits. This principle is often suggested as the basis for the "rule of thumb" reform in which a man was admonished not to beat his wife with a rod thicker than his thumb.

Perhaps we would even begin to develop theories of tort to compensate sexual affiliates for conduct endemic to family interactions but considered unacceptable among strangers. A tort for intentional infliction of emotional or psychological harm might emerge.[26] Norms that prohibit harassment (including stalking), verbal assault, and emotional abuse among strangers would be applied in defining appropriate conduct between sexual intimates. Other areas of law that would substitute for (or be supplemented by) the abolition of marriage and divorce rules would include bankruptcy, fiduciary responsibility, equity, and ethics.

In a completely different vein, the end of marriage as a state-regulated and state-defined institution would undermine, perhaps entirely erode, the state interest in controlling and regulating sexual affiliations. If no form of sexual affiliation were preferred, subsidized, and protected by the state, none should be prohibited. Same-sex partners and those forming other arrangements such as multiple-partner sexual affiliations would just be viewed as forms of privately chosen and individually preferred sexual connection. Such unions might be celebrated in religion or culture, but the state would have no regulatory interest. The substantial economic and other societal benefits currently afforded to certain heterosexual units would no longer be justified, and punishment of "deviant" sexual connections would no longer be permitted. The exceptions to this general principle should be obvious—rape and child molestation would still be prohibited and punished by law.

In addition, some other types of family formation that are currently interpreted through norms of heterosexual marriage would also be opened
up with the abolition of marriage. Single motherhood in particular would
be unregulated. Without marriage, motherhood would not be modified
by the existence of a legal relationship between heterosexual partners.
There would be no "single" mothers unfavorably differentiated in policy
and politics from "married" mothers—only the unmodified category of
"mothers." Women would be free to become pregnant without fear that
a paternity proceeding would be mandatorily begun, even against the
wishes of the parents and in disregard for their privacy, so that the state
could fill in the blank under "father's name" on a birth certificate. Sperm
banks and specialists in reproductive technologies, including artificial in-
semination and fertility treatments, would not feel that the martial status
of their patients was an appropriate item for ethical or professional concern. This method of reproduction might be preferred once such restraints were removed. It avoids any questions about "consent" vis-à-vis
the sperm donor, since he would have alienated his interest in his contribution of reproductive material by his donation to the sperm bank.

In addition to freeing women from the heterosexual marriage para-
digm in their reproductive lives, the abolition of marriage as a legal category would have other implications. Contract language is often used to
discuss the family, particularly in modern family law jurisprudence where
marriage is referred to as a "partnership," and some of the economic consequences may be tailored to individual preferences through prenuptial
contracts and/or separation agreements. However, the rules seem more
anchored in the role-defined common-law concepts of status. The status
of wife carries with it assumptions about what is owed—notions about
obligations and duties that arise merely from a woman's occupation of
that position. It is interesting to note, from the perspective of contract as a
metaphor for bargaining, that status encompasses and defines those
human activities in which women might be considered to have either a
"natural" monopoly or to possess more on the "supply" than the "demand" side of the equation. More specifically, these areas were set aside
and governed by special rules regulating marriage. Paying women for
reproduction, as with surrogacy contracting, is not allowed. Likewise, contracts or agreements to pay women for providing sexual services—that are
assumed in the marriage contracts—are also not allowed.

Thus, sex and reproduction (certainly significant areas of barter and
exchange) are not subject to negotiation and ordering through the private

process of contract, unless we are talking about the marital contract. Sex and reproduction are historically considered central to that contract. For example, a marriage can be annulled—declared to have been void all along—if the parties never sexually consummate it.[27] Further illustrating the centrality of sex to marriage is the traditional common-law marital exemption for rape, which was based on the idea that husbands had a right to the sexual services of their wives. Centuries ago, Lord Hale expressed the opinion that consent to marriage was consent to provide sexual services on demand.[28] The U.S. courts held, notably in *People v. Liberta,* that the marital exemption for rape no longer applies.

Why do we not allow enforceable individualized bargaining over sex outside of the marital contract? In fact, even outside of the contractual situation, we place sexual interactions as beyond the reach of the law, either as private interactions (the modern position) or by applying coercive criminal or civil rules to punish them. Rules, both criminal and civil, such as sodomy laws or laws against fornication and adultery, bolster and reinforce the institution of marriage by penalizing or prohibiting other sexual affiliations. These rules include not only the laws of marriage and divorce but also large areas of criminal and civil law that bolster the institution of marriage and penalize sexual affiliations that do not conform to the marriage model, such as laws against prostitution, fornication, adultery, and cohabitation, as well as inheritance and probate laws, property rules, and tax laws that treat economic exchanges between marital partners differently than those that occur between other members of society. There is no obvious reason that sex should be excluded from some contractual schemes (private bargaining) while it has been an explicit part of another contractual scheme (the services requirement in the marital contract).

Of course, as this discussion of regulating sex and reproduction through contract indicates, significant questions would arise with the abolition of marriage as a legal category and the placement of the relationship between sexual affiliates within contract and other areas of law. What would happen to those other areas of law if sexual affiliation, like other significant areas of social interaction, were not treated differently—if there were no special category of rules regulating consensual, adult sex exchanges, and all were subject to contract? A number of interesting legal process questions are also raised by this set of speculations about abolishing marriage as a legal category and relying on other areas of law to address the problems that might arise between sexual affiliates. These questions have to do with the process of transformation of law and the ability of doctrine to adapt to accommodate new patterns of behavior. Ideological as well as structural forces would have to be considered.

For example, pouring disputes that arise between sexual affiliates into the arenas of contract, tort, and criminal law would not leave the doctrines that now govern those areas of law untransformed. How would the content of contract, tort, and criminal law change? Would ideas about bargaining, consideration, and unconscionability be altered? The prospect of opening up all these areas to reconsideration presents exciting possibilities for reexamination of whole areas of substantive law where assumptions about interactions between independent, equal, and autonomous individuals govern terms and consequences. My concern in this chapter is with the institution of the family and the role marriage serves in society.

Outside of Contract

Of course, what is revealed if we take the relationship of husband and wife —the institution of marriage—out of the special category of family law is the dependency of the child (or any other family member who is incapable of caring for her- or himself). Even advocates of a restructuring of the relationship between women and men do not necessarily believe that every family relationship should, or could be, reducible to contract. Family law historically recognizes that the state maintains a protective interest in the well-being of children and that parental obligations in regard to them cannot be individualized and reduced to contract. This position is consistent with the arrangement in which family is the repository of dependency, performing an important public function in which the state maintains a regulatory and supervisory interest. And it seems that the state has not been deterred from defining, even reordering, relationships in order to preserve the family's role.

In regard to the state maintaining a primary interest in the dependency component of the parent-child relationship, the cases and legislation are very clear. The economics of the tie are for state determination. Husband and wife cannot negotiate child custody and support free from judicial scrutiny and approval (Mnookin and Kornhauser 1979). The state retains an interest in these arrangements and the right to assess and alter any settlement the spouses may reach upon divorce, even to modify existing arrangements in the best interests of the child.

Economic or dependency issues concerning the ongoing needs of children that are addressed in the divorce context can be compared with the nonmarital situation. Historically, marriage defined the status of children in relation to their parents and the claims they could make upon or through them. The presence or absence of marriage determined which children were labeled "legitimate" or "illegitimate" and, thus, either granted or denied benefits accrued by their parents under state insurance and compensation schemes.

The U.S. Supreme Court has reduced the significance of marriage in regard to the parent-child connection. It did so first in regard to mothers when, in *Levy v. Louisiana,* it held that denying damages to "illegitimate" children as a result of the wrongful death of their mother is a violation of the equal protection clause of the Fourteenth Amendment. But fathers' connection to children has also evolved so as to not require its mediation through the institution of marriage. Unmarried fathers now have rights and responsibilities for their children that were not part of the common-law scheme of things. Nonmarital children are entitled to benefits historically reserved for their marital counterparts, such as parental support, workers compensation benefits, and the right to recovery in the event of a parent's wrongful death.[29] Such improvements recognize the reality of dependency is more important than the status of the parents' relationship.

In fact, in *Clark v. Jeter,* the Supreme Court held illegitimacy to be a "suspect classification," which means that all distinctions made on this basis must be examined with a higher level of scrutiny than usual. Clearly, the state can express its interest in protecting children independent of the marital relationship of the child's parents. The label "illegitimate" and many of the disadvantages associated with this status were substantially altered in the waning years of the twentieth century.

Conclusion

The very existence of the marital family, as well as the ideology surrounding it as a societal structure, masks dependency. Marriage allows us to ignore dependency in our policy and politics because we can always safely refer that nasty subject to the waiting societal receptor.

This interaction between the institution of marriage and policy concerning dependency illustrates why it is important to clearly reject the idea that the marital family is a separate, private entity and, instead, to focus on the role that this family has been assigned and how that function can be best performed in the future. We have historically relied on the marital family to manage dependency. Yet changes in our expectations and aspirations for marriage have been profound. The institution does not have the same meaning to participants as it did decades ago.

Given that transition seems the current and likely future fate for marriage, it seems we can no longer rest assured that the marital family alone can continue to adequately provide for the emotional, physical, and developmental needs of all those in society who may be dependent. Concurrently, it is simply inaccurate to assume that nonmarital family units cannot provide for the dependency needs of their members.

However, the dominance of the image of the marital family in our political rhetoric means that it remains the constant vision of the family that underlies debates about public regulation and market autonomy. In spite of empirical evidence to the contrary, in our construction of social policy we assume this family's existence and vitality, as a complement to the public institutions we explicitly address. There are substantial costs to our refusal to face the changes in intimate behavior and patterns of family formation and function.

NOTES

1. *Prince v. Massachusetts*, 321 U.S. 158 (1994). Note that most of the debate about the state's interest in precluding same-sex couple from the institution of marriage concerned the negative effect this would have on children (in both the Hawaii and the Vermont cases). The other arguments focused on the possibility that same-sex marriage would weaken "real" marriage as an institution.

2. 127 U.S. 190 (1888) at 205–6: "Marriage, as creating the most important relation in life [has] more to do with the morals and civilization of a people than any other institution . . ."

3. 98 U.S. 145 (1878): "Upon it society may be said to be built, and out of its fruits spring social relations and societal obligations and duties, with which government is necessarily required to deal." At 165.

4. As the Hawaii Supreme Court noted in *Baehr v. Lewin*, benefits associated with marriage may include (1) a variety of state income tax advantages, including deductions, credits, rates, exemptions, and estimates; (2) public assistance from and exemptions relating to the Department of Human Services; (3) control, division, acquisition, and disposition of community property; (4) rights relating to dower, curtesy, and inheritance; (5) rights to notice, protection, benefits, and inheritance; (6) award of child custody and support payments in divorce proceedings; (7) the right to spousal support; (8) the right to enter into premarital agree-

ments; (9) the right to change one's name; (10) the right to file a nonsupport action; (11) postdivorce rights relating to support and property division; (12) the benefit of the spousal privilege and confidential marital communications; (13) the benefit of the exemption of real property from attachment or execution; and (14) the right to bring a wrongful death action. *Baehr v. Lewin*, 74 Hawaii 530 (1993).

5. Some of the critics of civil unions in Vermont, where they are legal, cite religious belief. See Julie Deardorff, "Vermont Is Front Line of Gay Marriage Fight," *Chicago Tribune*, April 3, 2001, 1. The use of history and tradition is more common. State court decisions in the 1970s limiting marriages to heterosexuals often assumed marriage was by definition between a man and a woman. Martha Chamallas, *Introduction to Feminist Legal Theory* (New York: Aspen Law and Business, 1999), citing *Baker v. Nelson*, 191 N.W. 2d 185 (Minn. 1971); *Jones v. Hallahan*, 501 S.W. 2d 588 (Ky. 1973); *Singer v. Hara*, 522 P. 2d 1187 (Wash. App. 1974) at 265–66.

6. See James A. Henderson Jr., Richard N. Pearson, and John A. Siliciano, *The Torts Process*, 5th ed. (New York: Aspen, 1999), regarding the duty to rescue as contrasted with strangers; and Krause et al., *Family Law: Cases, Comments and Questions*, 4th ed. (St. Paul, Minn.: West Group, 1998). See also *State v. Mally*, 139 Mont. 599 (1961); *State v. Smith*, 65 Me. 257 (1876) (spouses have an affirmative obligation to obtain medical assistance for each other); *McGuire v. McGuire*, 157 Neb. 226 (Neb. 1953) (duty to financially support one's spouse).

7. Jason Fields and Lynne M. Casper, "America's Families and Living Arrangements: March 2001," *Current Population Reports*, 20–37 (2001).

8. *Muhammad v. Muhammad*, 622 So. 2d 1239 (Miss. 1993). See also D. Kelly Weisberg and Susan Frelich Appleton, *Modern Family Law: Cases and Materials*, 2d ed. (New York: Aspen, 2002), 549. The supposed special nature of the marital family is also significant outside of family law. Many other areas of law incorporate and utilize the concept of the family: tort, criminal, and property laws have historically distinguished family relationships from those of "strangers" and established exceptions or alternatives to the general rules for family members. Marital rape exemption, spousal privilege, domestic violence, tort immunity, fornication, adultery, cohabitation, and so forth—these exceptions and alternatives are based on the belief that a family connection signifies a special relationship, one that justifies a different regulatory regime.

9. *Loving v. Virginia*, 388 U.S. 1 (1967) (the trial judge's opinion stated, "Almighty God created the races white, black, yellow, Malay and red, and he placed them on separate continents. And but for the interference with his arrangement there would be no cause for such marriages. The fact that he separated the races shows that he did not intend for the races to mix . . ."); *Potter v. Murray City*, 760 F.2d 1065 (10th Cir. 1985), cert. denied, 474 U.S. 849 (1988) ("monogamy is inextricably woven into the fabric of our society. It is the bedrock upon which our culture is built").

10. *Bradwell v. Illinois,* 83 U.S. 130, 141 (1873).

11. See generally *Graham v. Graham,* 33 F. Supp. 936, 938 (E.D. Mich. 1940) (holding that a contract between spouses to change the roles of husband and wife —the essential incidents of the marriage—is void).

12. See Weisberg and Appleton, *Modern Family Law,* 284–85. See also *Samuel v. University of Pittsburgh,* 375 F. Supp. 1119 (W.D. Pa. 1974), decision to decertify class vacated (invalidating, on equal protection grounds, university residency rules that assigned the husband's domicile to the wife for determination of tuition); *Restatement (Second) of Conflict of Laws* §21 (Supp. 1988) ("rules for the acquisition of a domicile of choice are the same for both married and unmarried persons").

13. *Edwardson v. Edwardson,* 798 S.W. 2d 941 (Ky. 1990). See also Uniform Premarital Agreement Act (UPAA), 9C U.L.A. 35 (2001) (premarital agreements are valid unless they are "unconscionable").

14. *Simeone v. Simeone,* 581 A. 2d 162, 165 (Pa. 1990).

15. *Edwardson v. Edwardson,* 798 S.W. 2d 941 (Ky. 1990).

16. Ibid., 944.

17. Ibid., 946.

18. American Law Institute, *Principles of the Law of Family Dissolution,* chap. 7 (Agreements), Topic 2 (Requirements for an Enforceable Agreement), §7.05 (Procedural Requirements), 88.

19. Ibid.

20. Ibid., chap. 6, Domestic Partners, § 6.05, Allocation of Domestic-Partnership Property ("Domestic-partnership property should be divided according to the principles set forth for the division of marital property in § 4.15 and § 4.16."), 55.

21. Ibid., chap. 6, Domestic Partners, § 6.01, Scope, 1.

22. Ibid., §§ 6.03, Determination that Persons are Domestic Partners.

23. www.promisekeepers.org/faqs/core/faqscore24.htm (visited June 17, 2002).

24. www.now.org/issues/right/promise/mythfact.html (visited June 17, 2002).

25. www.now.org/issues/right/promise/quotes.html (visited June 17, 2002).

26. There already are some moves to do this in the context of divorce. See *Ruprecht v. Ruprecht,* 599 A.2d 604 (N.J. Ch. Div. 1991) (allowing for suit for intentional infliction of emotional harm without physical injury in the context of a divorce). See also *Hakkila v. Hakkila,* 812 P.2d 1320 (N.M. App. 1991).

27. Historically, the reasons for annulment had to do with sex and reproduction—the "essential" aspects of the marriage relationship—such as consummation, ability to reproduce, pregnancy, and so on. Without sex and reproductive capacity the marriage was deemed "void," or not really to have taken effect. It's all about sex and reproduction.

28. 1 Hale P.C. 629, as quoted in *Warren v. State,* 336 S.E. 2d 221 (Ga. 1985).

29. *Gomez v. Perez,* 409 U.S. 535 (1973) (nonmarital child has a right to paternal support); *Weber v. Aetna Casualty & Surety Co.,* 406 U.S. 164 (1972) (state law that denied workers' compensation benefits to nonmarital dependent children is a

violation of the equal protection and due process clauses of the Fourteenth Amendment); *Levy v. Louisiana,* 391 U.S. 68 (denial of damages to "illegitimate" children as a result of the wrongful death of their mother is a violation of the equal protection clause of the Fourteenth Amendment).

REFERENCES

American Law Institute. 2002. *Principles of the Law of Family Dissolution.* Philadelphia: American Law Institute.

Blackstone, Commentaries 442–45.

Brand, Chad. 1998. "Christ-Centered Marriages: Husbands and Wives Complementing One Another." www.baptist2baptist.net/SBCLifeArticles/Sept_98/sept_98.html.

Carbone, June, and Margaret Brinig. 1991. "Rethinking Marriage: Feminist Ideology, Economic Change and Divorce Reform." *Tulane Law Review* 65:953.

Chamallas, Martha. 1999. *Introduction to Feminist Legal Theory.* New York: Aspen.

Cohen, Lloyd. 1995. "Rhetoric, the Unnatural Family, and Women's Work." *Virginia Law Review* 81:2275, 2286.

Deardorff, Julie. 2001. "Vermont Is Front Line of Gay Marriage Fight." *Chicago Tribune,* April 3.

Demos, John. 1979. "Images of the American Family, Then and Now." In *Changing Images of the Family,* ed. Virginia Tufte and Barbara Myerhoff, 43–60. New Haven, Conn.: Yale University Press.

Developments in the Law: Legal Responses to Domestic Violence. 1993. *Harvard Law Review* 106:1498, 1501–4, 1528–29, 1534–43.

Fields, Jason. 1996. "Living Arrangements of Children." *Current Population Reports.*

Fields, Jason, and Lynne M. Casper. 2001. "America's Families and Living Arrangements: March 2001." *Current Population Reports.*

Fineman, Martha Albertson. 1999. "What Place for Family Privacy?" *George Washington Law Review* 67:1207, 1209.

Friedman, Lawrence M. 1988. *A History of American Law.* 2d ed. New York: Simon and Schuster.

Gottlieb, Beatrice. 1993. *The Family in the Western World: From the Black Death to the Industrial Age.* New York: Oxford University Press.

Grossman, Joanna L. 1994. "Women's Jury Service: Right of Citizenship or Privilege of Difference?" *Stanford Law Review* 46:1115, 1131.

Hebard, Grace Raymond. 1913. "The First Woman Jury." *Journal of American History* 7:1293, 1302–3.

Henderson, James A., Jr., Richard N. Pearson, and John A. Siliciano. 1999. *The Torts Process.* 5th ed. New York: Aspen.

Krause, Harry D., Linda D. Elrod, Marsha Garrison, and J. Thomas Oldham. 1998. *Family Law: Cases, Comments and Questions.* St. Paul, Minn.: West Group.

Mnookin, Robert, and Lewis Kornhauser. 1979. "Bargaining in the Shadow of the Law: The Case of Divorce." *Yale Law Journal* 88:950–51, 954–57.

Nielsen, Linda. 1990. "Family Rights and the 'Registered Partnership' in Denmark." *International Journal of Law and Family* 4:297.

Olson, Frances E. 1983. "The Family and the Market: A Study of Ideology and Legal Reform." *Harvard Law Review* 96:1497, 1504–5.

Pham, Curt. 1996. "Let's Get Married in Hawaii: A Story of Conflicting Laws, Same-Sex Couples, and Marriage." *Family Law Quarterly* 30:727.

Riley, Glenda. 1991. *Divorce: An American Tradition.* New York: Oxford University Press.

Sanchez, Laura. 2001. "The Implementation of Covenant Marriage in Louisiana." *Virginia Journal of Social Policy and the Law* 9:194.

Sealey, Geraldine. 2002. "Marriage Proposal Debate Looms Over Bush Plan to Spend $300 Million Promoting Unions." At http://www.abcnews.com (last visited March 5, 2000).

Thornhill, Randy, and Craig Palmer. 2000. *A Natural History of Rape: Biological Basis of Sexual Coercion.* Cambridge, Mass.: MIT Press.

Wardle, Lynn D. 1996. "A Critical Analysis of Constitutional Claims for Same-Sex Marriage." *Brigham Young University Law Review* 1.

———. 2003. "The Bonds of Matrimony and the Bonds of Constitutional Democracy." Draft of comments made at Hofstra University, March 5. On file with author.

Weisberg, D. Kelly, and Susan Frelich Appleton. 2002. *Modern Family Law: Cases and Materials.* 2nd ed. New York: Aspen.

Weitzman, Lenore J. 1985. *The Divorce Revolution.* New York: Free Press.

TABLE OF CASES

Baehr v. Lewin, 74 Haw. 530 (1993).

Baker v. Nelson, 191 N.W. 2d 185 (Minn. 1971).

Baker v. State, 744 A.2d 864 (Vt. 1999).

Bowers v. Hardwick, 478 U.S. 186 (1986).

Bradwell v. Illinois, 83 U.S. 130 (1873).

Button v. Button, 388 N.W. 2d 546 (Wis. 1986).

Clark v. Jeter, 486 U.S. 456 (1988).

Edwardson v. Edwardson, 798 S.W. 2d 941 (Ky. 1990).

Feliciano v. Rosemar Silver Co., 514 N.E. 2d 1095 (Mass. 1987).

Gomez v. Perez, 409 U.S. 535 (1973).

Graham v. Graham, 33 F. Supp. 936, 938 (E.D. Mich. 1940).

Griswold v. Connecticut, 381 U.S. 479 (1965).

Hakkila v. Hakkila, 112 N.M. 172, 812 P.2d 1320 (App. 1991).

In Re Marriage of Greenwald, 454 N.W. 2d 34 (Wis. App. 1990).

J.E.B. v. T.B., 511 U.S. 127 (1994).

Jones v. Hallahan, 501 S.W. 2d 588 (Ky. 1973).

Levy v. Louisiana, 391 U.S. 68 (1968).

Loving v. Virginia, 388 U.S. 1 (1967).

Marvin v. Marvin, 557 P.2d 106 (Cal. 1976).

Maynard v. Hill, 127 U.S. 190 (1888).

McGuire v. McGuire, 157 Neb. 226 (Neb. 1953).

Muhammad v. Muhammad, 622 So. 2d 1239 (Miss. 1993).

People v. Liberta, 474 N.E. 2d 567 (N.Y. 1984), cert. denied, 471 U.S. 1020 (1985).

Potter v. Murray City, 760 F.2d 1065 (10th Cir. 1985), cert. denied, 474 U.S. 849 (1988).

Prince v. Massachusetts, 321 U.S. 158 (1994).

Reynolds v. United States, 98 U.S. 145 (1878).

Ruprecht v. Ruprecht, 599 A.2d 604 (N.J. Ch. Div. 1991).

Samuel v. University of Pittsburgh, 375 F. Supp. 1119 (W.D. Pa. 1974).

Simeone v. Simeone, 581 A.2d 162 (Pa. 1990).

Singer v. Hara, 522 P.2d 1187 (Wash. App. 1974).

State v. Mally, 139 Mont. 599 (1961).

State v. Smith, 65 Me. 257 (1876).

Stratton v. Wilson, 185 S.W. 522 (Ky. App. 1916).

Trammel v. United States, 445 U.S. 40 (1980).

Warren v. State, 336 S.E. 2d 221 (Ga. 1985).

Weber v. Aetna Casualty & Surety Co., 406 U.S. 164, 92 S.Ct. 1400, 31 L.Ed. 2d 768 (1972).

Wirth v. Wirth, 38 A.D. 2d 611 (N.Y. App. Div. 1971).

Chapter 2

Taking Government Out of the Marriage Business
Families Would Benefit

Dorian Solot and Marshall Miller

Marriage in the United States is a bundle of contradictions. Nine out of ten of us marry at least once in our lives (Kreider and Fields 2002, 16), and 96 percent of college freshmen say they hope to marry someday (Louis Harris and Associates 1998). We delight in throwing the most lavish, elaborate weddings of any culture in history, typically spending on the Big Day nearly as much as the average American earns in a year (Gillis 1996; Ingraham 1999). Weddings sell movie tickets and fuel an entire genre of glossy magazines thick with advertisements. More than three-quarters of people describe being married as the most satisfying lifestyle (Roper Starch Worldwide 1995).

Yet despite the steady stream of picture-perfect brides, 150 years of demographic trends paint a different picture: marriage does not play the central role it used to (Coontz 1992). Forty-six percent of American adults are not currently married (Fields 2001), and if the rate of increase of the last five decades continues, the bare-ring-finger crowd will be a majority in a few decades. The average American already spends the majority of his or her adult life unmarried, as the result of later first marriages, time spent unmarried after divorce and widowhood, and the small but growing number of people who never marry, by choice or circumstance (Kreider and Fields 2002, 15).

The conversation about whether to abolish marriage as a legal category swirls around these contradictions. To alarmists, the phrase "abolish marriage" conjures up images of bride and groom in handcuffs or, even more unsettling, divorce forced upon a husband and wife because the institution has been declared null and void. This scenario could not be further from the truth.

In this chapter we join those who advance a reasonable, thoughtful proposal to abolish marriage *as a legal category*. As both a personal decision and a public institution, marriage could and most likely would retain all its religious and symbolic significance, but not the legal meaning it has had in the United States in the last few centuries. We detail how disconnecting marriage from civil law would be a return to historical norms, and a wise approach to the ethical obligation to define and support families fairly and inclusively. We document the widespread public support that already exists for abolishing marriage as a legal category, and how real-world implementation is already under way. Far from a radical departure from current law, most of the groundwork for this change has already been laid. In her analysis of family law's shift in emphasis from marriage to parenthood and the care of dependent children, legal scholar June Carbone writes, "The state has, for all practical purposes, withdrawn from regulation of marriage" (2000, 142). Indeed, today the state acts as a hands-off licensing bureau and divorce granter, making marriage relatively easy to enter and exit, yet maintaining legal marital status as a key determinant of eligibility for more than one thousand federal rights and obligations. Cultural lag in family law leaves other kinds of family relationships dangerously ignored and penalized.

Our exploration of why marriage should not be the centerpiece of the country's family policy is grounded in demographic facts. Given the sheer number of people whose primary caretaking relationships exist outside of the institution of marriage, this subject is not only a theoretical matter but an eminently practical one. It has the potential to dramatically improve the lives of millions of adults and children currently being failed by the existing systems of law and policy. To better understand the lives behind demographers' data, we consider the wide variety of reasons why some people are not married, based partly on our own qualitative research on more than one hundred people in unmarried relationships around the country. Confronting these reasons makes it more difficult to dismiss our concerns by arguing that policy simply needs to do a better job of promoting and encouraging marriage, a strategy that relies on altering reality rather than addressing it.

We argue that abolishing marriage as a legal category is not a departure from history but a return to the way many past cultures and civilizations understood marriage and family life. We then turn to our nation's ethical duty to treat all families fairly and to respect people's right to choose the structure of their relationships in the absence of state-sanctioned penalties or rewards. Since it can be difficult to imagine how the system could function without the clear-cut arrangement of marriage licenses and divorce courts, the question of how the law would understand relationships in lieu of marriage often arises. To address this question, we consider a variety of proposals and policies that could offer a starting place for the United States. Finally, we point out that not only does considerable public support for the notion of shifting emphasis away from legal marriage already exist, but that the private sector is already implementing policies along these lines, providing a real-world testing ground for some of the ideas discussed in this volume.

As the founders of the Alternatives to Marriage Project, a national non-profit organization for unmarried people, we advocate within the existing system for fairness for diverse family structures. Here, we explore one potential way to address the growing problem of an outdated system that fails to capture the reality of contemporary intimate and caretaking relationships.

A Return to Historical Norms

Contrary to the claims of many marriage advocates, marriage as a legal category is a relatively recent invention. Throughout most of history, "family" was much more broadly defined and far less focused on state-registered marital status than is now the case. In many pre-marriage-license cultures it would have been difficult to distinguish between married couples and committed unmarried couples who only *acted* married, so even defining the institution is a challenge. Anthropologist Suzanne Frayser found that 28 percent of the societies she compared paid little or no attention to marriage and often had no way to distinguish between marriage and cohabitation (Frayser 1985). The word "family" comes from *familia*, a Roman word more akin to "household," which often included spouses, parents, children, servants, slaves, apprentices—in short, a collection of dependent relationships (Dixon 1992).

For thousands of years, formal marital status mattered only among the wealthy, for whom it affected power and property. Ancient Egypt had no word for marriage and no religious or civil marriage ceremony. Cohabitation was the way people formed valid families, and a marriage contract was optional. In ancient Babylon, the first legal system ever recorded, only the rich were allowed to marry, so most people in most communities functioned without it. The laws of ancient Rome provided for formal and informal marriages, the latter consisting of recognized unions without a ceremony or government approval (Graff 1999, 89, 210; Springer 2000; Duff and Truitt 1991, 37; Yalom 2001, 28).

Throughout medieval Europe, local community practices and traditions, not governmental bodies, determined which couples counted as married. Regardless of the role (or lack thereof) played by the church or state, couples made their own commitments, held their own rituals, and exchanged meaningful tokens of love. Well after the fourteenth century, when people first began to be married in churches, laws treated couples equally whether they formed their relationship in a church wedding or through private agreements among the individuals and families involved (Bohannan 1985; Gillis 1985, 7, 17, 84–105; 1996, 134–43; Graff 1999, 199–200).

These private promises were so common that in one fourteenth-century English town, 89 of the 101 marriages on record were created privately, much like today's cohabitations or the contract-based relationships that derive from what Martha Fineman proposes, rather than through a formal wedding. In the 1500s, between a third and half of European adults were officially unmarried (a statistic that mirrors marital status in the United States today), but just like today's legally "single" people, many of them were living with partners and raising children. Among eighteenth-century Scottish, English, and Welsh working-class families, long-term informally created relationships were perfectly acceptable. It was only in 1754 that England drew a clear line between married and unmarried relationships, by declaring the only valid marriages to be those established in churches by Anglican clergy. It was this system, in part, that later drove the Pilgrims to found a new country based on separation of church and state (Graff 1999, 199; Cott 2000, 35–36; Parker 1990, 18; Kiernan and Estaugh 1993; Gillis 1985, 140).

Even on our own continent, communities have long defined marriage and family without resorting to formal, government-established marital categories. Many Native American tribes, each with its own distinct culture, shared the idea that it was a couple's behavior and personal commitments that validated their relationship. We suggest that these same functional characteristics should govern legal presumptions about family. Colonial communities and courts accepted both self-made marriage promises and church-based weddings as equally valid, not requiring that couples formally register their relationships (Demian 2004; Cott 2000, 30–31; Mintz and Kellogg 1988, 39).

Only in the 1800s did the kind of marriage we take for granted today, in which a signed marriage license is necessary for a relationship to be granted legal recognition, became common. It took about a century for the state to take true control of the institution of marriage: it was the early 1900s before governments, enthusiastic about workplace regulation, decided to regulate marriage as well. Reformers narrowed the once-broad definition of family so that only married couples would count, and courts began to require proof that couples' marriages were formally created. The concept of common-law marriage, in which couples became married simply by living together and holding themselves out as husband and wife, came under attack because it allowed couples to form marriages without government intervention (Gillis 1996, 146; Katz 1995; Graff 1999, 204–5; Mintz and Kellogg 1988, 107–29).

Most historians agree that the 1950s, the decade Americans consider to have set the standard for "normal" married family life, was actually a historical anomaly caused by a unique set of social, economic, and political factors. Marriage rates hit an all-time high, while the average age at first marriage dropped to a hundred-year low (Mintz and Kellogg 1988, 177–201; U.S. Census Bureau 2003; Coontz 1992, 39). Television, the new medium, broadcast identical images of married life into living rooms across the country, branding the *Leave It to Beaver* and *Father Knows Best* style of family into the American consciousness. Describing the two-married-parents-with-their-biological-offspring household as "traditional" is historically inaccurate.

We may simply be seeing a return to the historical norms that preceded the post–World War II marriage-and-baby boom. Americans may not be marrying as young or staying married as long, but we are forming relationships at about the same rate we always have. The decrease in married couples is mostly offset by an increase in unmarried ones (Bumpass, Sweet, and Cherlin 1991). In fact, unmarried partners are one of the fastest-growing household types, increasing by 72 percent between 1990 and 2000, and growing 1,000 percent since 1960 (U.S. Census Bureau 1990, 2001c). These unmarried partner households do not necessarily fit the stereotype of a couple of recent college graduates sharing an apartment: nearly half are over age thirty-five, and a quarter are over age forty-five (U.S. Census Bureau 2001b). Since 43 percent of different-sex unmarried-partner households include children (compared with 46 percent of married couples), the childless image does not hold up either (Simmons and O'Connell 2003, 10). Both same-sex and different-sex unmarried partners have been overlooked in American discussions of family policy, yet both are "families" in every sense of the word *except* the legal one.

Straight and gay unmarried couples are not the only unmarried people who function as families yet fall outside most legal frameworks of family. The word "single" conjures up the image of someone eating cold pizza and reading the personals. To the contrary, many single people live within an extended network of close friends and family. They raise children (usually from a previous marriage or relationship, though also as "single parents by choice"), care for elderly parents and dependent siblings, and sometimes live with others as stable, interdependent "families of choice." The concept of "urban tribes," communities of interconnected unmarried adults, is gaining acceptance as one way to understand the family-like, friendship-based social structures that define the lives of growing numbers of young adults (Watters 2003). Still others of all ages form a myriad of supportive, complex, "nontraditional" relationships with others like former spouses, close friends who act as family, co-parents, committed partners who live in separate homes, formal and informal adoptive and foster children and parents, and many other family structures that can be described only in paragraphs, not phrases.

Defining Today's Family

Under the current law, "family" is defined by blood, marriage, and adoption. In the absence of marriage as a legal category, how would one define family? Some might even ask why family is a necessary legal concept at all; why not simply apply contract law and a basic ethic of fairness to all relationships? Although in this chapter we propose dismissing the legal notion of "marriage," we believe the concept of "family" retains significance and value. Family relationships often involve those with caretaker responsibilities and those who are dependent and vulnerable, such as children, some elderly, an adult partner who is supported financially by her partner while the couple's children are young, or an ill sibling who lives with and is cared for by a well one. It is in society's best interest to recognize these caretaking responsibilities as special and different than nonfamily caretaking arrangements, such as a paid nurse or nanny, or a neighbor who brings meals to a sick resident nearby. Broadly defining "family" to include not only blood, marriage, and adoptive relationships but also others who operate as caretakers in a significant way on a long-term basis protects both the vulnerable and the caretakers (whose responsibilities bring certain rights and protections). Given the increasingly frayed or nonexistent social safety net for the poor and vulnerable in the United States, our country has a moral obligation to provide recognition and protection to people who fulfill critical caretaking responsibilities and consider themselves family members, even if their relationship lies outside our current definition of family.

Even when dependents are not involved—for example, in the case of two adult partners who both work and have no children in their home—most people organize their lives, time, finances, priorities, and emotional life around a concept of family. They have someone, or several people, who are closest or most important to them, regardless of whether they represent traditional next of kin (e.g., a spouse, adult child, or parent); "nontraditional" family members (e.g., a longtime domestic partner); or members of a "family of choice" (close friends in nonintimate relationships who take on many of the roles of family members) or urban tribe.[1] If people were asked, "Who would you want to make medical or financial decisions for you if you were unable to do so? Who would you want nearby if you were ill or dying? Who would you choose to inherit the majority of your estate if you died?" most would name a person or people who fulfill the role of family members in their lives—regardless of whether existing law would recognize that person as "family."

Human relationships are inherently complex. They begin, evolve, and end; people die, and survivors eventually form new bonds; children are cared for by multiple adults in roles that change over decades. As much as the simplistic definitions of family appeal to the desire to categorize and compartmentalize, they are an inadequate match for human needs and serve them poorly. Why should a couple who marry in Vegas after knowing each other for a week gain more legal recognition than an unmarried couple who have shared their lives for thirty years and raised children together? Small wonder that "marriage fraud" is increasingly widespread. More people are willing to marry friends or strangers to get a green card or a football ticket (Duffy and Kane 2002), or to stay legally married to someone even if the relationship ended years or decades before to continue to share a health insurance policy. An entire genre of reality television shows match up total strangers, who, if they marry, receive all the benefits and legal protections as couples who approach the institution with considerably more care and reverence. Maintaining and reinforcing the legal distinctions between married and unmarried has become an increasingly farcical exercise, as was evident when pop star Britney Spears concluded her first fifty-five hours of legal marriage in the same month that President Bush called upon Congress to "defend the sanctity of marriage" to exclude loving same-sex couples in his State of the Union address. As the American Law Institute wrote in its recommendations regarding the law of family dissolution:

> As the incidence of cohabitation has dramatically increased and cohabita-
> tion has become more socially acceptable at all levels of society, it has
> become increasingly implausible to attribute special significance to the par-
> ties' failure to marry. . . . Normatively, [we] take the view that family law
> should be concerned about relationships that may be indistinguishable
> from marriage except for the legal formality of marriage. The more fre-
> quent such relationships become, the more the law should be concerned.
> (American Law Institute 2002, 33)

Removing marriage from legal consideration, and instead recognizing people's real, privately made commitments and caretaking responsibilities, would be a return to a system closer to the way most people conceive of their own families, and more in line with the way families have been recognized throughout history.

To reiterate, we are not proposing that marriage disappear. Quite the contrary, we expect that most people would continue to marry in a social and religious sense, and that a minority would form long-term, intimate unmarried relationships as they have across time and culture. Some have argued that legal marriage must be protected because of the benefits it allegedly confers, but there is no reason to believe these benefits would be lost if marriages were formed in the context of communities, rather than in the context of the state. We suggest that shaping law to match the long-standing existence of many family forms would strengthen a diversity of family types without detracting from the strength many find in marriage. In countries that have crafted policies that recognize unmarried partners, cohabitation has fewer of the negative effects that are attributed to it in the United States. Their own argument supports the conclusion that expanding the legal definition of family would likely strengthen both married and unmarried relationships.

In the absence of legal marriage as the primary way to trace family relationships, how should the myriad issues currently handled by family law be approached? Rather than beginning with a few categories of relationships recognized by the state, the proposed system would begin with contract law, allowing any two people to agree on their own expectations and intentions. As with wills, individuals would be encouraged to craft their own documents, which could range from simple to extremely complex. With rare exceptions (for instance, to protect the rights of children and other dependents) these would be respected regardless of whether the intentions set forth were considered "traditional" or "nontraditional." As with wills, there could be a variety of freely available boilerplates for people to use and modify. For instance, they could choose a contract agreeing to joint or separate ownership of property and assets, a shorter relationship contract with the option to renew, or a long-term commitment. Unlike the existing marriage contract—a contract people cannot read before they sign—private agreements would allow individuals to craft an understanding that meets their specific needs.

In the absence of a contract, the state would presumably need a set of working assumptions. Rather than falling back on marriage, it could rely on broader definitions of family. Three-quarters of Americans today believe a "family" is a group of people who love and care about each other, not limited to those bound by blood and marriage. Yet it is difficult to imagine how to make such an inclusive definition legally meaningful. How does one measure love and caring? How much love do you have to demonstrate before you become a family? Does the love have to be mutual? Does duration factor in? What if you used to care for each other but you do not anymore? Questions like these induce cold sweats in lawyers and policymakers, making the tidy marriage license seem that much more appealing—even if it does not match reality.

However, more workable existing and proposed models do exist. Canada is one source of ideas, since its legislators have made far more progress at writing diverse family forms into their legal codes. The Vanier Institute for the Family, a Canadian think tank, offers the following definition of family:

Any combination of two or more persons who are bound together over time by ties of mutual consent, birth and/or adoption placement, and who, together, assume responsibilities for variant combinations of some of the following:

- physical maintenance and care of group members
- addition of new members through procreation or adoption
- socialization of children
- social control of members
- production, consumption, and distribution of goods and services
- affective nurturance, love.

The American Law Institute suggests defining domestic partners (a category narrower than what we are discussing here, yet still illustrative of a way to define relationships without relying on marriage licenses) as "[t]wo persons of the same or opposite sex, not married to one another, who for a significant period of time share a primary residence and a life together as a couple." The ALI recommends determining whether two people "share life together as a couple" by factors such as

- their oral or written promises or statements to each other
- the extent to which they intermingle their finances
- the extent to which their relationship fosters economic dependence or interdependence
- the extent to which they assume specialized or collaborative roles to further their life together
- the extent to which the relationship has brought change in either person's life
- the extent to which they acknowledge responsibility for each other, such as naming each other as a beneficiary of a life insurance policy or employee benefits plan
- the extent to which they treat their relationship as qualitatively distinct from the relationship they have with anyone else
- their emotional and physical intimacy
- their community reputation as a couple
- their participation in a commitment ceremony or registration as domestic partners
- their giving birth to, adopting, or assuming joint parenting responsibilities for a child
- maintenance of a common household. (American Law Institute 2002, 917–18)

Many Canadian provinces and the country of Norway allocate certain rights to couples who cohabit continuously for a certain length of time (usually ranging from one to three years, depending on the country or province), or who have a child together. In Canada, these laws create a category of common-law spouses for which the United States has no equivalent. (In the few states where common-law marriage persists, legal recognition of these unions follows different criteria.)[2] Sweden allows same-sex and different-sex unmarried couples to become registered partners and assumes an equal division of property in the event their relationships end, unless the couple has agreed otherwise (Probert and Barlow 2000; International Lesbian and Gay Association 2000). We include these other definitions here not to argue that the United States should follow these examples by recognizing unmarried couples as married ones, but to demonstrate that new, more concrete ways to define which relationships are worthy of certain protections and assumptions have been thriving in real life. One of the challenges in creating these kinds of policies is how to draft legislation that ensures protections for children and those with less power within relationships, while also allowing adults to "opt out" of basic governmental presumptions, if they wish, to define their own legal relationship (or lack thereof).

The two-part process we propose, based first on individuals' own contracts, and second on a set of legal assumptions if there is no contract, could function equally well for the government rights and responsibilities currently associated with marriage, and also for families' private matters. Some governmental matters, like income tax, would no longer need to be linked to marriage. Income taxes would be based on income, not relationship status. This innovation, lining up the United States with most of the world, would have the added benefit of resolving the contentious debates about the marriage bonus and marriage penalty, and the less-discussed unmarried bonus and unmarried penalty.[3] Inheritance would function similar to the existing system, with people using wills to designate heirs, and a set of (improved) governmental assumptions about next of kin for situations with no will. For private matters, like a couple's agreements with each other about property ownership in case the relationship ends, again, couples could be encouraged to write their own agreement based on widely available boilerplates, and if no such written agreement existed, relationship dissolution guidelines like those recommended by the American Law Institute would take effect for couples who met the guidelines' criteria.

Rather than add another demographic slice of people into the "married" category through common-law unions, this approach would make it possible to eliminate legal marital status categories and instead depend solely on criteria like the ones listed earlier. Given the demographics set forth at the beginning of this chapter, this would be a logical step. It would shift the law's emphasis from the formal structure of marriage to the reality of people's relationships of emotional and financial interdependence. Using these broader definitions as the centerpiece of family policy, rather than as a way to tweak exactly who counts as a spouse, satisfies two needs. First, it is the most accurate way currently available to match law and policy to real relationships. Broader definitions allow us to treat fairly a far more varied range of relationships, both "traditional" and "nontraditional," without creating the need for a never-ending list of eligibility requirements to enter the privileged ground of recognized family structures.

Second, it eliminates the archaic notion that legally married families are superior to unmarried families. Unmarried families should not be granted rights by squeezing them under the "married" umbrella. One would not, for example, say that women have the right to vote by making them honorary men at the ballot box. Instead, we say that gender is irrelevant when it comes to voting rights. Similarly, formal marital status should be irrelevant when it comes to family policy.

"Why Don't They Just Get Married?"

Those resistant to the definition of family offered here might furrow their brows and wonder, "Why don't they just get married?" At the heart of the debates about marriage is a misguided belief that unmarried people can easily gain access to family protections by merely acquiring a marriage license. This is often used to rationalize why it is not necessary for policies to be changed to recognize unmarried families alongside married ones. Television and radio hosts seem to take particular delight in trying to solve the inequities by advising us (an unmarried couple), or the individuals whose stories we tell, simply to tie the knot and stop complaining. There seems to be a widespread belief that with a little straightforward encouragement, the right incentive carrot dangled, or a proverbial kick in the pants, unmarried people can be brought to their senses and married off.

The reality is not so simple. Understanding the sheer number of reasons that unmarried people are not married can be a useful step toward understanding the demographic picture and developing equitable approaches to family policy. Even if a given talk show host could convince that day's guest that getting hitched would really solve his or her problems, it would take a lot of talk shows to convert all 94 million unmarried adults into married ones (Fields 2001).

Marriage-promoting pundits seem to hope that extolling the value of the institution will send couples scampering for the closest marriage license bureau. The truth is that the United States already has one of the highest marriage rates in the world, and that by their late twenties most Americans have already married (by their forties, 88 percent have; Eurostat 2000, 2001; U.S. Census Bureau 2003; Kreider and Fields 2002, 4). The most common reason people are not married, or are not married yet, is that they have not found the right person to marry. No media campaign, counseling session, or research statistic about an alleged benefit of marriage is likely to convince someone to marry if he or she is not already in a relationship. Most incentive policies are similarly useless—although the country's marriage-centered immigration policies have inadvertently and ironically generated a flood of marriages between people who have no intimate relationship.

Others in the sizable "unmarried by circumstance, not by choice," category include people who have been widowed or abandoned by a spouse or partner, or who have made a courageous decision to leave an abusive or dysfunctional relationship. (One of the reasons cohabitors have a higher breakup rate than married couples is because people are putting cohabitation's screening function to use, and not entering marriages that would be likely to end in divorce.) A visitor to the Alternatives to Marriage Project Web site wrote:

> I have a live-in boyfriend of two years who just proposed. I feel that . . . living together first (thank God) has enabled me to realize he is not the one I want to spend the rest of my life with. I believe if we hadn't lived together first, I might be making a big mistake. You never truly know someone until you have lived with them.

Others, especially senior citizens and the disabled, would lose significant financial benefits if they married. As long as legal marriage exists, policies that penalize people for marrying need to be updated, so people can have the freedom to personal decisions unobstructed by arbitrary penalties. It is an issue of fairness for the millions of people who currently cannot afford to marry, whether they would like to or not. One woman we interviewed said she and her partner wished they could marry but could not afford to:

My previous husband was killed in a coal-mining accident, and the state compensates us for that loss with workers' compensation benefits. If I remarry, my children and I lose those benefits. They increase our income by about $24,000 a year. It's a big difference. Between the two of us we have six children—car insurance alone is unreal. Without those benefits, there's no way that we could live.

In the vast majority of states and municipalities in the United States, same-sex couples are not legally allowed to marry or claim the benefits or civil unions or government-recognized domestic partnership. Some different-sex couples have decided not to marry until their gay, lesbian, bisexual, and transgender (GLBT) friends and relatives have equal marriage rights. Exactly how many different-sex couples have taken this stance is unknown, but given the number of people who contact our organization having decided against marriage in solidarity with the GLBT community, we suspect the public would be surprised by how many heterosexual people feel strongly enough about this issue to take part in this "marriage boycott."

Most unmarried couples in male-female relationships are simply delaying matrimony temporarily for varying reasons. The most common reason is to be sure they are a good match for a lifetime commitment. As premarital cohabitation and engagement periods stretch longer—in a high-profile example, Oprah Winfrey has now been "engaged" but not married to her partner, Steadman Graham, for more than a decade—many of these couples adopt all the characteristics of married couples, yet they lack any legal recognition. Some are unwilling to marry a partner whose potential future income is unlikely to improve their own situation. Many low-income people delay marrying until they can afford a vision of married life that may include a steady job, a house, a car, children, a fancy dress, and a big party.

A small minority of couples have chosen not to marry for the long term. Some cite political, philosophical, or personal beliefs about the institution of marriage or its relationship to government, religion, or gender. Many women express profound discomfort with the "wife" role, sometimes based on their own past experience with what author Dalma Heyn calls "marriage shock," a powerful shift in expectations of the woman's role after getting married.[4] One woman we interviewed married her partner of six years in response to parental pressure; she and her partner (interviewed separately) both believe they would still be together had they not married. She explained:

> We had the same bills as we had before, and we had the same kids, lived in the same place, but it was just harder. I had to become a wife. I was expected to make dinner. Before, it was like, "Oh, want to eat? Well, go ahead." But now I was expected to make dinner, I was expected to do the laundry, expected to keep an immaculate house. Not necessarily by Kyle, but by my mother, his mother: "Oh, you're a wife now." Kyle and I have not always been the conventional parents or the conventional couple, but we were expected to suddenly become this conventional husband and wife. It became hard.

Many who are not religious say they are unable to separate marriage from religion in their minds, and see no appeal in having a civil ceremony for an institution they feel belongs in the hands of clergy. On the other end of the continuum, some extremely religious couples have sought our organization's support for their decision not to get legally married, because civil marriage brings the option of divorce. Since they believe God does not allow divorce, they prefer to be married in the eyes of God alone. Growing numbers are questioning why government has the power to regulate marriage, or to decide who can marry and who cannot. Many libertarians, holding a belief in an extremely limited role for the state in people's lives, are offended by the idea that any relationship requires outside "authorization" in the form of a marriage license from city hall. In thousands of conversations with those in long-term unmarried relationships, we have heard many explain thoughtful, heartfelt beliefs, including the ones outlined here, that make their relationship incompatible with the many meanings encompassed in the institution of marriage. Other simply see no reason to marry, especially if they have been married in the past or do not expect to have children.

Whether one celebrates the diversity of contemporary families or grieves late twentieth-century changes in family life, it is clear that the reality of unmarried lives is complex. While a small minority of unmarried people may be "convincible," trying to eliminate inequities by converting unmarried adults into married ones is unrealistic and ineffective. If, instead, we face the demographic facts, we will be called to reconsider what constitutes a family today. Whatever the factors that underlie their unmarried status, these people's relationships need legal protections so that they may best support and care for each other.

Is Marriage Better?

Proponents of marriage point to marriage as distinct from, and measurably better than, cohabitation. These arguments are often grounded not in law but in social science research. If marriage is better, some worry about what will happen to the benefits claimed to be associated with it if it is eliminated as a legal category. Yet many of the social science benefits claimed to be associated with marriage are less than straightforward. For instance, nearly any statistic that compares "average" cohabitations with "average" marriages is misleading, since the cohabitation category encompasses everyone from casually dating couples who moved in together last week to save on rent to couples who have shared their lives for decades. No wonder the "average" cohabitation does not last as long as the "average" marriage, since the latter group is made of those who have planned, in theory at least, for a long-term relationship. Using facts like there as a basis to exclude all cohabiting couples from recognition would be like saying the government should discourage dating, since the majority of dating couples split up; dating is far less stable than marriage. The key question is not whether marriage is somehow "better" than cohabitation, but whether we need a measure more accurate than legal marital status to distinguish significant family-like relationships from other kinds of interpersonal relationships.

The idea that cohabitors who marry have a higher divorce rate is another reason frequently offered for why the government has a stake in discouraging unmarried couples from living together. In fact, this statistic is far less dramatic than it first appears. First, researchers who have approached the question in a more nuanced way have learned that the higher divorce rate applies only to those who live with more than one partner before they marry,[5] a small percentage of all cohabitors (DeMaris and MacDonald 1993; Teachman 2003).

Second, many researchers examining this phenomenon have concluded that the selection effect accounts for most or all of the difference. That is, it is well established that the minority of couples who marry without having lived together first tend to be more religious, more conservative, and more strongly opposed to divorce. That these couples also tend to have a lower divorce rate is not to say that cohabiting is somehow ruining other couples' relationships, but that the *non*-cohabitors are a distinct group whose behaviors differ from those of the general population (Clarkberg, Stolzenberg, and Waite 1995; Thomson and Colella 1992; Lillard, Brien, and Waite 1995; Schoen 1992; Seltzer 2000). As a report on the subject commissioned by the U.S. Department of Health and Human Services concluded, "The most sophisticated studies have found that, although cohabitation engenders somewhat more liberal attitudes toward divorce, it does not increase the likelihood of marital disruption" (Fein et al. 2003, iv).

Perhaps most telling, researchers who reexamine this question with succeeding cohorts of cohabitors conclude that the finding appears to be diminishing (Schoen 1992). The claim of a cohabitation-divorce link is simply insufficiently robust for the government to use it as a justification for maintaining its sharp legal distinction between married and unmarried.

Finally, there are reams of claims that marriage is superior when it comes to health, wealth, happiness, lack of domestic violence, longevity, sexual satisfaction, and countless other factors, and that these differences necessitate government intervention to encourage couples to choose wisely. These claims, too, often mislead. Many of these benefits, such as positive health effects, have also been found to accrue to unmarried partners; they seem to result from being in a supportive relationship, whether married or not (Anson 1989; Graff 1999, 46–47; Joung et al. 1994; Peters and Liefbroer 1998). Some alleged benefits of marriage may be the direct result of the social, legal, and economic benefits granted to married couples in the United States. Other straightforward explanations abound to explain what are often presented as mysterious riches of marriage. Couples' incomes often rise around the time they get engaged and marry, for instance, because couples commonly marry when they finish school or get a stable job (and delay marrying until economic stability is within their grasp). In the case of the higher rate of domestic violence among cohabitors—one of the most disturbing claims made—researchers have found that in an initial pool of cohabitors, there is no higher rate of domestic violence as compared with married people. Over time, though, cohabitors in nonviolent relationships are more likely to marry, while those whose partners are abusive wisely choose not to make a lifetime commitment to that partner. These abusive ones "accumulate" in the cohabitor population (Kenney and McLanahan 2001). This does not mean, of course, that violence develops as a bizarre side effect of having lived together for too long.

Sorting through the research is a never-ending and necessary task, but it should not be used to overlook a fundamental question: Even if there are real differences between different kinds of relationships and legal marital statuses, do the differences justify government regulation or intrusion? Any comparison of two groups will reveal variables where one seems more favorable: people who live in cities versus rural areas, parents versus the childfree, those who are religious or not, vegetarians versus meat eaters, people who watch lots of television and those who watch little. Most people do not believe the government should interfere with people's freedom to make these types of personal decisions. Haggling over the nuances in the latest social science research bogs us down in differences that ultimately bear little relevance to how public policy can treat a diversity of family forms more fairly.

Legal Rights and Protections

The most significant difference between married and unmarried couples lies not in the quality of their relationships but in the way they are treated under federal, state, and local laws. Most people want the people they consider their family members, whether "traditionally" defined or not, to have access to certain rights and protections. Bookstore shelves and law journals are filled with mass-market guidebooks, professional articles, and court cases that revolve around the legal rights of unmarried partners and others who fall outside the blood, marriage, or adoption definition of family. When the two of us teach adult education classes for unmarried couples, legal concerns always top our students' lists of questions. Family lawyers have had to become proficient at crafting sets of contracts, wills, durable powers of attorney, and other documents for their unmarried clients. Without the bundle of legal rights that marriage provides, unmarried people are forced to read and research their options, hire a lawyer, or just take their chances. The last option is the road too many unmarried people take, usually unaware that they have any other options or naively assuming the law will protect them, particularly if their relationship is loving and long-lasting. Too often, they or their loved ones are in for a rude surprise.

Every day, the laws intended to protect families harm unmarried people and their families simply by leaving them outside the shelter of protections. People are shut out of hospital rooms, lose their homes when their partner dies without a will, are denied access to joint health insurance, pay higher income taxes, are ineligible to receive a longtime partner's Social Security benefits, are prevented from filing suit when a partner is killed by a drunk driver, have no recourse when they encounter discrimination in employment and housing, are charged extra to insure their homes or rent a car, and are forcibly separated from partners who are not U.S. citizens. In some states poor unmarried families are penalized because of their marital status, eligible for fewer public safety net benefits in an attempt to create a "marriage incentive."[6]

Although many of these inequities primarily affect adults, children in these families are unquestionably harmed as well when a family must spend a significantly greater portion of the household budget for basic needs like health insurance (or leave family members uninsured) than an identical married family will spend. The Alternatives to Marriage Project occasionally receives calls from unmarried parents in the most extreme situations, forced to live apart and break up their families because of anti-cohabitation laws or anticohabitation custody agreements. One recent caller explained how she and her male partner, in an intimate relationship for seven years with plans to marry sometime in the future, are now living separately while their biological child travels back and forth between their two homes. Because her state still has an anticohabitation law on the books, a judge announced she would lose custody of her first child (from a previous marriage) if she continued to live with her unmarried partner (the parent of her second child). Despite their seven-year loving relationship, their plans to marry in the future, and the fact that they are co-parenting two children (her first child and their joint biological child), this family has been disrupted because of the legal assumption that cohabitation is dangerous for children. Although the law no longer explicitly penalizes "bastards" or "illegitimate children," it does cast a cloud over their field of opportunities by preventing their families access to the same rights and protections—and, in the most appalling examples, tearing their families apart.

If one accepts the notion that community support and public recognition are key ingredients to strengthening families, it becomes clear that the legal exclusion of unmarried families from recognition weakens these social units. Unmarried couples with children are frequently forced to buy two separate health insurance policies or risk going uninsured, confront slurs about "illegitimacy" from conservative groups—still!—and constantly battle the perception that their families lack commitment or have some hidden dysfunction simply because they lack a marriage license. They often feel unwelcome in religious communities that are a great source of support for married families. Other relatives, like grandparents, aunts, and uncles, often take unmarried families less seriously and may provide less child care or exclude a partner from family gatherings. Unmarried parents spend more time explaining their relationship, confirming their different last names, filling out extra forms at the hospital or at their children's school. While each example is small, unmarried families often describe the cumulative effect as exhausting. Even though many of the issues mentioned here are interpersonal ones, not legal ones, they are the result of a society that has only one way to recognize families: legal marriage.

Despite the hopes of marriage-promoting pundits and politicians, the demographic reality is stark. An ever-growing percentage of families in America are unmarried, and therefore vulnerable in an increasingly outdated system that still relies primarily on marital status to legitimize family relationships. The marriage divide roughly follows the class divide. As marriage becomes what demographer Frank Furstenberg (2000) famously called "a luxury consumer item," the poor are disproportionately likely to cohabit or become single parents, the "budget" approaches to family formation. Since the poor have little political power, the marriage divide, like other issues that disproportionately affect low-income families, receives little serious political attention.

An Ethical Obligation

As a nation, we have a fundamental ethical duty to treat families fairly, even when family forms fall outside our imagined norms or ideals. Just as the law was once interpreted to exclude women and African Americans from equal consideration, today discrimination on the basis of marital status is an institutionalized and largely unquestioned element of our legal system. A variety of feeble justifications prevail. Most often we hear that marriage must be privileged to ensure the well-being of children. Yet there seems less concern for the 20 million children—28 percent of children in the United States—who are already living in unmarried families (U.S. Census Bureau 2001a). (Similarly, some pundits seem unaware that the majority of married-couple households do not include minor children [Simmons and O'Connell 2003, 10].) Some defenders of the current system argue essentially that recognition of marriage should not be changed because "it's always been this way," a claim that family historians and anthropologists have frequently repudiated (see Rosen, this volume; Graff 1999). In many policy discussions, there is no explanation offered for why marriages should be privileged above other family types. The primacy of marriage is simply assumed as a given, and public policy built from that assumption. We see a logical progression of ethics-based arguments that marriage should *not* be the centerpiece of our country's family policy:

1. As we began by suggesting, it is our nation's ethical obligation to treat families fairly.
2. Most people believe that "family" is a group of people who love and care for one another, not limited to people related by blood, marriage, or adoption. Ninety percent of survey respondents agreed that society "should value all types of families" (Seligman 1990, 38; Coontz 1997, 94).
3. An ever-growing number of families fall outside the existing legal definition of family.
4. This broader definition of family is consistent with the way family has been defined in most places and times throughout history.
5. In a democratic society, people should be free to form intimate relationships and families in ways that work best for them.
6. Therefore, society has an ethical obligation to treat these "nontraditional" families as well as it treats "traditional" ones. A straightforward way to move toward this goal would be to stop making legal distinctions based on marital status.

Public policy debates in recent years have swirled around the question of how to define family. Same-sex marriage and domestic partnership registries and benefits are major news in states and municipalities across the country, with debate hinging on the issue of which relationships should count as "families" for legal purposes. In 2001, the terrorist attacks of September 11 highlighted the sheer number of victims' family members who were not legally considered family: long-term unmarried partners, both gay and straight, and these partners' children; fiancés with wedding dates approaching; dependent relatives who lived with and were supported by someone who was killed that day. A few months after the attacks, an Associated Press article about the aftermath read:

From among the nearly 3,000 victims of September 11, at least one had two wives, some were married, but had children out of wedlock, while many were divorced and remarried. Others, heterosexual and homosexual, lived with long-term partners now in legal limbo. While the varied family structures reflect the remarkable diversity of American society, they also are creating plenty of complications for lawyers sifting through claims for compensation and inheritances. (Crary 2002)

Because of the high profile of the crisis, charities scrambled to expand policies that had been exclusionary for decades, agreeing to recognize some in "nontraditional" relationships as surviving family members. New York governor George Pataki issued an executive order suspending existing state law in order to expand relationship recognition for crime victim awards—but only for those whose loved ones were killed in the attacks of September 11. The order included its own definition of family for survivors:

A person shall be eligible for awards upon a showing of unilateral dependence or mutual interdependence . . . which may be evidenced by a nexus of factors, including but not limited to common ownership of property, common householding, shared budgeting and the length of the relationship between such person and the victim. (State of New York 2001)

We are heartened by this generous reunderstanding of family, but also note that it was written as a narrow exception to an unchanged governmental stance. Governor Pataki gave less than he should have. The limited nature of the order reveals the state of public policy denial about the state of the law for "nontraditional family members" unlucky enough to die by other means on any other day of the year.

Removing legal marriage from consideration in these debates, as Governor Pataki's executive order essentially did for one small portion of the law, would have clarified the issues enormously, allowing policymakers to consider relationships directly. Without marriage as a legal category, people who considered themselves family members of those who were killed would be on equal footing. Those who had written contracts and agreements would easily be able to demonstrate the deceased's intentions regarding the relationship. After implementation of the changes we recommend here, presumably there would be many more of these documents, given a public education campaign that would need to accompany a policy change of this kind.

In the absence of such a contract, policies would rely on a set of criteria similar to the one used in Pataki's executive order, allowing a variety of ways for people to establish themselves as next of kin. Most couples who are today legally married would easily meet such criteria; a few would not, raising the question of whether we want our policies to recognize, say, a married couple who do not live together and are unable to produce any evidence of financial or emotional interdependence. No criteria to define "family" could be perfect, and drafting them would generate heated debate. But nearly any thoughtful set of criteria, including the Vanier Institute for the Family and American Law Institute proposals outlined earlier in this chapter, could do a far better job of capturing the real ways people live, care for, and think about their relationships than the current marital status–centric system. As one British analysis of Britain's approach put it, "Basing a policy of supporting families almost entirely upon marriage as an institution seems to leave the government with its head rather deep in the sand" (Barlow and Duncan 2000, 141).

But Would It Fly?

One might assume the general public is unaware of any theoretical debate about this issue, but evidence suggests there is already considerable mainstream public support for abolishing marriage as a legal category, particularly among younger generations. A recent Gallup poll funded by the National Marriage Project, a pro-marriage advocacy group, found that 45 percent of unmarried adults in their twenties believe government should not be involved in licensing marriages. "A high percentage" (details not reported) of young adults say the government should not give special privileges to married couples, and 80 percent view marriage as "nobody's business but the two people involved" (Whitehead and Popenoe 2001, 13).

This generation of young adults is not antimarriage. Most still marry by their late twenties, and 96 percent of college freshmen say they want to marry someday (U.S. Census Bureau 2003; Sweet and Bumpass 1992; Louis Harris and Associates 1998). But they see marriage as a private relationship, one kind among many. Fewer of them see the need for public institutions to make a distinction between the relationships of married people, those of gay, lesbian, bisexual, and transgender people, or other forms of interdependent, consensual, adult relationships. Most think marriage is tremendously significant and hope to find a spouse who can be their best friend or even soul mate (Whitehead and Popenoe 2001). But this quest for a partnership that yields a lifetime of happiness is also seen as deeply personal. Just as they would not expect government to interfere with dating or childbearing behavior, they are uncomfortable with government control over the institution of marriage.

Beyond young adults, people of all ages are interested in separating symbolic, spiritual marriage from legal recognition of relationships and families. While the public is decidedly split on whether same-sex marriage should be legalized, there is strong support for the idea that committed gay and lesbian relationships should receive the same rights and protections as married couples (Henry J. Kaiser Family Foundation 2001; Newport 2003). Torn between what they see as a question of fairness for their gay and lesbian loved ones and a reluctance to change what they perceive as an institution with a stable historic definition, many intuitively conclude that same-sex relationships should receive legal recognition without being called "marriages." When the Vermont Supreme Court required the state's legislature either to give same-sex couples access to legal marriage or to provide the equivalent rights and benefits, the legislators came to this same conclusion. The resulting law created civil unions, an invention that gives same-sex couples the state-granted legal standing usually associated with marriage—without using the M word. Like reciprocal beneficiary laws in Hawaii, civil unions are yet one more attempt to separate the legal category of marriage from the legal rights and protections needed by real people in real relationships and families. Most GLBT activists see civil unions as an unacceptable substitute for marriage rights, since they fail to provide the federal benefits of marriage, may be meaningless outside state borders, and lack the symbolic meanings of marriage. Yet civil unions' presence in the public discourse, confirmed when Connecticut adopted this legal category in 2005, shows that the distinction between marriage and legal rights is becoming ever clearer in the public mind.

Interestingly, those who are thinking deeply about the implications of legalizing same-sex marriage often arrive at the logical conclusion: abolishing marriage as a legal category is the next step. In 1997, libertarian author David Boaz sketched out these ideas in "Privatize Marriage" in the online magazine *Slate:*

Why should the government be in the business of decreeing who can and cannot be married? Proponents of gay marriage see it as a civil-rights issue. Opponents see it as another example of minority "rights" being imposed on the majority culture. But why should anyone have—or need to have—state sanction for a private relationship? . . . And what of gay marriage? Privatization of the institution would allow gay people to marry the way other people do: individually, privately, contractually, with whatever ceremony they might choose in the presence of family, friends, or God. Gay people are already holding such ceremonies, of course, but their contracts are not always recognized by the courts and do not qualify them for the 1049 federal laws that the General Accounting Office says recognize marital status. Under a privatized system of marriage, courts and government agencies would recognize any couple's contract—or, better yet, eliminate whatever government-created distinction turned on whether a person was married or not. (Boaz 1997)

In Canada, columnist Russell Smith drew similar conclusions:

Why not eliminate marriage as a legal category altogether, and leave it as a religious one? . . . Marriage is, as the homophobes consistently and vociferously point out, fundamentally a religious tradition. That's exactly why I personally don't want to have much to do with it. And we have, at least nominally, a separation of church and state here. . . . Maybe it's time for the state to get entirely out of the business of sanctioning or defining religious rituals. Maybe marriage is a legal category we no longer need. (Smith 2003)

Eliminating marriage's legal standing has been suggested by columnists and radio hosts across the country, and even by a Massachusetts state representative. In a last-minute bid to block same-sex marriages in his state, Republican Paul Loscocco proposed that the state offer only civil unions to both same-sex and different-sex couples, and leave marriage to churches, synagogues, and mosques (see Shanley, this volume). "A lot of people can't put their finger on why they're opposed to gay marriage, but when it comes down to it they're confusing the civil with the religious acts," he said. "We have two concepts using the same word" (Frost 2004).

Some religious conservatives would like to see the government get out of the marriage business for the same reasons they prefer home schooling over public schools. And plenty of people do not see any logical reason why the government should be licensing intimate relationships. One woman we interviewed who had a wedding without getting legally married commented, "The whole idea of making a contract with the state so that you have the right to have sex with somebody, and then when you want to stop having sex with them you have to pay a whole bunch of money, doesn't seem to be very smart." Another said she is uncomfortable with a potentially arbitrary system in which the government can decide who marries:

> By engaging in this act you are basically saying that someone has the right to decide who can get married and who can't. I mean, technically, we could go into City Hall and ask for a marriage license, and they could say, "No, you can't have one." They could say, "Well, she's too short and he's too tall, and we want five foot five, blond-haired, blue-eyed people, and we don't think you should get married." I mean, it doesn't happen that way, fortunately, but it says that they have the power to decide.

Even if it seems outlandish to think marriage licenses could actually be denied on this basis, the U.S. government does have a checkered history on this issue. Prior to the Civil War, slaves were not allowed to marry in slaveholding states (see Davis, this volume). Marriage between blacks and whites was once illegal in the United States: sixteen states still had antimiscegenation laws on the books when the Supreme Court finally declared them unconstitutional in 1967, and an Alabama law barring interracial marriage was repealed only as recently as 2000. Other governments across history have prevented students from marrying before graduation, artisans from marrying before completing their apprenticeships, peasants from marrying noblemen, and disabled and blind people from marrying at all, and have set the minimum legal age for marriage as high as thirty years for men and twenty-five for women (Graff 1999, 201–2). Access to marriage for incarcerated persons and persons seeking plural marriage has continued to be debated in the courts. Government control over marriage has always been, and perhaps will always continue to be, an exercise in inclusion and exclusion.

It is important to be clear that potential support exists for eliminating marriage as a legal category, not for abolishing marriage itself. Most people probably agree that marriage is a personal, religious, or spiritual matter (about three-quarters of weddings are performed by clergy [Gross

1999]), not a subject for state intrusion or control. The public is likely to support reforms that would keep the institution of marriage where it belongs—in the domain of the private relationship of couples to each other, their families, and their faith communities—while increasing fairness for all families involved in the legal system. Advocates would undoubtedly be branded as "promoting the homosexual agenda," a favorite conservative rallying cry. Supporters would need to be prepared to respond that, yes, reforms of this kind will treat gay people more fairly (most Americans favor fair treatment for gay people in many policy areas [Henry J. Kaiser Family Foundation 2001; Newport 2003], but that they would help single people, senior citizens, stepfamilies, married people, and children just as much. Rather than an antimarriage project, what we are proposing is a family justice movement, a movement for a family-friendly legal system.

Real-World Implementation

Driven by public demand, the private sector has already widely implemented changes that define family more broadly. Although these changes do not usually eliminate the "marriage" category entirely, they demonstrate that policies based on other definitions can be written and implemented with positive results, and without negative fiscal or public-relations repercussions. In businesses where these policies are already in place, replacing legal marital status with the new criteria would be a simple transition, and would change nothing for most legally married people.

The massive growth in employers' adoption of domestic partner health benefits policies (a 50 percent jump in the two years from 1999 to 2001 [Human Rights Campaign Foundation 2001, 18]) is perhaps the best example. The change has come about in response to employees' complaints that compensating married employees more generously than unmarried ones, by providing expensive joint health insurance for spouses but not for partners or other dependents, violates the principle of equal pay for equal work. One labor union made the point using a mock want ad:

WANTED—ACCOUNT CLERK
Starting wage of homosexual or unmarried worker $9.02 per hour. For married worker $10.33 per hour. Apply at the County Personnel Office. Alameda County Is An Equal Opportunity Employer. (Local 616 of the Service Employees' International Union)

Attuned to the need to attract and retain top employees, a growing number of employers are revising their benefits policies accordingly. Today, about a third of Americans work for an employer that has a domestic partner health benefits plan, making what were once "spousal benefits" available to (in the vast majority of cases) both same-sex and different-sex unmarried couples (U.S. Census Bureau 2002, 3; Society for Human Resource Management 2002, 6; Human Rights Campaign Foundation 2003, 23).[7] Some employers take this concept even further, allowing employees to add an even broader range of types of dependents and household members to their health plans. Nearly 90 percent of employers that offer domestic partner benefits have added them since 1995 (Hewitt Associates 2000).

In drafting their policies, private employers, along with the smaller number of public entities that have also begun to offer domestic partner benefits, have been forced to reexamine which kinds of relationships should be entitled to benefits equivalent to those received by married couples. Who counts as family? Most employers with domestic partner policies have created some kind of affidavit containing the criteria that will make partners, dependents, or household members eligible for benefits. Although the specific criteria vary widely from employer to employer, they often include some of the following: coresidence, a minimum length of time the people must have been in the relationship, financial interdependence, and a requirement that the relationships be close, caring, or "for mutual support and benefit." Employees who wish to add a nonspouse to their health plan sign the affidavit, indicating that their relationship meets the criteria set by the employer. Although a few managers reportedly worry that "people will sign up their roommates," the affidavit makes fraud a punishable offense. (It is worth noting that one rarely hears concern expressed that people could claim someone as their spouse who is not really, despite the fact that married couples are almost never required to present their marriage licenses as proof.)

Domestic partner and family recognition benefits policies have been implemented smoothly in more than seventy-four hundred workplaces around the nation, including more than two hundred Fortune 500 companies (Human Rights Campaign Foundation 2004). At the same time, other kinds of businesses have quietly made similar policy changes. Many membership-based businesses like museums, health clubs, grocery cooperatives, and even the American Automobile Association (AAA) have changed their membership eligibility systems, now providing joint memberships based on who shares a household or meets other functional family criteria, rather than on legal marital status. In most cases the changes have been introduced with little fanfare, and the transitions have been imperceptible for most members and patrons. But for that minority of employees, patrons, or members who had family members previously excluded by too-narrow definitions of "family," the changes can result in savings of thousands of dollars a year, health care for family members previously uninsured, and other significant gains. With few exceptions, married couples also meet the eligibility criteria, meaning the new systems operate fairly without reliance on legal marital status.

In effect, these thousands of businesses have tested the idea of allocating rights and benefits based on characteristics of human relationships, rather than, or in addition to, basing eligibility on legal marriage. There have been few, if any, negative repercussions, a negligible fiscal impact (Kohn 1999; Badgett 2002), and few complaints from customers, clients, investors, other employees, or the human resources or membership staff who process the benefits paperwork. Implementing similar changes in the legal system would obviously be more complex, and changing marriage's legal status would be different from adding a "separate but equal" category like domestic partnerships. But a parallel exists. As in so many areas, the private sector's flexibility, responsiveness to the market, and focus on public demand put it ahead of the public sector. The legal questions with which it has already grappled, the policies it has tested and refined, and the public education that has already taken place could all be valuable in the public sector.

Members of the religious community have also embraced these changes. Small but growing numbers of ministers and rabbis have continued to perform marriage ceremonies but decline to sign marriage certificates for heterosexual couples until they can legally sign them for gay and lesbian ones. The movement was inspired at least in part by a journal article by the Reverend David Pettee, who wrote, "I came to the awareness that the willingness of clergy to assist with legalizing marriage ceremonies carries grave repercussions. . . . The seemingly neutral act of signing a marriage license actually represents a silent collusion with the state's position to extend the many privileges and benefits of marriage only to certain couples—heterosexual couples" (*UU World* 2003).

On the surface, this is a high-profile protest of the exclusionary legal politics of marriage. But a more fundamental shift is occurring. "It seems to me to be a pure religious position for a minister to say, 'I will marry people before God, but their business with the state is up to them,'" said the Reverend Fred Small, a minister in Littleton, Massachusetts (*UU World* 2003). Likewise, Reverend F. Jay Deacon, whose congregation is in Northampton and Florence, Massachusetts, commented that given the separation of church and state, "I have been wondering for a long time why I am signing a legal document at all," and said that he might never sign marriage licenses again. "I might sign a few just to celebrate [if same-sex marriage were legal], but probably no more after that" (Giampetruzzi 2003). In other words, boundaries are being redrawn not only in the private sector but also in the religious sphere. The reasons are different, but the result is the same: real-world reenvisionings of marriage-the-legal-institution, marriage-the-religious-institution, and caretaking relationships.

Families Win If the State Gets Out of the Marriage Business

There is no inherent reason that one kind of structure for relationships between adults should receive government sanctions and others not when effects on children are considered. Those who advocate that the state should promote marriage often say this is because, on average, children of married parents have higher well-being than children of unmarried parents, and that government has a stake in the well-being of children. Two major flaws mar this argument. First, as we mentioned earlier, 54 percent of married-couple households have no minor children, according to the 2000 census (Fields 2001). More than one-third of divorces from first marriages involve no children (National Center for Health Statistics 1995). Yet government-in-marriage "for the sake of the children" advocates are unlikely to accept the logical proposal that follows from their own argument, that government be involved only in marriages that involve children, not in regulating the relationships of couples who marry in their fifties or older, child-free couples, or those whose children are grown.

Second, children's well-being varies dramatically by an infinite number of factors: rich versus poor families, urban versus rural households, parents in high-conflict versus low-conflict relationships, families with fewer versus more children, planned versus unplanned births, families of various ethnic and racial groups. Yet most policymakers agree it would be offensive, and perhaps even unconstitutional, to have a different set of laws that affect the "preferred" families (well-off white couples in low-conflict relationships with no more than three children, for instance). Like these other factors, legal marital status is an option for some but not for others, and as personal a choice as whether to have one child, ten children, or none at all. No rational explanation tells us why we need to have legal distinctions between married and unmarried, any more than we would have legal distinctions between urban and rural.

The most compelling reason to end legal interest in marital status is the simple ethical obligation to treat the wide variety of caretaking relationships fairly. Although marriage proponents often speak of marriage as the fabric of society, this fabric is actually woven of caretaking relationships of all kinds, with strands held by parents and children, siblings, spouses, partners, friends, and neighbors. These human relationships—some simple and easy to understand, others "messy" and nontraditional—are what truly matter when it comes to ensuring that individuals, families, and communities are healthy and strong and receive the support they need. Ending the practice of arbitrarily elevating some human relationships above others would benefit all of us.

NOTES

1. The concept "family of choice" was pioneered by anthropologist Kath Weston in *Families We Choose: Lesbians, Gays, Kinship* (New York: Columbia University Press, 1991).

2. In the United States, only twelve states recognize new common-law marriages, and couples must hold themselves out as married in order to be considered common-law spouses.

3. Despite the uproar about the "marriage tax penalty," the majority of married couples actually receive a "married bonus" (*Seattle Times* 1999).

4. For more on this subject, see Dalma Heyn, *Marriage Shock: The Transformation of Women into Wives* (New York: Villard, 1997); and Susan Mausart, *Wifework: What Marriage Really Means for Women* (New York: Bloomsbury, 2002).

5. These are usually referred to as "serial cohabitors," a term we feel compelled to argue should be dropped from the social science lexicon. The only other situation in which the word "serial" is commonly used to describe a person is when it precedes "killer." We do not call people who marry more than once "serial spouses." "Multiple cohabitors," "repeated cohabitors," or simply "people who have cohabited more than once" would be vastly preferable.

6. In others, benefits bring marriage penalties that inadvertently discourage poor couples from marrying. We believe safety net benefits should be based on income and need, neither rewarding nor penalizing couples for marrying, in order

to respect that couples are likely to make the best decisions about marriage when this is unrelated to financial gain or loss.

7. Calculation by Dorian Solot.

REFERENCES

American Law Institute. 2002. *Principles of the Law of Family Dissolution.* Philadelphia: American Law Institute.

Anson, Ofra. 1989. "Marital Status and Women's Health Revisited: The Importance of a Proximate Adult. *Journal of Marriage and the Family* 51:185–94.

Badgett, M. V. Lee. 2002. "Calculating Costs with Credibility: Health Care Benefits for Domestic Partners." *Angles.* Washington, D.C.: Institute for Gay and Lesbian Strategic Studies, November.

Barlow, Anne, and Simon Duncan. 2000. "New Labour's Communitarianism, Supporting Families and the 'Rationality Mistake': Part II." *Journal of Social Welfare and Family Law* 22:129–43.

Boaz, David. 1997. "Privatize Marriage." *Slate,* April 25. http://slate.msn.com/?id= 2440 (visited May 29, 2003).

Bohannan, Paul. 1985. *All the Happy Families: Exploring the Varieties of Family Life.* New York: McGraw-Hill.

Bumpass, Larry, James Sweet, and Andrew Cherlin. 1991. "The Role of Cohabitation in Declining Rates of Marriage." *Journal of Marriage and the Family* 53: 913–27.

Carbone, June. 2000. *From Partners to Parents: The Second Revolution in Family Law.* New York: Columbia University Press.

Clarkberg, Marin, Ross Stolzenberg, and Linda Waite. 1995. "Attitudes, Values, and Entrance into Cohabitational versus Marital Unions." *Social Forces* 74:609–34.

Coontz, Stephanie. 1992. *The Way We Never Were: American Families and the Nostalgia Trap.* New York: Basic Books.

———. 1997. *The Way We Really Are: Coming to Terms with America's Changing Families.* New York: Basic Books.

Cott, Nancy. 2000. *Public Vows: A History of Marriage and the Nation.* Cambridge, Mass.: Harvard University Press.

Crary, David. 2002. *Associated Press.* February 17.

DeMaris, Alfred, and William MacDonald. 1993. "Premarital Cohabitation and Marital Instability: A Test of the Unconventionality Hypothesis." *Journal of Marriage and the Family* 55:399–407.

Demian. 2004. "Marriage Traditions in Various Times and Cultures." *Partners Task Force for Gay and Lesbian Couples.* February. http://www.buddybuddy.com/mar-trad.html (visited April 30, 2004).

Dixon, Suzanne. 1992. *The Roman Family: Ancient Society and History.* Baltimore: Johns Hopkins University Press.

Duff, Johnette, and George Truitt. 1991. *The Spousal Equivalent Handbook: A Legal and Financial Guide to Living Together.* Houston: Sunny Beach Publications.

Duffy, Jamie, and Brad Kane. 2002. "Students Rush to Marry for Bowl Tickets." *The Lantern.* (Ohio State University), December 5.

Eurostat. 2000. "First Results of the Demographic Data Collection for 1999 in Europe." *Statistics in Focus.*

———. 2001. "100 Basic Indicators from Eurostat Yearbook 2001." *Eurostat Yearbook 2001.*

Fein, David, Nancy Burstein, Greta Fein, and Laura Lindberg. 2003. "The Determinants of Marriage and Cohabitation among Disadvantaged Americans: Research Findings and Needs." Marriage and Family Formation Data Analysis Project. Cambridge, Mass.: Abt Associates.

Fields, Jason. 2001. "America's Families and Living Arrangements: March 2000." Washington, D.C.: U.S. Census Bureau.

Frayser, Suzanne. 1985. *Varieties of Sexual Experience: An Anthropological Perspective on Human Sexuality.* New Haven, Conn.: HRAF Press. As cited in Burton Pasternak, Carol Ember, and Melvin Ember. *Sex, Gender, and Kinship: A Cross-Cultural Perspective* (Upper Saddle River, N.J.: Prentice-Hall, 1997).

Frost, Greg. 2004. "Lawmaker Eyes Simple Fix to Gay Marriage Spat." *Reuters,* April 15.

Furstenberg, Frank, Jr. 2000. "The Future of Marriage." *American Demographics,* June, 34–40.

Giampetruzzi, Tony. 2003. "Second Clergy Takes Dramatic Stand in Favor of Same-Sex Marriage." *Newsweekly,* March 5.

Gillis, John. 1985. *For Better, for Worse: British Marriages, 1600 to the Present.* New York: Oxford University Press.

———. 1996. *A World of Their Own Making: Myth, Ritual, and the Quest for Family Values.* Cambridge, Mass.: Harvard University Press.

Graff, E. J. 1999. *What Is Marriage For?* Boston: Beacon Press.

Gross, Judy. 1999. "Church, State Join Struggle to Save U.S. Marriages." *National Catholic Register,* September 17.

Henry J. Kaiser Family Foundation. 2001. *Inside-OUT: A Report on the Experiences of Lesbians, Gays, and Bisexuals in America and the Public's Views on Issues and Policies Related to Sexual Orientation.* Menlo Park, Calif.

Hewitt Associates. 2000. *Domestic Partner Benefits 2000.* Lincolnshire, Ill.

Human Rights Campaign Foundation. 2001. *The State of the Workplace for Lesbian, Gay, Bisexual and Transgender Americans 2001.* Washington, D.C.

———. 2003. *The State of the Workplace for Lesbian, Gay, Bisexual, and Transgender Americans 2002.* Washington, D.C.

———. 2004. "Domestic Partner Benefits." http://www.hrc.org/Template.cfm?

Section=The_Issues&Template=/TaggedPage/TaggedPageDisplay.cfm&TPLID =26&ContentID=13399 (August 16, 2004).

Ingraham, Chrys. 1999. *White Weddings: Romancing Heterosexuality in Popular Culture.* New York: Routledge.

International Lesbian and Gay Association. 2000. *World Legal Survey.* June 6. www.ilga.org/Information/legal_survey/europe/sweden.htm (visited November 21, 2002).

Joung, I., H. van de Mheen, K. Stronks, F. van Poppel, and J. Mackenbach. 1994. "Differences in Self-Reported Morbidity by Marital Status and by Living Arrangement." *International Journal of Epidemiology* 23:91–97.

Katz, Jonathan, ed. 1995. *The Invention of Heterosexuality.* New York: Penguin.

Kenney, Catherine, and Sara McLanahan. 2001. "Are Cohabiting Relationships More Violent Than Marriage?" Working Paper no. 01-02. Princeton, N.J.: Center for Research on Child Well-Being, Princeton University.

Kiernan, Kathleen, and Valerie Estaugh. 1993. *Cohabitation: Extra-marital Childbearing and Social Policy.* London: Family Policy Studies Centre.

Kohn, Sally. 1999. *The Domestic Partner Organizing Manual for Employee Benefits.* Washington, D.C.: Policy Institute of the National Gay and Lesbian Task Force.

Kreider, Rose, and Jason Fields. 2002. "Number, Timing, and Duration of Marriages and Divorces: 1996." *Current Population Reports.* Washington, D.C.: U.S. Census Bureau.

Lillard, Lee, Michael Brien, and Linda Waite. 1995. "Premarital Cohabitation and Subsequent Marital Dissolution: A Matter of Self-Selection?" *Demography* 32: 437–57.

Local 616 of the Service Employees' International Union. Quoted in Patti Roberts, "Comments," in *Women and Unions: Forging a Partnership,* ed. Dorothy Sue Cobble (Ithaca, N.Y.: ILR Press, 1993), 352.

Louis Harris and Associates. 1998. "Generation 2001: A Survey of the First College Graduating Class of the New Millennium," 8.

Mintz, Steven, and Susan Kellogg. 1988. *Domestic Revolutions: A Social History of American Family Life.* New York: Free Press.

National Center for Health Statistics. 1995. *Monthly Vital Statistics Report.* Vol. 43, no. 9, Supplement. Washington, D.C.: Centers for Disease Control and Prevention, March 22.

Newport, Frank. 2003. "Six Out of 10 Americans Say Homosexual Relations Should Be Recognized as Legal." Gallup News Service, May 15.

Parker, Stephen. 1990. *Informal Marriage, Cohabitation and the Law 1750–1989.* New York: St. Martin's Press.

Peters, Arnold, and Aart Liefbroer. 1998. "Beyond Marital Status: Partner History and Well-Being in Old Age." *Journal of Marriage and the Family* 59:687–99.

Probert, Rebecca, and Anne Barlow. 2000. "Cohabitants and the Law: Recent European Reforms." *Deutsches und Europäisches Familienrecht* 2:76–81.

Roper Starch Worldwide Inc. 1995. "The 1995 Virginia Slims Opinion Poll: A 25-Year Perspective on Women's Issues." Available at tobaccodocuments.org.

Schoen, Robert. 1992. "First Unions and the Stability of First Marriages." *Journal of Marriage and the Family* 54:281–84.

Seattle Times. 1999. "With This Wedding Ring, the IRS Thee Taxes." Editorial, April 15.

Seligman, Jean. 1990. "Variations on a Theme." *Newsweek* (special edition) Winter/Spring.

Seltzer, Judith. 2000. "Families Formed Outside of Marriage." *Journal of Marriage and the Family* 62:1247–68.

Simmons, Tavia, and Martin O'Connell. 2003. "Married-Couple and Unmarried-Partner Households: 2000." Washington, D.C.: U.S. Census Bureau.

Smith, Russell. 2003. "Marriage: Who Needs It Anyway?" *Globe and Mail,* May 14.

Society for Human Resource Management. 2002. *2002 Benefits Survey.* Alexandria, Va.

Springer, Ilene. 2000. "The Egyptian Bride." *Tour Egypt Monthly.* September 1. http://www.egyptmonth.com/mag09012000/magf4.htm (visited April 29, 2004).

State of New York. Governor. 2001. Executive Order. *Suspension of Provisions Relating to Crime Victim Awards for Persons Dependent upon Victims of the World Trade Center Attack and Redefining the Term Principal Support for Persons Dependent upon Victims Who Die as a Result of a Crime.* No. 113.30, October 10.

Sweet, James, and Larry Bumpass. 1992. "Young Adults' View of Marriage, Cohabitation, and Family." In *The Changing American Family,* ed. S. J. South and S. E. Tolnay. Boulder, Colo.: Westview Press.

Teachman, Jay. 2003. "Premarital Sex, Premarital Cohabitation, and the Risk of Subsequent Marital Dissolution among Women." *Journal of Marriage and the Family,* 65:444–55.

Thomson, Elizabeth, and Ugo Colella. 1992. "Cohabitation and Marital Stability: Quality or Commitment?" *Journal of Marriage and the Family* 54:259–67.

U.S. Census Bureau. 1990. "Profile of General Demographic Characteristics for the United States: 1990." Table DP-1. Washington, D.C.

———. 2000. "Profile of General Demographic Characteristics for the United States: 2000." Table DP-1. Washington, D.C.

———. 2001a. "Detailed Living Arrangements of Children by Race and Hispanic Origin, 1996." Washington, D.C.

———. 2001b. "H3. Households with Two Unrelated Adults of the Opposite Sex, by Presence of Children under 15 and Age, Marital Status, and Race and Hispanic Origin/1 of Householder and Partner: March 1999." Washington, D.C.

———. 2001c. "UC-1. Unmarried-Couple Households, by Presence of Children: 1960 to Present." Washington, D.C.

———. 2002. *County Business Patterns 2000.* Washington, D.C.

————. 2003. "Table MS-2. Estimated Median Age at First Marriage, by Sex: 1890 to the Present." Washington, D.C.

UU World. 2003. "UU Clergy Won't Sign Licenses." May/June.

Vanier Institute for the Family. "What Is a Family?" *Family Facts.* http://www.vifamily.ca/library/facts/facts.html (visited April 30, 2004).

Watters, Ethan. 2003. *Urban Tribes: A Generation Redefines Friendship, Family, and Commitment.* New York: Bloomsbury.

Whitehead, Barbara Dafoe, and David Popenoe. 2001. *The State of Our Unions 2001.* Piscataway, N.J.: National Marriage Project.

Yalom, Marilyn. 2001. *A History of the Wife.* New York: HarperCollins.

Chapter 3

What Place for Marriage (E)quality in Marriage Promotion?

Linda C. McClain

I don't want to play Cupid. This isn't about telling anybody who should marry who. But when you have a couple who say, we're interested in getting married, or who are already married, it's about helping them develop the skills and knowledge necessary to form and sustain healthy marriages.

—Dr. Wade Horn, assistant secretary, Department of Health and Human Services (Henary 2002)

Men think that piece of paper says they own you. You are their personal slave. Cook their meals, clean their house, do their laundry. Who did it before I came along, you know? That's why they get married. A man gets married to have somebody take care of them 'cause their mommy can't do it any more. Most mothers don't want to be owned or slave for their husband. They want a partnerships of equals.   —Quoted by Kathryn Edin (2001)

Marriage Promotion and the Missing Dimension of Marriage (E)quality

The place of marriage in a just and fair constitutional democracy reverberates as one of the most challenging questions posed in debates over family law and policy. What is government's interest in intimate affiliation and in families? Should the fate of the institution of marriage be government's central concern in regulating the family? On the one hand, some voices urge that government should properly support and promote marriage, defined as the union of one man and one woman, as the proxy for the form of family best able to undergird our polity by allowing realization of the goods associated with family life and carrying out the important functions society assigns to families. On the other hand, critics of marriage's privileged place contend that it is an imperfect and inadequate proxy for these purposes: it fails to represent the full range of forms of intimate affiliation capable of fostering family members' capacities for self-government; of allowing the realization of such goods as interdependence, mutual support, and friendship; and of performing the vital function of nurturing children and other dependents (Solot and Miller, this volume). On this view, government should look beyond marriage—even if expanded to include same-sex marriage—to recognize a broader range of forms of families, such as the (single) parent-child bond, the bonds of extended and complex families, and the bonds of friendship.

As this anthology implicitly asks, Why marriage? Or, perhaps, Why *only* marriage? My answer to these questions is that marriage should continue to have a place in governmental regulation of families. As I elaborate in a longer work, there are two dimensions of family life that warrant governmental support and regulation: (1) the intergenerational dimension of families, that is, the role of families in carrying out the vital task of orderly social reproduction—nurturing children and preparing them to take their place as capable, responsible members of society (as well as attending to other dependency needs within the family); and (2) the dimension of intimate association between adults who form families, that is, the place of families in allowing the realization of such goods as love, friendship, sexual pleasure, commitment, interdependency, mutual responsibility, and the like (McClain 2005). Marriage, I contend, deserves governmental support because it is a social institution that may facilitate both of these dimensions of family life.

Thus, to the question, Should family law and policy move beyond marriage? my response is yes and no. I embrace moving beyond marriage in three relevant ways: (1) moving beyond "traditional" marriage to embrace more firmly sex equality, or equality *within* families, as a guiding norm for governmental efforts to support and encourage marriage; (2) moving beyond "traditional" marriage, defined as the union of one man and one woman, to recognize and support same-sex marriage as a step toward greater equality *among* families; and (3) as a further step toward equality *among* families, moving beyond an exclusive governmental focus upon marriage toward recognition and support of a broader array of families that afford a place for carrying out the tasks assigned to and realizing the goods associated with families. Along with this "yes" is a "no": society should not, as contributor Martha Fineman has proposed, move wholly beyond marriage to abolish it as a legal category, relegating all adult intimate relationships to the realm of private contract.

In the confines of this chapter, I will take up only the first of these three proposed moves beyond—but not wholly beyond—marriage: governmental efforts to support marriage should embrace and support equality within families, specifically, sex equality. Respect for sex equality does not require that marriage be abolished. Rather, such equality must feature in any governmental effort to support marriage. I will contend that, measured against this requirement, contemporary proposals to promote marriage and shore up a "marriage culture" made by the social movement known as the "marriage movement" and by politicians who seek to use marriage promotion as a central tool of welfare policy fall short. Although such proposals are also inattentive to the issue of equality generally within families (Young 1995), I defer that critique to another forum and in this chapter focus on the problem of inattention to sex equality within families.

Marriage promoters contend that shoring up the institution of marriage is vital to social health and that the best way for government, at all levels, to support families is to promote marriage and stem the tide of cohabitation, nonmarital childbearing, and divorce. Concern for declining levels of marital happiness and high levels of marital conflict leads to calls for government to help reduce the number of "unhealthy marriages" and to promote "healthy marriages." Although the most immediate arena in which politicians propose to use law to promote "healthy marriages" is welfare reform, as concern is the most acute over low-income unmarried families, the rhetoric sweeps more broadly. Various state initiatives aim to equip their citizens with the skills and knowledge to have happy, long-lasting marriages. The social movement known as the "marriage movement" seeks reform in our culture itself, aiming to reverse a "divorce culture" and "nonmarriage culture" and to renew a "marriage culture."

This chapter will examine the social health argument for marriage promotion set forth in key documents of the marriage movement, including the reasons offered for why marriage promotion is a legitimate governmental interest. Do the social health benefits argued to flow from marriage justify a governmental program of marriage promotion? Or, as some popular sentiment holds, is marriage really a private choice with which government, particularly the federal government, has "no business" interfering? What special concerns arise from using welfare reform as a vehicle to promote marriage among low-income (disproportionately minority) members of society, who have lower rates of marriage and higher rates of nonmarital family forms? Will government's agenda of promoting "healthy" marriage include a normative commitment to certain values? If so, will they include sex equality and economic interdependence as elements of healthy marriage (rather than women's traditional economic vulnerability and dependence within marriage)?

The marriage movement and governmental actors seeking to promote "healthy marriage" have paid insufficient attention to the relationship between marriage *quality* and sex *equality.* Proposals to promote marriage and a "marriage culture" fail, for the most part, to reckon with whether a commitment to sex equality is in tension with these ends or, by contrast, is a vital component of pursuing them. These proposals invite two questions: To what extent does the marriage movement's program of promoting healthy marriage rest on and seek to shore up fixed gender roles or gender stereotypes like those of an earlier regime of family law, condemned in our constitutional jurisprudence as inconsistent with contemporary norms of sex equality? And if this gender retrenchment is not a purpose of the movement, are the policies proposed likely to undermine gains in sex equality? I will conclude by suggesting how norms of sex equality should shape any governmental program of supporting marriage.

Marriage Promotion: From Social Movement to a "Central Pillar" of Welfare Policy

On the premise that most Americans desire a happy, long-lasting marriage, but this goal eludes them, the marriage movement seeks to restore a "marriage culture."[1] Various organizations affiliated with this movement have issued "calls" or "reports" to the nation, urging that reinvigorating marriage is our most urgent social challenge.[2] For example, the National Marriage Project releases annual reports titled "The State of Our Unions."[3] Since the 1990s, a related social movement has sought to promote "responsible fatherhood" through, among other things, fortifying marriage and affirming the unique and irreplaceable role of fathers in the emotional and moral development of children (Blankenhorn 1995).[4] Other social movements, such as the Alternatives to Marriage Project,[5] and the movement for recognition of same-sex marriage, argue for support of a broader range of family forms (Solot and Miller, this volume).

Promoting marriage animates not only social movements but also governmental actors. As a social movement, the marriage movement aims at transforming "culture," and yet it also urges federal, state, and local governments to "make supporting and promoting marriage an explicit goal of domestic policy" (Marriage Movement 2000). Moreover, within the last decade, promoting "responsible fatherhood" has become not only a social movement but also a governmental imperative. Indeed, Wade Horn, former head of the National Fatherhood Initiative, became assistant director of the Administration for Children and Families (ACF) at the Department of Health and Human Services (DHHS). In his writings and public appearances, Horn has stated that government cannot be "neutral" about marriage, a social good, and that the nation needs to be convinced that supporting marriage is a legitimate function of government (Toner 2002). Testifying before the Senate in support of President Bush's marriage promotion proposals, Horn appealed to research showing the greater benefits for children of healthy marriages and stated: "What we seek to do in our proposal [for welfare reauthorization] is increase the number of children who grow up in healthy marriages, and decrease the number of children who grow up in unhealthy marriages" (Horn 2002).

The most immediate vehicle for promoting a governmental "message" about marriage is welfare policy, as is evident in the unfolding debates over reauthorizing the Temporary Assistance for Needy Families (TANF) component of the Personal Responsibility and Work Opportunity Reconciliation Act of 1996 (PRWORA). In that act, Congress found that "marriage is the foundation of a successful society" and included as a purpose of TANF encouraging the formation and maintenance of two-parent families (PRWORA 1996). When TANF came up for reauthorization, Congress held hearings on welfare and marriage, on the assumption that welfare law should do far more to promote marriage, and that government, at various levels, might successfully encourage people who would otherwise have children outside of marriage to marry and to remain married. In support of proposals to promote skills and knowledge needed for successful marriage, legislators cite data from the Fragile Families and Child Well Being Survey, which reports that 80 percent of unmarried parents are romantically involved at the time of their child's birth, and that the majority say there is a good or almost certain chance that they will marry (although few in fact do go on to marry).[6]

The Bush administration's welfare plan, "Working toward Independence," includes "strengthening families" as a central pillar, which it defines in terms of "promoting healthy marriages" (Bush 2002). Praising PRWORA's devolution of authority and responsibility to the states to find ways to move persons from welfare to work, the plan identifies the federal government's role in marriage promotion as providing financial incentives to states to "find new and effective ways to encourage healthy marriages in appropriate circumstances." The plan also envisions that state governments will be "working together with private and faith-based organizations" to develop successful programs that will be "disseminated" to other states (Bush 2002, 2).

Some members of Congress have voiced caution about whether the federal government has any business to use welfare policy as a vehicle to promote marriage, "which is a personal and private choice" (Baucus 2002). Nonetheless, as of this writing it appears likely that a final reauthorization bill approved by Congress will be similar to the Bush plan and legislation approved by the House of Representatives in making the promotion of healthy marital families and responsible fatherhood the express purpose of TANF and in including funds for demonstration projects aimed at promoting those ends.[7]

State and local governments also seek to promote healthy marriage and responsible fatherhood and to use partnerships with nongovernmental actors (especially faith-based groups) to do so. For example, in Oklahoma, a Bible Belt state with a self-described "family-values culture"—as well as the second-highest divorce rate in the nation—Governor Frank Keating created the Oklahoma Marriage Initiative and allocated $10 million of TANF funds to meet his pledge to reduce the divorce rate by one-third (Anderson 2002, 335, 336). Several governors have signed marriage proclamations, proclaiming the importance of marriage to the public (U.S. DHHS 2002). Florida passed the Florida Marriage Preparation and Preservation Act of 1998, becoming the first state to require teaching marriage skills as part of the high school curriculum.[8] The act also gives a discount on marriage licenses to couples who take a premarital education course, couples who do not have a three-day waiting period. And Florida and some other states have created premarital education materials to be distributed to all marrying couples (U.S. DHHS 2002; Ooms, Bouchet, and Park 2004). Other state efforts aim more directly at legal reform to "reinstitutionalize" marriage and foster marital permanence: Arkansas, Arizona, and Louisiana, for example, have "covenant marriage" statutes, which permit couples to opt for a form of marriage in which divorce is more difficult to obtain; similar legislation is under consideration in other states (Ooms, Bouchet, and Park 2004).

All these governmental efforts to promote marriage draw on the social health arguments advanced by the marriage movement. As a video provided by Utah's Governor's Commission on Marriage puts it: "The duty of government is to protect and foster the common good. Strong marriages are key to improving both personal and social well-being."[9] There is a basic optimism that there is a set of skills, values, and knowledge needed to have a strong, healthy marriage and reduce conflict and divorce, and that these skills can be taught (Hendrick 2002; Horn 2002).

The Marriage Movement: How Marriage Promotes Social Health

The social health argument for marriage holds that families play a vital role in social reproduction, that is, nurturing and raising children to become good citizens and lead good lives. As Wade Horn puts it, "Families are the primary institutions through which we protect and nurture our children, and upon which free societies depend for establishing social order and promoting individual liberty and fulfillment" (Horn and Bush 1997). The vital role of families in social reproduction is not a new insight or one that is unique to the marriage movement. Indeed, there is considerable common ground among feminist, liberal, and civic republican views about the important place of families in fostering the preconditions for self-government (McClain 2001a). However, like the civil society argument, the social health argument stresses that it is not families as such but the institution of marriage and the marital family that are the "seedbed from which healthy children and, ultimately, a healthy society spring" (Horn 2001). For example, Florida's legislature found: "Just as the family is the foundation of society, the marital relationship is the foundation of the family."[10] Marriage promoters argue that marriage is "not just a private relationship" but also a "social institution," indeed, a "social good and therefore a legitimate concern of the state" (Marriage Movement 2000, 6). Thus government has a legitimate interest in strengthening marriage and in favoring it over other forms of family.

The marriage movement offers several justifications for why society should restore a marriage culture and government should promote mar-

riage. I glean these from a variety of books and reports written by prominent figures in the marriage movement and sponsored by affiliated organizations, such as the Institute for American Values; the Center for the
American Experiment; the University of Chicago's Religion, Culture, and
Family Project; and the Coalition for Marriage, Family and Couples Education (Waite and Gallagher 2000; Marriage Movement 2000; Whitehead
and Popenoe 2001).[11] Governmental pronouncements echo many of these
claims:

1. "Married adults, women as well as men, are happier, healthier, and
   wealthier than their unmarried counterparts" (Horn 2001). Put in the
   currency of social capital: Marriage is "a unique generator of social and
   human capital" (Marriage Movement 2000, 10). In referring to benefits
   for "women as well as men," marriage promoters seek to refute the common claim that men benefit from marriage, but women do not, and to
   highlight newer social science literature indicating mutual benefit (Waite
   and Gallagher 2000).

2. "Marriage protects the well-being of children"; "Children do better, on
   average, when they are raised by their two own married parents" (Marriage Movement 2000, 8). Marriage promoters contend that abundant
   social science evidence supports this claim.[12] This argument might suggest that marriage in and of itself is the key to comparative benefit for
   children, but the claim is more refined: current rhetoric about promoting marriage claims that children fare better in "healthy" marriages than
   in "unhealthy marriages" and that the goal is "loving," "healthy," or "low
   conflict" marriages (Horn 2002). Therefore, if protecting the well-being
   of children should be the primary goal of family policy, government
   should favor and promote healthy marriage.

3. "Divorce and unwed parenting generate large taxpayer costs." This is
   a point about the externalities generated by particular family forms:
   "higher rates of crime, drug abuse, education failure, chronic illness,
   child abuse, domestic violence, and poverty among both adults and children." Such problems bring "higher taxpayer costs in diverse forms
   including: more welfare expenditure; increased remedial and special
   education expenses; higher day-care subsidies; and additional child-sup-
   port collection costs." (Marriage Movement 2000, 9–10)

4. "Marriage is society's way of engaging the basic problem of fatherhood
   —how to hold the father to the stronger mother-child bond" (Popenoe 2001). Why is marriage necessary? "Being a father is universally

problematic for men in a way [motherhood] is not for women. Put simply, as marriage weakens, fathers stray" (Popenoe 2001).[13] Otherwise,
"left culturally unregulated, men's sexual behavior can be promiscuous,
their paternity casual, their commitment to families weak" (Popenoe
2001). The gender-neutral version of this argument is that marriage
offers "the only realistic promise of permanence": married couples stay
together more often and longer than cohabiting couples. (Marriage
Movement 2000, 11)

One additional proposition serves as an overarching justification for government and society to renew a "marriage culture": the idea that government should help people fulfill their deepest human desire, which
otherwise might be thwarted or "shattered" (Marriage Movement 2000,
22). "Although Americans haven't stopped seeking or valuing happy and
long-lasting marriages as an important goal, they are increasingly likely to
find that this goal eludes them" (Whitehead and Popenoe 1999, 3–4). Evidence of this gap between goals and experience includes several phenomena: the high divorce rate, the prevalence of cohabitation and nonmarital
child rearing, the declining percentage of people who say they are in "very
happy" first marriages, and increasing pessimism among young people,
especially young women, about the chances for a happy and long-lasting
marriage (Whitehead and Popenoe 1999).

Justifying Government's Role: The Pursuit of Happiness or Child Well-Being?

The marriage movement uses the language of personal happiness as a
motivating reason for society and government to take steps to shore up
marriage. But its call to renew a marriage culture also entails a changed
understanding of marriage, one more compatible with the civic virtue
ideal of a strengthened marriage culture, or "familial culture." Indeed,
marriage promoters suggest a paradox: in a "high-divorce society," because
Americans view marriage as a private contract for personal happiness,
rather than as a permanent commitment, this happiness proves elusive
because "we become less willing to invest ourselves fully—our time, resources, dreams, and ultimate commitments—in the institution of marriage" (Popenoe, Elshtain, and Blankenhorn 1996, 293, 300). Moreover, a
related claim is that too many married couples divorce merely because

they are unhappily married. A better course, at least in low-conflict marriages in which there are children, is to stay together and work things out. Indeed, marriage promoters reassure readers that research shows that many unhappy couples who stay together, instead of divorcing, find themselves happy several years later (Waite and Gallagher 2000).

The marriage movement focuses both on teaching skills to increase marital happiness and reduce divorce and on "reinstitutionalizing" marriage in the sense of strengthening marriage's place as the central public institution for ordering sexuality, reproduction, and child rearing. Carl Schneider (1992) speaks of family law's "channeling function" in using marriage as a social institution to order these human activities; marriage molds men and women to limit individual freedom for the sake of achieving family bonds. Channeling techniques include social approval and reward for marriage, and social disfavor of competing institutions. Thus, the marriage movement favors reinstitutionalizing marriage through reversing the trend of extending legal protections and marriage-like benefits to nonmarital relationships, a trend argued to make marriage less important or attractive. Another important component of reinstitutionalizing marriage is to renew the idea of the *permanence* of marriage. The marriage movement, through such measures an covenant marriage, seeks to restore a thicker social meaning of marriage, one that reintroduces the idea of marriage as an important, indeed vital, *social institution,* with norms of commitment and self-sacrifice, not merely a personal, private contract, terminable when it no longer makes one happy (Gallagher 1996; Spaht 2002).

An important goal of the marriage movement is not so much helping people achieve their deepest desires as it is to reconstruct those desires, to change the way they think about finding happiness through and within marriage. That is, the marriage movement supports the pursuit of happiness, rightly understood. At stake is the social meaning of marriage, as well as the reconstruction of social norms and social roles within marriage. Thus, education in the "skills and knowledge" important to "healthy marriage" might include not simply conflict resolution tips but also education in social norms, such as that marriage means a commitment to work things out, rather than divorce, and a willingness to invest in one's family even at personal cost. As such, this goal of the marriage movement raises intriguing issues about government's proper role in fostering the pursuit of happiness and in shaping social institutions and steering the behavior of persons within such institutions.

An animating premise of the marriage movement is that the gap between most persons' desire for a happy, long-lasting marriage and their ability to have such a marriage provides a good reason for government to promote marriage. But beside the appeal to the pursuit of happiness is the claim that government should promote marriage because it is a *social good* that fosters human capital and leads to increased health, wealth, and community well-being: "Healthy marriages benefit the whole community. Conversely, when marriages fail, huge personal and public costs are generated" (Marriage Movement 2000, 16). Thus, this claim grounds government's interest both in promoting goods and in avoiding harms and views government's proper role as helping people pursue human goods—a view with a long history in political philosophy.[14] Contemporary treatments of marriage also appeal to the human goods and the ends it fosters, such as intimate association, love, relational responsibility, commitment, and the nurture of children (Regan 1993).[15] Some arguments for why marriage should extend to same-sex couples emphasize allowing them to partake in the goods marriage provides (Ball 1997; Wriggins 2000).

One common public reaction to discussion about government seeking to promote marriage is to claim that marriage and family life are wholly "private" matters and none of government's business. This view is wrong, both as a matter of practice and as a matter of principle. In our constitutional order and in the law of domestic relations, there are two strands in tension with each other: first, the tradition that government has a proper interest in families, and, second, the tradition of governmental noninterference, that is, that families enjoy a protected realm of privacy that government should not enter. These strands reflect the dual nature of families as having both a private and a public dimension. Because of the important social functions associated with families, families cannot be left wholly free of regulation, and thus marriage cannot be viewed purely as a private contract (Bix 2000). Thus, in our constitutional order parents and government are dually responsible for children: parents enjoy a fundamental liberty—both a right and a responsibility—to direct their children's rearing and education, yet government also has the authority and responsibility to foster the healthy development of children (McClain 2001b). Addressing feminist critiques that privacy rights create spheres of dangerous unaccountability that leave women and children subject to private violence, I have argued that it is a misconception of the principle of governmental noninterference with personal decision making about intimacy and family to conclude that government may not regulate intimate and family relations to protect individuals against abuse (McClain 1998, 1999). This reflects the basic tension between viewing families as a unit and as composed of individuals who may have rights against each other and rights to be protected by the state.

Governmental regulation of families, in my view, is a component of government's responsibility to undertake a formative process (or formative project) to foster persons' capacities for democratic and personal self-government.[16] Such a formative process requires both governmental action (e.g., supporting families through providing resources and benefits) and governmental restraint (e.g., noninterference with the exercise of rights of intimate association and parental rights). The capacity to form and sustain intimate relationships is an important component of self-government. Similarly, the human capabilities approach posits a responsibility of government to help persons achieve (as Amartya Sen puts it) certain "functionings" that they have "reason to value" (Sen 1992, 4–5). Martha Nussbaum, for example, includes "affiliation," that is, "being able to live for and in relation to others," as a central human "functional capability" that should be a goal of public policy (Nussbaum 1999, 41).

In principle, I find the idea of government making available education to foster relationship skills to be compatible with the idea of fostering the capacities for personal self-government. No doubt, this type of relationship education for children and adolescents is more readily defensible than for adults, given the state's traditional educative and *parens patriae* powers regarding children and adolescents. Indeed, proponents of relationship training speak of it as a needed "fourth R," joining "Reading, wRiting, and aRithmetic" as basics of the curriculum, training in the "emotional literacy" needed to succeed in life.[17]

What if relationship education for adults may help them achieve happier, less conflictual, more stable intimate relationships, and (as some proponents argue) may even have more general application to such domains as the workplace and civic life?[18] There is good evidence, for example, that too much conflict and arguing are a reason both men and women frequently give for their decisions to divorce; disproportionately for low-income couples and for women across the economic spectrum, domestic violence is also a frequent reason. Another reason is a lack of premarital preparation (Johnson 2001, 15–16, 28–30, 33–34). Marital education proponents claim that training in relationships skills, such as how to handle inevitable stress and conflict, can reduce levels of unhappiness as well as divorce. If it is true that many relationship problems stem from a lack of knowledge about how to handle conflict, then government facilitating education in these skills seems acceptable. Similarly, stress and conflict can result in domestic violence, which is a major barrier to its target's well-being and self-government (particularly for women, who are disproportionately its victims). If government seeks to foster training in how to handle stress and conflict to reduce domestic violence, this goal certainly seems legitimate.

Why not encourage more thoughtful, reflective decisions to marry and help people toward more successful relationships? Nussbaum speaks of government's interest in helping foster persons' capabilities so they can "choose well" (Nussbaum 1990, 203), just as Ronald Dworkin's model of ethical individualism supports government fostering persons' capacity for reflective decision making (Dworkin 1996, 26). Dworkin also defends the idea of government encouraging responsible decision making when intrinsic values (such as the sanctity of life) are at stake (Dworkin 1993). Are such intrinsic values at stake in forming families and pursuing marriage? Or, short of that, are there public values at stake that would justify government fostering persons' capacity for reflective, responsible decision making?

If relationship skills are generally valuable to persons' lives going well, and even to good citizenship, why make marriage the occasion for such education? Also, while in principle the idea of premarital education is compatible with the sort of formative project I endorse, there may be issues raised by the content of the curriculum, both when government writes it, and when it leaves the script to nongovernmental actors (Yudof 1983; Greene 2000). Facilitating the relationship decisions of persons considering marriage differs from trying to persuade persons who may not be seeking to marry to do so. Facilitative premarital education aimed at helping persons make a thoughtful decision may result in some couples deciding not to marry, particularly when this process reveals risks of a conflict-filled or dangerous relationship (Stanley 2001). By contrast, creating a "pro-marriage" welfare office, on the premise that marriage leads to "independence," likely sends a message that government takes the view that those who apply for public assistance should work *and* marry. This message could feel coercive and also be harmful, given the high percentage of welfare recipients who have experienced physical violence and nonviolent abuse within marriage or intimate relationships, especially at the point that they try to move from welfare to work (Burt, Zweig, and Schlichter 2000).

Is marriage's supposed role in fostering adult happiness sufficient to render educating citizens about marriage an urgent imperative, or, as the Florida legislature puts it, "a compelling interest"?[19] Neither the marriage movement nor state marriage initiatives rest governmental authority merely on this basis. Instead, it is society's interest in the successful rearing of children—and the negative consequences of failure—that makes marriage a public institution: "The need of every society for successful childrearing is why marriage has been a public institution and a focus of religious concern. . . . Without children, it is much more difficult to envision the institution of marriage as something that requires public attention and regulation" (Popenoe 2002, 200).[20]

Thus, the structure of the social health argument for marriage seems to be that government has a legitimate interest in helping people achieve an important personal goal—and even steering others toward that goal if they do not seek it—when achieving it benefits society and failing to achieve it has serious personal and social costs.[21] Not surprisingly, some marriage proponents make an analogy between the marriage crisis and public health crises. They use the language of epidemics to refer to the rates of nonmarital births and divorce and to the negative health consequences of the marriage crisis.

Ultimately, the public health argument, with its claims that intact marriage between two biological parents is the best proxy for child well-being, is an empirical one, and I disclaim any attempt to evaluate the social science evidence on which it rests. But because it relates to the question of equality among families—both marital and nonmarital—I should mention that there is not the unanimity or consensus among social scientists that the marriage movement suggests. Rather, a phenomenon may be at work that is reminiscent of the phenomenon sociologist Judith Stacey described in the "neo–family values campaign" of the 1990s: a group of social scientists cite repeatedly each other's work in what becomes a feedback loop, so that a certain set of claims is presented as "uncontested" and the consensus view, even if there is credible social science to the contrary (Stacey 1996, 83–104).

That the social science underlying the case for marriage—and against divorce—is not uncontested, and that the stakes are high for establishing a consensus position, became clear from the media attention given to eminent psychologist Mavis Hetherington's book *For Better or for Worse: Divorce Reconsidered.* Hetherington argues, based on a thirty-year study of families, that "much current writing on divorce—both popular and academic—has exaggerated its negative effects and ignored its sometimes considerable positive effects" (Hetherington and Kelly 2002, 5). Voices in the marriage movement were quick to caution of a "backlash" against taking divorce seriously and to take issue with some of the book's claims, even as other social scientists praised Hetherington's rigorous research (Peterson 2002, 1A; Duenwald 2002, F6). Thus, while social scientists across the spectrum agree with the proposition that "on average" children fare better in an intact, two-parent family, this "on average" may be misleading as a prediction about particular children in a range of circumstances and may encourage a false determinism (Cherlin 1999). Overemphasis on family form as such misses the importance of variables like the emotional tenor of families and the quality of the parent-child relationship. Rather than using (heterosexual) marriage as the sole proxy for child well-being, a better approach is to learn what sorts of family conditions contribute to child well-being and consider how government and civil society may help to foster them.

Should Government Promote Marriage to Civilize Men?

Marriage promoters contend that one justification for promoting is that society needs marriage to socialize, or civilize, men. A common assumption in discourse in the marriage movement is that the mother-child bond is less fragile and less dependent upon marriage than is the father-child bond. For example, *The Marriage Movement: A Statement of Principles* observes that "as a matter of mere biology, men can sire a virtually unlimited number of children, but a man can provide daily care, protection, love, and financial support to only a few children." Marriage "closes this gap between a man's sexual and fathering capacities" (Marriage Movement 2000, 7). James Q. Wilson's book *The Marriage Problem* draws on evolutionary biology to argue that "[m]arriage is a cultural contrivance designed to prevent weak paternal roles" (Wilson 2002, 30).

The gender role assumptions about the danger posed by unsocialized men and the domesticating role of women are striking. They also invite the question: If men need marriage more than women do, what cost will a marriage promotion program have in terms of women's equality and self-government? Wilson and others speak of a "male problematic" that promoting marriage is thought to address: father absence, or men's inclination (rooted, in part, in evolutionary biology) toward procreating without taking responsibility for children. By contrast, the "female problematic" is women's inclination toward procreating and rearing children, even in the absence of adequate resources and commitment by fathers and at the expense of self (Browning et al. 2000, 68–69). This, too, is a problem that promoting marriage is thought to address (Wilson 2002, 62–63). The disaggregation of marriage, reproduction, and parenting, the marriage movement contends, threatens to undo the socially useful role of fatherhood and unleash men in more destructive directions (Popenoe, Elshtain, and Blankenhorn 1996, 303). Of course, this argument about socializing men ultimately relates to the well-being of children, since the fear is that without marriage, society lacks an effective glue to bind fathers to children.

This domestication argument, as a justification for governmental promotion of marriage, has several flaws. First, feminist analysis urges skepticism about appeals to "nature" or to sex differences as a justification for policy, given a long history of such appeals to justify sex-based restrictions on women's citizenship and of gender hierarchy in families and civil society. Second, this portrait of men insults their capacity to be morally responsible agents and reinforces women's familiar role of being morally responsible for themselves and for men in the areas of sexuality and family (Cornell 1998, 131–40).[22] Third, evidence of some men's practices of responsible fathering outside of marriage cast doubt on the claim that only marriage can secure such commitment. Fourth, as I shall discuss later, if men need not only marriage but such hallmarks of masculinity as being the head of household, then marriage promotion directly conflicts with women's equality.

There is a long history in the United States of government fostering sex inequality within marriage, through the sex-linked duties and rights associated with the status of being a husband or wife. In addition, underlying state domestic relations law, as well as federal marriage policy, was a public philosophy that viewed proper gender ordering and performance of these sex-linked duties within the "republican family" as contributing to public order and good citizenship. In particular, the idea of domesticating men through establishing them as responsible heads of households was an animating premise of much marriage policy (Cott 2000).

Today, the rhetoric appeals more to social health, to evolutionary biology, and to a "male problematic," but the common thread is domesticating, or taming, men. Indeed, even those voices in the marriage movement most supportive of sex equality, such as theologian Don Browning, who calls for a "critical" marriage culture, identifies this "male problematic" (acknowledged in theology as well as evolutionary biology). He views marriage as the best institutional framework for anchoring male commitment (Browning et al. 2000).

Would a contemporary public philosophy about marriage rest on traditional gender role assumptions? I agree with Browning that *if* government is to play a role in creating a "critical marriage culture," then sex equality should inform such a public philosophy. But can the supposed "male problematic" be solved in a way compatible with sex equality? And is solving the "female problematic" done only through promoting marriage? For example, one logical inference from the claim that the mother-child bond is strong, even apart from marriage, and less precarious than the connection between women and men, might be that we should premise family policy (as Fineman argues) on supporting that bond (Fineman, this volume, 1995).

Masculinity and Marriage: Do Men Need "Traditional" Marriage?

The social health argument suggests that men need marriage to be productive, responsible fathers and citizens, in a way that women do not need it to be responsible mothers and citizens. It also acknowledges that men benefit more than women from marriage. Sociologist Steven Nock concludes, in his book *Marriage and Men's Lives:* "Men reap greater gains than women for virtually every outcome affected by marriage." Men seem to benefit "by simply *being married.*" By contrast, he finds: "When women benefit from marriage, it is because they are in a satisfying relationship" (Nock 1998, 3), While some authors suggest that it is the solicitude of wives for husbands' well-being that makes the difference (Wilson 2002; Waite and Gallagher 2000), Nock stresses a different factor: marriage's role in conferring masculinity. In societies around the world, Nock argues, marriage plays a unique role in helping men achieve and establish masculinity, a precarious task in all societies (Nock 1998, 43–52).

If men need marriage to establish masculinity, do they need traditional or "normative" marriage as Nock defines it, in which "[t]he husband is the head, and principal earner, in a marriage" (Nock 1998, 6) to do so?[23] If being the head of household and principal earner is necessary for men to develop and sustain masculinity, should government promote such marriages and such masculinity? What relationship does this "normative marriage" bear to "healthy marriage"? As Philip Blumstein and Pepper Schwartz's well-known study, *American Couples,* found, decision-making authority usually correlates with income earning, and thus the term "head of household" also connotes leadership and authority within the household (Blumstein and Schwartz 1983), Indeed, in more recent work, Schwartz concludes: "The linchpin of marital inequality is the provider role—or, to be precise, the provider complex, a combination of roles that give the man the responsibility for financially supporting the family's life-style and the woman all the auxiliary duties that allow the man to devote himself to his work." Schwartz reports that the provider role brings with it an expectation of appreciation, which is akin to obedience: "The more the provider provides or the harder he works to do so, the more he feels entitled to emotional returns and provision of services" (Schwartz 1994, 111–13), Thus, as a legal matter, marriage no longer entails a status relationship in which husbands have a duty to provide and may expect from wives services and obedience, but the "provider complex" carries with it this type of expectation.

Certainly some contemporary research about men and marriage bears out the thesis that men's role in "normative marriage" continues to be viewed as that of "provider and protector," and that men's failure to live up to that role plays a part in men's flight from marriage and fathers' absence from their children (Anderson, Browning, and Boyer 2002, 269–70). In particular, some scholars identify this dynamic among inner-city, low-income African American men (Wilson 1996).[24] Elijah Anderson's ethnographic studies of inner-city African American men's values suggest the salience of the inability to fulfill the provider role—an ideal of manhood —in explaining why young men do not marry and why they separate fathering children from marrying. Anderson's book *Code of the Street* gives dramatic testimony to an expectation that accepting the responsibility for the breadwinner role—being a "decent daddy"—brings with it a normative entitlement to another traditional masculine role, "head of household," that is, the perk of being in control within the family (Anderson 1999). The report *A Statement from the Morehouse Conference on African American Fathers: Turning the Corner on Father Absence in Black America* contends that slavery and its legacy have robbed African American men of a chance to fill the role of provider and breadwinner and describes men's contemporary debilitating bitterness, anger, and pain over their continuing inability to be providers and their living at the margins of family life and society (Morehouse Research Institute and Institute for American Values 1999).[25]

By contrast, research on low-income men's and women's views of responsible fatherhood indicates that the provider role is not the defining
trait of what makes a "good father": "Both married and unmarried parents
rank emotional involvement and guidance above economic support"
(Waller 2002, 67). This research suggests that inability to be a patriarch in
the home does not lead to abdication of paternal responsibility and that it
would be constructive to support models of fatherhood premised more
centrally on nurture (Dowd 2000).

While shoring up men to be providers features prominently in the
general discourse of responsible fatherhood, when the subject is black
fathers (who are disproportionately poor), the task is seen as urgent. For
example, Congress aims, through promoting "responsible fatherhood" and
marriage among low-income men, to help such men become better providers for their families, a traditional hallmark of masculinity and fatherhood. And yet, left unexamined is whether it is possible to do this without
(consciously or unwittingly) shoring up male dominance and control
within the household. An unanswered question is the connection between
traditional marriage—and the male provider/head of household role—
and healthy marriage. What if traditional marriage directly conflicts with
many women's aspirations for equality and economic independence within marriage? Is inequality within marriage a reason for the "decline" of
marriage? Is equality within marriage antithetical to promoting a marriage culture?

Marriage (E)quality, Women's Independence, and the Marriage Crisis

The marriage movement, generally, recognizes that women's expectations
of sex equality (or gender equity) and their diminished reliance upon
marriage for economic survival have contributed to the weakening of a
marriage culture. For example, in the documentary *Marriage: Just a Piece
of Paper?* the narrator, Cokie Roberts, reports that women's greater independence creates "tremendous confusion" about men's roles. She poses the
question: "Can men and women be reconciled to each other? Is marriage
part of the work of reconciliation?"[26] Concerns for equality and economic
independence may also be one explanation for why women disaggre-
gate motherhood and marriage. Thus, Kathryn Edin (2000) found that a
reason low-income mothers separated childbearing from marriage was

that, while they viewed their early twenties as the best time to have children, they did not wish to marry until later in their twenties, when they had established enough economic independence *through market work* to ensure bargaining power within marriage and to avoid economic dependency. Rather than viewing marriage as a means to achieve economic independence (as Bush's welfare plan does), they viewed some degree of economic independence as a necessary precondition for a successful marriage, that is, one in which they had sufficient power to avoid subservience and economic dependency. This strategic behavior among low-income mothers has a parallel in the poll data reported by the National Marriage Project: in both cases, young women associate marriage with economic vulnerability and gender inequality, and they try to take measures, either delaying or avoiding marriage, to secure equality and independence within marriage (Whitehead and Popenoe 2002).

Thus, women's expectations of gender equality and marriage quality, and their experience of gender inequality in marriage, appear to be significant factors leading to disenchantment with marriage and ultimately to divorce. These factors seem to hold true across class lines and across race. Surveys often point out the fact that most married people accept the premise of equality within marriage, for example, with respect to domestic labor, but that the actual practice falls short. When wives view this as unfair—but husbands do not—this can lead to marital instability (Nock 2001; Nock and Brinig 2002).[27] For example, in the growing number of marriages in which spouses are equally dependent upon one another's earnings, such economic interdependence without a fairer division of labor may lead to more marital instability *unless* husbands change by doing more housework and recognizing their wives' greater efforts (Nock 2001).

It should not be denied, as Schwartz recognizes, that many women seem content to bargain for what she calls the provider complex, giving men the primary responsibility for breadwinning and giving themselves a supporting role. And yet even in these more traditional relationships, evolving notions of equality may lead to wives' resentments because of contradictory expectations of husbands: even as such wives expect their husbands to be good providers—which requires men to invest in employment—their absorption of cultural ideals of equality leads wives to expect men to contribute more to sustaining family life (Schwartz 1994, 125).

There is a practical dilemma that the marriage movement must confront: if women decreasingly marry to secure economic independence through affiliation with a husband's income, what will induce women to marry and stay married? If women's ability to achieve economic independence without marriage leads some women not to marry, what public policies to promote marriage—short of rendering women less economically independent—could respond to this change in women's behavior? For example, the tougher work requirements in the 1996 welfare reform law seem to be lowering low-income women's rates of marriage, and researchers suggest that one reason may be women's increased economic independence (Bernstein 2002, A1).

In an earlier, coauthored article, Wade Horn identified a sharp tension between women's economic independence and marriage:

> The problem is that strategies for promoting fatherhood and marriage are, to a very large extent, in conflict with those that seek to help single mothers achieve self-sufficiency through work. Indeed, a welfare system that helps single mothers become employed, but ignores the need to promote fatherhood and marriage, may serve only to enable unmarried women to rear children without the presence of the father. (Horn and Bush 1997)[28]

At the time of his appointment to the Department of Health and Human Services, Horn distanced himself from the position (taken in that article) that government should address this problem by favoring married low-income couples over single mothers for means-tested benefits. He went on to suggest that the tension may dissolve if government promotes both women's work *and* marriage. Critics of current welfare proposals have offered many practical reasons that marriage promotion is not sound antipoverty policy and will not foster poor women's economic security (Coontz and Folbre 2002). But there is also a normative conflict: as some feminist scholars argue, if marriage-promoting welfare policies "instantiate[] marriage as the *sine qua non* of worthy citizenship," they directly inhibit some women's construction of motherhood as "independent" from marriage (Mink 2002). This sort of independence conflicts with the marriage promotion goals of welfare reformers and of the marriage movement.

Will Sex Equality Be in the Recipe for Promoting "Healthy Marriages"?

The marriage movement appears to recognize that sex equality is a feature of the contemporary landscape, as the coinage "equal regard marriage" indicates. Yet prescriptions that take sex equality seriously are in short supply. Illustrative of ambivalence about sex equality, *The Marriage Movement: A Statement of Principles* reassures that "supporting marriage . . . does not require turning back the clock on desirable change, promoting male tyranny, or tolerating domestic violence" (Marriage Movement 2000, 3). And it seeks to help "more men and women achieve a caring, collaborative, and committed bond, rooted in *equal regard* between spouses" (3). But the rest of the statement offers no guidance as to the relationship between "equal regard" and sex equality, and it provides no concrete proposals for how to understand or constitute "healthy marriages" in light of contemporary expectations of sex equality and fairness. Its guiding principles for a plan of action make no mention of addressing gender inequity and make no admonitions to married couples to quest for more egalitarian marriage as a means of strengthening marriage.

In the one passage directly addressing household division of labor, the statement urges:

> Do not discourage marital interdependence by penalizing unpaid work in homes and communities. Couples should be free to divide up labor however they choose without pressure from policies that discriminate against at-home parenting and other activities that serve civil society. (Marriage Movement 2002, 18)

This gender-neutral appeal says nothing about who should perform the unpaid labor. Feminists might readily suspect that, without any cultural transformation, this division of labor is a coded affirmation of women's role as unpaid caregivers.

Popenoe is more explicit in resolving the gender crisis, or "gender confusion," by advocating a model of modified traditional gender roles, whereby although both men and women invest in education and career, once children are born, women are encouraged to leave work for the first few years of a child's life and to work part-time until the teenage years. Popenoe roots this proposal in sex differences; indeed, critiquing an ideal of androgyny, he reports a concern that men may avoid marrying and having children "if they are going to be asked to give up their independence and over-engage in 'unnatural' nurturing and caretaking roles" (Popenoe, Elshtain, and Blankenhorn 1996, 254–61).

This appeal to gender specialization brings to mind economic models of marriage and the idea that men and women bring different capacities

and skills to marriage and differentially invest in it. Some marriage promoters argue that role specialization in domestic versus market activities
benefits children, parents, and society. But the person who makes this
investment in domestic activities, sacrificing other forms of investment,
may be vulnerable at divorce. Hence, they argue, the key is to reform
divorce laws to reward such investment and to shift power to those who
are committed to permanence (Parkman 2002, 74–77; Gallagher 1996, 233).

That "equal regard" marriage may also be consistent with belief in gender-differentiated roles is clear from frequent statements by persons in
the marriage movement—such as Wade Horn himself—who embrace
"equal regard" but reject, and even mock as "androgyny," a notion that
mothers and fathers should share equally in all child-rearing activities
(Pear 2001; Blankenhorn 1995, 117–23).[29] And yet some in the marriage
movement, notably Browning, interpret "equal regard" as requiring "equal
access" by mothers and fathers to "the responsibilities and privileges of
both the public and domestic realms" (Browning et al. 2000, 328). Although Browning, like Popenoe, draws on evolutionary biology for identi-
fying the "male problematic," his solution does not appeal to "natural"
differences to justify different roles. While Browning and his associates,
like others in the marriage movement, advocate achieving work-family
balance through a sixty-hour workweek (in a two-parent family), they
make clear that equality should be a guiding principle (Browning et al.
2000, 327–28).

Since much of the focus in policy discourse about marriage promotion
is on the low rates of marriage among African Americans, the Morehouse
statement's approach to the "crisis" in gender relations between African
American women and men warrants attention. It recognizes the importance of marital *quality,* calls for "gender and family healing," and embraces "equal regard between husband and wife" (Morehouse Research
Institute and Institute for American Values 1999). The statement, however,
gives no guidance on how *equality* is to feature in a program of gender
healing.

Studying gender conflict between black women and men, Donna
Franklin identifies genuine equality and mutuality between men and
women as a goal not easily achieved in general, but made even more difficult in America by the experience of being black (Franklin 2000). Measured against cultural norms of femininity and female deference, African
American women—who, historically, have worked both for the survival of
African American families and communities and for wages—appear too

"independent" and matriarchal. Parallel to male bitterness and anger over inability to fill the cultural ideal of the provider role is female anger and distrust toward men. Franklin argues that "the issue of male dominance remains one of the primary sources of tension in black marriages, especially when the wife is the principal wage earner" (Franklin 2000, 210).[30] Wives typically are wage earners and also shoulder the burden of the "second shift" of home and family work. Franklin suggests that this strain in black marriages may explain why black women and men report less marital happiness than other groups.

A governmental program of teaching skills and knowledge will likely fail to address these problems if it does not include some attention to the issues of gender conflict, to the link between marital quality and equality, and to supporting models of marriage not premised on male provider/female caregiver. Similarly inadequate will be programs focusing on making men more "marriageable," another goal of marriage promoters. On the one hand, public policy aimed at fostering economic empowerment of low-income men *and women* on the premise that it might facilitate their marrying is not objectionable, since research finds that one significant reason that people do not marry is a lack of economic resources, either their own or that of their potential partner (Waller 2002). On the other hand, economic empowerment aimed at making men more "marriageable" will not address the other reasons identified by Edin for mothers not marrying, such as women's lack of trust in potential marriage partners (for instance, due to infidelity), domestic violence, and the desire for sex equality within marriage. She concludes that, although enhancing labor market opportunities for low-skilled men would address the affordability and respectability concerns of these mothers, "other factors, such as the stalled sex-role revolution at home (control), the pervasive mistrust of men, and the high probability of domestic abuse, probably mean that marriage rates are unlikely to increase dramatically" (Edin 2000, 30).

Why Government Should Foster Marriage (E)quality

If government is to promote "healthy marriages," will it take any position on whether equality is an ingredient in the recipe for such marriages? Given the link between marriage quality and equality, a model of marriage as equal partnership would seem to be a promising way to avoid the problems of dominance and hierarchy that have impaired women's equal citizenship and have contributed to the marriage "crisis." Not only is this a just corrective to a long history of governmental promotion of sex inequality within marriage, but it also may be a practical approach to some of the tensions facing contemporary families in juggling domestic, market, and other responsibilities.

There is considerable evidence that a new, more egalitarian model of intimate relationships may be emerging both as a practical and as a normative matter. The legal structure of marriage has evolved to embrace norms of gender equality. And some family law scholars argue that, even though role differentiation continues in practice, there is an emerging social norm of equality, or equal partnership (Carbone 2001; Scott 2000). Francine Deutsch's *Halving It All: How Equally Shared Parenting Works* (1999) finds that those husbands and wives across the economic spectrum who adopt a model of equal parenting view it as the fair thing to do, as well as the most practical arrangement. Feminist ideology is neither a necessary nor a sufficient requirement for reaching an arrangement of equality. Thus, couples may adopt an equal parenting arrangement out of a sense of fairness, or to avoid repeating the patterns of their parents' marriage or their own prior marriage(s). Moreover, a powerful motivator leading men to agree to an equal partnership is love for, and a desire to preserve the relationship with, a female partner who insists on equality. Pepper Schwartz found similar motivations in her study *Love between Equals:* "People seek an egalitarian relationship because they want fair treatment, respect, and the right to have equal voice in creating and maintaining a fulfilling marriage" (Schwartz 1994, 125–26).

One recent survey of American attitudes toward marriage, conducted by Browning and his associates, found that 55 percent of persons surveyed thought that a model of marital love as a matter of "equal regard and mutuality between husband and wife" best correlated with a successful marriage; "only 38 percent hold that love as self-sacrifice is the key." But the survey also found some striking gender differences: women chose the equal regard and mutuality model more often then men (61 percent to 48 percent); men (44 percent) chose the self-sacrifice model more often than women (33 percent). Moreover, the survey notes that the gender differences in the black community were "stunning": "76 percent of women in contrast to 33 percent of men selected mutuality, whereas only 14 percent of women in contrast to 48 percent of men thought love as self-sacrifice correlates with good marriages" (Browning 2001, 49–50). Addressing these gender and race-gender differences, the surveyors were not sure *whose* self-sacrifice the male respondents had in mind in embracing sacrifice.

From these data, Browning concludes that for Americans "mutuality is in; self-sacrifice is going out," and that mutuality is more important to women, "possibly as a consequence of both feminism and the entry of women into the workplace." But, he further cautions, it is not clear whether Americans "have the skills to live a love ethic of equal regard" or have the "supporting social conditions to live this ethic." Indeed, he posits that the high rates of divorce, nonmarital birth, and cohabitation suggest that the skills and social conditions are not in place. Significantly, he further concludes that women and mothers want "equal regard marriages more than men," and they may not be getting it, which may be "one explanation of why more women then men are initiating divorce" (Browning 2001, 50–51).

This gender difference is intriguing, given the historic and cultural equation of women's care (especially maternal care) with self-sacrifice. Indeed, even as her groundbreaking book, *In a Different Voice* (1982), urged attention to the missing dimension of care in models of moral reasoning, moral psychologist Carol Gilligan cautioned that society must learn to resist the equation of female identity and caring with self-sacrifice.[31] Perhaps women themselves are resisting that model in the context of marriage. This again underscores the importance of focusing on the link between marriage quality and equality.

However, the marriage movement identifies the decreasing willingness to sacrifice (e.g., to invest in family life at personal cost or to stay together despite personal unhappiness) as evidence of the decline of a marriage culture and a cause for more divorce (Marriage Movement 2000, 18–19; Whitehead and Popenoe 2001). Another tenet of the marriage movement is that many divorces occur in "low-conflict" marriages, and that children would fare better if parents in such marriages would stay together. In a renewed marriage culture, one assumes, couples would stay together despite unhappiness, and more people would affirm (as only a small minority do today) that it would be better for children if unhappily married parents stayed together, except in cases of high conflict and abuse. These discussions do not address whether discontent with gender inequity is just another example of low-level conflict and unhappiness to be borne for the sake of the children, or whether a renewed married culture would aspire to less inequity.

Thus, if government's goal is to promote healthy marriages, and if it is interested in disseminating effective ways to do so, then it would seem that promoting equality within marriage, or equal regard, is likely to be effective and "get results." But if this is so, then perhaps the rhetoric should be not simply of restoring a marriage culture, but of promoting a transformed and reconstructed marriage culture. Indeed, Schwartz argues that peer marriage, a more egalitarian model than traditional marriage, is a vanguard for a new model of marriage and could be a promising way to improve marital stability, since it rests on deep friendship and on male engagement with children, and avoids the sorts of resentments that may arise from the provider complex (Schwartz 1994, 1998, 48). Support for this "do what works," or functional, argument for the link between marriage quality and equality is found in Hetherington's study of the relative stability of various types of marriages: a type she describes as "the cohesive/individuated marriage," expressive of the value of "gender equity" and the cultural ideal of the baby boomer generation, had the second lowest divorce rate in her study (Hetherington and Kelly 2002, 30–31).

Hetherington's study also found that the lowest divorce rates were found in traditional marriages, with the male breadwinner/female homemaker roles. This kind of marriage, she observes, "still works very well if a couple shares a traditional interpretation of gender roles" (31). Moreover, research in states with covenant marriage statutes finds that couples who are most attracted to this model of marriage, which is supposed to signify a deeper commitment to marriage permanence, are those who have more traditional attitudes about gender roles (Nock and Brinig 2004) But Hetherington also finds that "the Achilles heel of traditional marriage is change," and when one or the other partner begins to behave untraditionally, "trouble follows" (Hetherington and Kelly 2002, 31–32). Thus, traditional marriage is not conducive to stability if expectations change.

What implications follow from the foregoing analysis for public policy about "healthy marriages"? Should government "take sides" in favor of equality? In favor of tradition, or a "cultural script" of modified traditional gender roles? One gambit some in the marriage movement take is to avoid taking any express position on this issue and urge that good marriages depend upon a basic "tool kit" of communication skills that can be learned and used all across the political and religious spectrum.[32] Is this tool kit approach likely to be the position of DHHS as it helps people acquire necessary "skills and knowledge"? As noted earlier, Wade Horn has espoused the goal of "healthy, *equal regard* marriages," but his own critique of androgyny indicates that many forms of gender-differentiated roles, or complementarity, are compatible with equal regard.

What approach are states taking in materials prepared in connection with marriage promotion and preservation efforts? Beyond the common claim that government has an interest in "whether [a couple's] marriage is long lasting and happy," because successful marriages are the "backbone" of society, there is little said about the normative content of healthy marriage. The minimum content seems to be: a healthy marriage includes good communication and conflict resolution skills, and does *not* include domestic violence.[33] This minimum content in itself suggests an important recognition of the place of equality within marriage, since one salient feminist critique of the legal regulation of families has been its traditional toleration of domination and violence within families. Indeed, language of "public health" and of an "epidemic" accompanied feminist and legislative efforts to address domestic violence.

On gender roles and equality within marriage, in terms of distribution of decision making and household labor, the materials take different approaches. In Texas's glossy brochure, "When You Get Married . . . ," similar to a premarital counseling questionnaire, ideas about gender roles and gender expectations appear as discussion items for which there is no "right" answer, just "whatever works for you" (Attorney General of Texas 2002). (For example: "A mother should not work outside the home unless her children are in school: agree, disagree, or undecided?"; and "the father should discipline the children: agree, disagree, or undecided?" [9]). By contrast, the video provided by Utah's Governor's Commission on Marriage, *Marriage News You Can Use*, features a clinical social worker expressing the view that, although mothers carry the baby, after birth, parenting should be an equal responsibility for mothers and fathers.[34]

Current marriage promotion proposals envision that a primary means of promoting marriage is funding the efforts of nongovernmental actors, especially faith-based groups. If so, it seems unlikely that these skills will be delivered in a "neutral" manner devoid of other value commitments. Some religious groups may share the sort of commitment to "critical familialism" urged by Browning; others may support a model of male "headship" and leadership. To bring up the obvious, not-so-hypothetical, concern for feminists and other proponents of marriage equality, what if government contracts with a faith-based group that believes, as one Catholic bishop expresses it, that it is crucial "to reach out to men and indicate to them that they have a special place in the eyes of the Lord as being the head of their families" (Anderson, Browning, and Boyer 2002, 368–69)? Or contracts with Promise Keepers, whose leader instructs husbands that they must inform their wives that they are reclaiming their proper role of "leading the family," and that, if wives object, "there can be no compromise here"; to wives, such instruction is to give the leadership back: "For the sake of your family and the survival of our culture, let your man be a man if he's willing. . . . God never meant for you to bear the load you're carrying" (Browning et al. 2000, 233–34).[35]

A pluralistic approach to governmental funding would open the purse to Promise Keepers and the Nation of Islam, along with feminist marriage advocates, domestic violence activists, and religious groups that reject a patriarchal model of family self-government for one premised on gender equality. In this way, government could be neutral about the division of power and roles within marriage. And, one might argue, given that not all couples seek to embrace an egalitarian model of marriage, this pluralism allows for persons with different values to find the kind of service provider that best comports with their own values. But I believe that direct funding of groups that espouse sex inequality as a model of family governance conflicts with government's commitment to sex equality.

Sex equality, as I explain in other work, is a constitutional principle and a normative commitment of antidiscrimination laws (McClain 2001b). It is a "sovereign virtue"[36] guiding how government must treat its female and male citizens. The repudiation of coverture in family law and the ascent of a more gender-neutral model of rights and responsibilities of spouses evidence the reach of this public value into the realm of family governance. Moreover, sex equality is a norm in international human rights law.

Sex equality not only is relevant to public life but also has implications for family governance. At a minimum, it is inappropriate for government to embrace models of marriage premised on gender hierarchy (Case 2002). Furthermore, direct government funding of groups with a model of family governance premised on gender hierarchy and male leadership/female deference would be inappropriate and violate equality norms. Thus, if "armies of compassion"—faith-based groups—are to help in promoting marriage, there should be some attention to how important public values of sex equality feature in this enterprise.

Arguably, government may and should go farther and ensure that a commitment to sex equality is part of its educative efforts about healthy marriage. The minimal content of equality begins with a rejection of patriarchal governance in favor of mutual self-governance. Thus, rejecting domestic violence and any male entitlement to exclusive decision-making power within the household come within this minimum content. Beyond this, as a general guiding principle, family law holds parents equally responsible for the material support and nurture of their children. In light of women's disproportionate responsibility for caregiving work and domestic labor, and the importance of this work to orderly social reproduction, I believe that if government engages in education about marriage, then it is appropriate to espouse an ideal of equal responsibility and inappropriate to steer couples to the sort of "natural" gender role specialization urged by some in the marriage movement.

Some may object that this would impose a governmental orthodoxy and thwart pluralism. In calling for sex equality as a constitutive principle in a public philosophy about families, I am not suggesting that government should dictate a particular division of labor within families (as it did with the sex-linked status of husbands and wives of an earlier era). Government may educate and persuade in favor of important public values; it may espouse an ideal of shared parental responsibility but not *dictate* who does the dishes or feeds the baby (Nussbaum 2000, 279–80). Government may and should promote the public value of sex equality and embrace it as relevant to family self-governance. But respect for intimate association, autonomy, and reasonable moral pluralism counsels some governmental restraint. Also, practical and prudential concerns about the monitoring of family life caution against using coercive measures and in favor of using facilitative and persuasive measures.

Nor am I suggesting that embracing equality means that gender becomes a meaningless category with respect to how persons understand themselves. My argument is that government may facilitate equality by offering a framework of family regulation within which one's sex does not carry with it gender-based entitlements and responsibilities. This framework allows individuals within families to work out in their own relationships what equality means to them.

Finally, cultural support for equality is also important. The social meaning of gender exerts a powerful pull even when couples try to achieve equal partnership. Whether or not they can find social support for equal partnerships affects their success in resisting what feels "natural," familiar, and expected (Deutsch 1999; Schwartz 1994). If the social meaning of gender is at work in how people choose family roles, then there are limits to what governmental efforts alone can accomplish in fostering equality. Fostering equality also depends upon cultural reinforcement of emerging models of equality. Unfortunately, to date, such cultural reinforcement is not a feature of most calls to renew a marriage culture.

Conclusion

In this chapter, I have argued that government may support marriage, as part of its facilitative role in regulating families. However, contemporary calls to promote marriage fail to reckon seriously with the issue of equality within families. I have not argued that respect for such equality requires that marriage be abolished. Rather, if government is to play a role in supporting marriage, then equality must feature in such a program. Measured against this requirement, contemporary proposals for governmental promotion of "healthy marriage" fall short.

I have confined my focus in this chapter to equality within families. Yet another relevant dimension of equality, equality among families, should also guide a governmental program of supporting marriage. This dimension of equality rules out the solution of reinstitutionalizing marriage by denying recognition to other forms of committed intimate relationships. It is appropriate for government to support marriage, but it may not use marriage as a proxy for the only family form worthy of governmental support and respect. Respect for equality among families—and for women's and men's personal self-government in the areas of intimacy and family—should inform a policy of supporting not only marriage but also other forms of family that can foster orderly social reproduction and allow realization of the values and goods associated with families.

NOTES

1. The declaration "The Marriage Movement: A Statement of Principles," written in 2000 and available at http://www.marriagemovement.org/html, calls for and explains the basic principles of the "marriage movement." Its sponsors are the Institute for American Values; the Religion, Culture, and Family Project (University of Chicago); and the Coalition for Marriage, Families, and Couples Education.

2. In addition to "The Marriage Movement: A Statement of Principles," other examples include the Council on Families in America, "Marriage in America: A Report to the Nation" (Popenoe, Elshtain, and Blankenhorn 1996, 293–318), and "Final Report of the Ninety-seventh American Assembly" (Browning and Rodriguez 2002, 181–99).

3. Barbara Dafoe Whitehead and David Popenoe are the codirectors of the National Marriage Project, located at Rutgers University, New Brunswick. The annual reports are available at the project Web site, http://marriage.rutgers.edu.

4. Some groups in this movement include the National Fatherhood Initiative (of which David Blankenhorn, prominent in the marriage movement, is a former chair, and in which two current members of the Bush administration, Don Eberly and Wade Horn, have held leadership roles) and the Institute for Responsible Fatherhood and Family Revitalization (headed by Charles Ballard). Religious groups like Promise Keepers also stress responsible fatherhood.

5. Alternatives to Marriage Project, *Affirmation of Family Diversity,* and *Let Them Eat Wedding Rings,* available at http://www.unmarried.org/family.html.

6. For information on the study, see http://crcw.princeton.edu/fragilefamilies.

7. At this writing, Congress has extended TANF several times pending enactment of a reauthorization bill. The House of Representatives passed a bill, "The Personal Responsibility, Work, and Family Promotion Act of 2003," H.R. 4, which echoes the president's plan in including funding for promoting marriage and responsible fatherhood.

8. A handbook for marrying couples prepared by the Florida Bar Association reproduces some of the legislative findings in this act.

9. The statement appears on the jacket of the *Marriage News You Can Use* video provided by the Governor's Commission on Marriage and the Utah Department of Workforce Services. A Texas handbook, *When You Get Married . . . ,* puts it: "Your commitment to your marriage is the backbone of our society." *When You Get Married . . . ,* 2002 edition including updates from the Seventy-seventh Legislature, prepared by the attorney general of Texas under Texas Family Code Section 2.104, available at www.oag.state.tx.us/newspubs/publications.html.

10. Chapter 98-403, included in a handbook prepared by the Florida Bar Association for marrying couples.

11. For example, as was noted (see note 1) "The Marriage Movement: A Statement of Principles" was sponsored by the Institute for American Values; the Religion, Culture, and Family Project (University of Chicago); and the Coalition for Marriage, Family, and Couples Education. The booklet "Why Marriage Matters: Twenty-one Conclusions from the Social Sciences" (2002) was produced by the Center of the American Experiment; the Coalition for Marriage, Family, and Couples Education; and the Institute for American Values. The Religion, Culture, and Family Project sponsored the television documentary *Marriage: Just a Piece of Paper?* and a related book (Anderson, Browning, and Boyer 2002). The Institute for American Values joined with the Morehouse Research Institute on African American Fathers on the report *A Statement from the Morehouse Conference on African American Fathers: Turning the Corner on Father Absence in Black America* (Morehouse Research Institute and Institute for American Values).

12. The Bush administration's welfare plan, "Working toward Independence,"

invokes this "abundant body of research" concerning outcomes for children in support of its claim that "it is simply wise and prudent to reorient our policies to encourage marriage, especially when children are involved (Bush 2002, 2, 19).

13. James Q. Wilson draws similar contrasts between (natural) motherhood and (problematic) fatherhood (Wilson 2002, 24–32).

14. For example, Aristotle's work is a root of this idea (Barker 1958, 284).

15. John Witte finds that in the several theological traditions of Western Christianity, the goods of marriage are friendship, reproducing and caring for children, and channeling sexuality and deterring sin (Witte 1997).

16. There are many theoretical supports for this view of government's role, including the human capabilities approach and strands of feminism, liberalism, and civic republicanism (McClain 1998, 2000). In my book *The Place of Families* I develop its application to the regulation of families (McClain 2005).

17. So states a pamphlet by the widely used PEERS program (Practical Exercises Enriching Relationships Skills), "It's Time to Fully Prepare Our Youth for Life!"

18. One defense of this skills training draws on the philosopher Jürgen Habermas's model of "discourse ethics" to support an argument that training in communication and conflict facilitates the sort of "communicative competence" needed in family life and other spheres of life, including the workplace and politics (Browning and Rodriguez 2002, 137–38).

19. Chapter 98-403.

20. The Council on Families in America expresses a similar conviction: "What brings us together is our concern for children. This concern leads us to focus on the state of marriage and family life in America" (Popenoe, Elshtain, and Blankenhorn 1996, 293–94).

21. As such, to invoke John Stuart Mill's familiar distinction in *On Liberty,* it is an argument that society has jurisdiction over marriage because persons' decisions and behavior concerning marriage may cause harm to others, and not merely to themselves.

22. This point has been made by feminists in the debate over regulating pornography and in analysis of the law of rape and of approaches to sex education.

23. Among the other elements are: "Marriage is a free personal choice, based on love"; "Marriage is a heterosexual relationship"; "Marriage typically involves children"; and "Sexual fidelity and monogamy are expectations for marriage" (Nock 1998, 6).

24. The report *Turning the Corner on Father Absence in Black America* makes this argument, invoking the work of William Julius Wilson (Morehouse Research Institute and Institute for American Values 1999).

25. This is also James Q. Wilson's view (Wilson 2002). However, as some scholars observe, until the 1960s, marriage rates among African Americans were as high as and even higher than rates among whites, so slavery alone is not a sufficient explanation for contemporary differentials.

26. *Marriage: Just a Piece of Paper?* was a documentary shown on many PBS stations on February 14, 2002, produced at the initiative of the University of Chicago Divinity School's Religion, Culture, and Family Project. *Turning the Corner on Father Absence in Black America* declares: "The conclusion is inescapable: there is a crisis in gender relations in the Black community" (Morehouse Research Institute and Institute for American Values 1999, 17).

27. One study presents the notable finding that "marriages are strained when either partner does more traditionally female housework," while "marriages are strengthened by time spent in traditionally male tasks" (Nock and Brinig 2002, 186).

28. Feminist analysis of welfare policy reveals its reinforcement of women's dependency on marriage (Law 1983).

29. Feminist scholar Nancy Dowd (2000) reports findings that when fathers spend as much time nurturing as mothers, there are no significant differences in what they do; but generally, fathers do far less than mothers.

30. Orlando Patterson (1998) contends that studies find black women's attitudes on gender issues egalitarian and feminist, and black men's patriarchal.

31. More recently, Gilligan has applied this analysis to marriage dynamics (Davis and Gilligan 2002).

32. One prominent voice in the marriage movement, Diane Sollee, Coalition for Marriage, Family, and Couples Education, expresses this "tool kit" view (Anderson, Browning, and Boyer 2002, 372, 380–81).

33. For example, this is true of materials used in Florida, Texas, and Utah. What is absent, at least in the state materials I have seen, is any explicit embrace of marriage movement claims that couples should stay together in low-conflict marriages and divorce only in high-conflict and abusive marriages.

34. The jacket for the video indicates it is "provided by the Governor's Commission on Marriage and the Utah Department of Workforce Services." For information on Utah's marriage initiative, see www.utahmarriage.com.

35. Browning and his associates critique this view, attributed to pastor Tony Evans.

36. Ronald Dworkin (2000) describes equality—but not specifically sex equality—in these terms.

REFERENCES

Anderson, Elijah. 1999. *Code of the Street.* New York: Norton.

Anderson, Katherine, Don Browning, and Brian Boyer, eds. 2002. *Marriage: Just a Piece of Paper?* Grand Rapids, Mich.: Eerdmans.

Attorney General of Texas. 2002. "When You Get Married . . ."

Ball, Carlos. 1997. "Moral Foundations for a Discourse on Same-Sex Marriage." *Georgetown Law Journal* 85:1871–943.

Barker, Ernest, ed. and trans. 1958. *The Politics of Aristotle.* Oxford: Oxford University Press.

Baucus, Max. 2002. "Statement by Chairman Max Baucus." Senate Committee on Finance, Hearing on TANF Reauthorization: Building Stronger Families. May 16.

Bernstein, Nina. 2002. "Strict Limits on Welfare Benefits Discourage Marriage, Studies Say." *New York Times,* June 3.

Bix, Brian H. 2000. "State of the Union: The States' Interest in the Marital Status of Their Citizens." *University of Miami Law Review* 55:1–30.

Blankenhorn, David. 1995. *Fatherless America: Confronting Our Most Urgent Social Problem.* New York: Basic Books.

Blankenhorn, David, Steven Bayme, and Jean Bethke Elshtain, eds. 1990. *Rebuilding the Nest: A New Commitment to the American Family.* Milwaukee, Wis.: Family Service America.

Blumstein, Philip, and Pepper Schwartz. 1983. *American Couples.* New York: Morrow.

Brinig, Margaret F., and Steven L. Nock. 2004. "What Does Covenant Mean for Relationships?" *Notre Dame Journal of Law, Ethics, and Public Policy* 18:137–88.

Browning, Don S. 2001. "What Kind of Love? The Equal-Regard Marriage and Children." *American Experiment Quarterly* 4:47–52.

Browning, Don S., and Gloria C. Rodriguez. 2002. *Reweaving the Social Tapestry: Toward a Public Philosophy and Policy for Families.* New York: Norton.

Browning, Don S., Pamela D. Couture, Bonnie J. Miller-McLemore, K. Brynolf Lyon, and Robert M. Franklin, eds. 2000. *From Culture Wars to Common Ground: Religion and the American Family Debate.* (2nd ed.) Louisville, Ky.: Westminster John Knox Press.

Burt, Martha R., Janine M. Zweig, and Kathryn A. Schlichter. 2000. "Strategies for Addressing the Needs of Domestic Violence Victims within the TANF Program." The Urban Institute (http://www.urban.org/welfare/dv_tanf.pdf).

Bush, President George W. 2002. "Working Toward Independence." Available at www.whitehouse.gov/news/releases/2002/02/20020212-7.html.

Carbone, June. 2001. "Has the Gender Divide Become Unbridgeable? The Implications for Social Equality." *Journal of Gender, Race, and Justice* 5:31–86.

Case, Mary Anne. 2002. "Reflections on Constitutionalizing Women's Equality." *California Law Review* 90:765–90.

Cherlin, Andrew. 1999. "Going to Extremes: Family Structure, Children Well-Being, and Social Science." *Demography* 36:421–28.

Coontz, Stephanie, and Nancy Folbre. 2002. "Marriage, Poverty, and Public Policy." *Poverty Research News* 6 (May–June): 9.

Cornell, Drucilla. 1998. *At the Heart of Freedom.* Princeton, N.J.: Princeton University Press.

Cott, Nancy. 2000. *Public Vows: A History of Marriage and the Nation.* Cambridge, Mass.: Harvard University Press.

Davis, Peggy Cooper, and Carol Gilligan. 2002. "Reconstructing Law and Marriage." *Good Society* 11:57–67.

Deutsch, Francine M. 1999. *Halving It All: How Equally Shared Parenting Works.* Cambridge, Mass.: Harvard University Press.

Dowd, Nancy. 2000. *Redefining Fatherhood.* New York: NYU Press.

Duenwald, Mary. 2002. "Two Portraits of Children of Divorce: Rosy and Dark." *New York Times*, March 26.

Dworkin, Ronald. 1993. *Life's Dominion.* New York: Knopf.

———. 1996. *Freedom's Law.* Cambridge, Mass.: Harvard University Press.

———. 2000. *Sovereign Virtue.* Cambridge, Mass.: Harvard University Press.

Edin, Kathryn. 2000. "What Do Low-Income Single Mothers Say about Marriage?" *Social Problems* 47:112–33.

———. 2001. "Testimony of Kathryn Edin" before House Ways and Means Committee Hearing on Welfare and Marriage. May 22.

Fineman, Martha Albertson. 1995. *The Neutered Mother, the Sexual Family, and Other Twentieth Century Tragedies.* New York: Routledge.

———. 2001. "Why Marriage?" *Virginia Journal of Social Policy and the Law* 9: 239–72.

Franklin, Donna L. 2000. *What's Love Got to Do with It?* New York: Simon and Schuster.

Gallagher, Maggie. 1996. "Re-creating Marriage." In *Promises to Keep: Decline and Renewal of Marriage in America,* ed. David Popenoe, Jean Bethke Elshtain, and David Blankenhorn, 233–46. Lanham, Md.: Rowman and Littlefield.

Gilligan, Carol. 1982. *In a Different Voice.* Cambridge, Mass.: Harvard University Press.

Greene, Abner. 2000. "Government of the Good." *Vanderbilt Law Review* 53:1–69.

Hawkins, Alan J., Lynn D. Wardle, and David Orgon Coolidge, eds. 2002. *Revitalizing the Institution of Marriage for the Twenty-first Century.* Wesport, Conn.: Praeger.

Henary, Beth. 2002. "Mother and Father Know Best: A New Role for Bush's Health and Human Services Department." *Weekly Standard,* March 4, 18.

Hendrick, Howard H. 2002. "Testimony of Howard H. Hendrick, Oklahoma Secretary of Health and Human Services" before Senate Finance Committee in Hearing on Issues in TANF Reauthorization: Building Stronger Families. May 16.

Hetherington, E. Mavis, and John Kelly. 2002. *For Better or for Worse: Divorce Reconsidered.* New York: Norton.

Horn, Wade F. 2001. "Wedding Bell Blues." *Brookings Review* 19 (3).

———. 2002. "Statement by Wade F. Horn, Assistant Secretary for Children and Families, Dept. of Health and Human Services, before the Committee on Finance, U.S. Senate." May 16.

Horn, Wade, and Andrew Bush. 1997. "Fathers, Marriage, and Welfare Reform."

Washington, D.C.: Hudson Institute. Available at www.action.org (visited May 6, 2005).

Johnson, Christine A. 2001. *Marriage in Oklahoma: 2001 Baseline Statewide Survey on Marriage and Divorce.* Oklahoma City: Oklahoma State University Bureau for Social Research.

Law, Sylvia. 1983. "Women, Work, and the Preservation of Patriarchy." *University of Pennsylvania Law Review* 131:1249–339.

Marriage Movement. 2000. www.marriagemovement.org (visited May 6, 2005).

McClain, Linda C. 1998. "Toleration, Autonomy, and Governmental Promotion of Good Lives: Beyond 'Empty' Toleration to Toleration as Respect." *Ohio State Law Journal* 59:19–132.

———. 1999. "Reconstructive Tasks for a Liberal Feminist Conception of Privacy." *William and Mary Law Review* 40:759–94.

———. 2000. "Toward a Formative Project of Securing Freedom and Equality." *Cornell Law Review* 85:1221–58.

———. 2001a. "Care as a Public Value: Linking Responsibility, Resources, and Republicanism." *Chicago-Kent Law Review* 76:1673–731.

———. 2001b. "The Domain of Civic Virtue in a Good Society: Families, Schools, and Sex Equality." *Fordham Law Review* 69:1617–66.

———. 2005. "The Place of Families." Unpublished manuscript.

Mink, Gwendolyn. 2002. "From Welfare to Wedlock: Marriage Promotion and Poor Mothers' Inequality." *Good Society* 11:68–73.

Morehouse Research Institute and Institute for American Values. 1999. *A Statement from the Morehouse Conference on African American Fathers: Turning the Corner on Father Absence in Black America.* Atlanta: Morehouse Research Institute.

Nock, Steven. 1998. *Marriage and Men's Lives.* New York: Oxford University Press.

———. 2001. "The Marriage of Equally Dependent Spouses." *Journal of Family Issues* 2:756–77.

Nock, Steven L., and Margaret F. Brinig. 2002. "Weak Men and Disorderly Women: Divorce and the Division of Labor." In *The Law and Economics of Marriage and Divorce,* ed. Antony W. Dnes and Robert Rowthorn. New York: Cambridge University Press.

———. 2004. "What Does Covenant Mean for Relationships?" *Notre Dame Journal of Law, Ethics, and Public Policy* 18:137.

Nussbaum, Martha. 1990. "Aristotelian Social Democracy." In *Liberalism and the Good,* ed. R. Bruce Douglass, Gerald M. Mara, and Henry J. Richardson, 203–52. New York: Routledge.

———. 1999. *Sex and Social Justice.* New York: Oxford University Press.

———. 2000. *Women and Human Development.* Cambridge: Cambridge University Press.

Ooms, Theodora, Stacey Bouchet, and Mary Park. 2004. *Beyond Marriage Licenses:*

Efforts in States to Strengthen Marriage and Two-Parent Families. Center for Law and Social Policy, April.

Parkman, Allen M. 2002. "Good Incentives Lead to Good Marriage." In *Revitalizing the Institution of Marriage for the Twenty-first Century,* ed. Alan J. Hawkins, Linda J. Waite, Lynn D. Wardle, David Coolidge, and David Orgon Coolidge, 69–77. Westport, Conn.: Praeger.

Patterson, Orlando. 1998. *Rituals of Blood: Consequences of Slavery in Two American Centuries.* Washington, D.C.: Civitas/Counterpoint.

Pear, Robert. 2001. "Human Services Nominee's Focus on Married Fatherhood Draws Both Praise and Fire." *New York Times,* June 7.

Personal Responsibility and Work Opportunity Reconciliation Act of 1996, Pub. L. No. 104-193, 110 Stat. 2105.

Peterson, Karen S. 2002. "Kids, Parents Can Make Best of Divorce." *USA Today,* January 14.

Popenoe, David. 2001. "Testimony of David Popenoe, National Marriage Project." Hearing on Welfare and Marriage, House Ways and Means Committee, May 22.

———. 2002. "A Marriage Research Agenda for the Twenty-First Century: Ten Critical Questions." In *Revitalizing the Institution of Marriage for the Twenty-first Century,* ed. Alan J. Hawkins, Linda J. Waite, Lynn D. Wardle, David Coolidge, and David Orgon Coolidge. Westport, Conn.: Praeger.

Popenoe, David, Jean Bethke Elshtain, and David Blankenhorn. 1996. *Promises to Keep: Decline and Renewal of Marriage in America.* Lanham, Md.: Rowman and Littlefield.

Regan, Milton C., Jr. 1993. *Family Law and the Pursuit of Intimacy.* New York: NYU Press.

Schneider, Carl E. 1992. "The Channeling Function in Family Law." *Hofstra Law Review* 20:495–532.

Schwartz, Pepper. 1994. *Love between Equals.* New York: Free Press.

———. 1998. "Peer Marriage." *Responsive Community* 8 (Summer): 48–60.

Scott, Elizabeth. 2000. "Social Norms and the Legal Regulation of Marriage." *Virginia Law Review* 86:1901–70.

Sen, Amartya. 1992. *Inequality Reexamined.* New York: Russell Sage Foundation.

Spaht, Katherine Shaw. 2002. "Why Covenant Marriage May Prove Effective as a Response to the Culture of Divorce." In *Revitalizing the Institution of Marriage for the Twenty-first Century,* ed. Alan J. Hawkins, Linda J. Waite, Lynn D. Wardle, David Coolidge, and David Orgon Coolidge, 59–67. Westport, Conn.: Praeger.

Stacey, Judith. 1996. *In the Name of the Family: Rethinking Family Values in the Postmodern Age.* Boston: Beacon Press.

Stanley, Scott M. 2001. "Making a Case for Premarital Education." *Family Relations* 50:272–80.

Toner, Robin. 2002. "Welfare Chief Is Hoping to Promote Marriage." *New York Times,* February 19.

U.S. Department of Health and Human Services. 2002. *State Policies to Promote Marriage: Preliminary Report.* Prepared by the Lewin Group, Inc. Available at www.lewin.com (visited May 6, 2005).

Waite, Linda, and Maggie Gallagher. 2000. *The Case for Marriage: Why Married People Are Happier, Healthier, and Better-Off Financially.* New York: Doubleday.

Waller, Maureen R. 2002. *My Baby's Father: Unmarried Parents and Paternal Responsibility.* Ithaca, N.Y.: Cornell University Press.

Whitehead, Barbara Dafoe, and David Popenoe. 1999. "The State of Our Unions: 1999: The Social Health of Marriage in America." Rutgers, the State University of New Jersey: The National Marriage Project.

———. 2000. "The State of Our Unions: The Social Health of Marriage in America, 2000: Sex without Strings, Relationships without Rings." Rutgers, the State University of New Jersey: The National Marriage Project.

———. 2001. "The State of Our Unions: The Social Health of Marriage in America, 2001: Who Wants to Marry a Soulmate?" Rutgers, the State University of New Jersey: The National Marriage Project.

———. 2002. "The State of Our Unions, 2002: Why Men Won't Commit." Rutgers, the State University of New Jersey: The National Marriage Project.

Wilson, James Q. 2002. *The Marriage Problem.* New York: HarperCollins.

Wilson, William Julius. 1996. *When Work Disappears.* New York: Random House.

Witte, John., Jr. 1997. *From Sacrament to Contract.* Louisville, Ky.: Westminster John Knox Press.

Wriggins, Jennifer. 2000. "Marriage Law and Family Law." *Boston College Law Review* 41:265–325.

Young, Iris Marion. 1995. "Mothers, Citizenship, and Independence: A Critique of Pure Family Values." *Ethics* 105:535–56.

Yudof, Mark. 1983. *When Government Speaks: Politics, Law and Government Expression in America.* Berkeley: University of California Press.

Part II

Some Perils of Attempting Abolition

Chapter 4

Anthropological Perspectives on the Abolition of Marriage

Lawrence Rosen

Every discipline has its own conceit. And every discipline has attributed to it by others its presumed utility to the latters' own designs. The anthropological conceit is that it is the universal donor of academe: there is an anthropology of everything. And, perhaps as a sign of its success in promoting this conceit, other disciplines seem to think that there is almost always an anthropological perspective that can assist in the furtherance of their own claims. The resulting merger of conceits naturally has its benefits and its liabilities. Anthropologists get invited to everything, but like the too-traveled cousin or resident divine often receive a respectful if uncomprehending nod at their end of the table from hosts who take the inclusion of these odd guests as proof of their own broad-mindedness. If, however, the anthropologists cannot reinforce the expectations of their host or, worse yet, undermine the universal claims or specific premises of the host, the anthropologists' contribution may be treated as proof of their marginal importance or boorish ingratitude.

Such is the case with almost all considerations of kinship. Seen as the natural domain of the anthropologist, issues of marriage, family form, and sexuality often prompt those coming from other disciplines to seek confirmation of their assumptions or universal claims through anthropology's own array of exotic instances. But if one understands that anthropology is not just a listing of curious traits and conventions but a distinct set of approaches to seeking the linkages among a culture's diverse domains, the contribution of anthropology to discussions about kinship, sexuality, marriage, and the state may, perhaps, be placed on a more realistic and desirable footing.

In this chapter I will, therefore, be trying to point out what anthropology can and cannot confirm in the perspectives taken by those who seek in our material and our theories support for their own working assumptions about marriage and the family. By surveying—admittedly, from my own perspective within the discipline—the limitations on our ability to corroborate certain views, we may, perhaps, see that assertions based on anthropology may not always be as supportive as some might wish them to be but may, properly seen, add in a far more theoretical than iterative way to discussions about the relation of marriage and family to religion and the state.

Specifically, when issues are raised about marriage, family, and sexuality, questions often fall into several categories. Thus, to borrow the phrasings of several recent articles, one asks: Is marriage a necessary legal concept? Is kinship necessarily based on heterosexuality? Does family form matter? Do parents matter? Or, What is "marriage-like" like (Cossman and Ryder 2001)? The turn to anthropology prompts responses that may themselves be placed in several overlapping categories: the link (if any) between sexuality and kinship structures; the assessment of biology as a basis for such supposed universals as infant-parent bonding and the "brute facts" of sexual dimorphism; the functions played by family forms and the impact on these functions of alternative sexual orientations; the relation of marriage, however public or privatized, to the broader aspects of a culture; the cultural and political role of legitimization; and the problematic nature of political forms and their relation to conjugal life. Thus as we move through the questions about marriage and its "abolition," we will, at each point, consider the uses being made of anthropological information and interpretations in an overall attempt to situate the claims to universality and function that often seek support from a discipline that has invested itself quite heavily in the comparative study of such matters.

Nature versus Nurture

The debate over the respective importance of nature or social context has, in the course of American history, moved primarily from the domains of theology, racial discrimination, and educational policy to that of the legal status of sexuality and the family. The suitability of alternative forms of marriage and the family, the place of reproductive technology in the very idea of kinship, and the rationale for governmental involvement in the

sexual lives of its citizens have become the new terrain for applying biological and anthropological information. The two predominant orientations of current debate center on questions of natural law and evolutionary biology.

To some the issue is quite simple: like Lucretius, they believe that if you
cast nature out the door, it will come flying back in through the window.
Thus the neo–natural law proponents, particularly those who draw their
jurisprudential inspiration from religious sources, often argue, to use the
phrasing of Mary Ann Glendon, that "underneath the mantle of equality
[and freedom] that has been draped over the ongoing family, the state of
nature flourishes."[1] To these thinkers, common sense dictates that while
marital and familial forms have obviously varied with time and place,
there remain certain invariant "facts"—that only women get pregnant,
that conjugal relations occupy a unique place in the realm of human emotions, that children need recognizable and enduring parental attachments
in order to develop healthy personalities—which no stable system can
afford to ignore. By contrast the biologists, particularly the sociobiologists,
see human nature as founded on a set of biological conditions that effectively constrain the range of possibilities human communities may create
for themselves. Whether it is cast in terms of cognitive or psychological
evolution, or the unity of biological forces with those of human behavior,
the thrust is clearly toward seeing cultural practices as secondary to,
indeed (at the analytic level said to be of greatest import) wholly dependent on, the factors associated with the kind of animal that we are.[2] Whatever the merits of these arguments as philosophical positions, the occasional reliance on anthropology in each of these arguments is at least open
to question.

Take first the uses of anthropology in the various natural law arguments. Working mostly from classical and Roman Catholic philosophers,
contemporary proponents of a natural law approach see in the human situation a built-in disposition to seek marital ties as a way of achieving the
common good of two persons through their unity in both a biological
(sexual) bond and the formation of new life. While such issues as same-
sex marriage and adultery are, for most of these thinkers, violations of the
goodness that flows from the unity of husband and wife, and while the
question of nonprocreative marriage is said to be finessed by claiming that
such unions are not actively contrary to the possibility of unity, external
support for natural law theories is difficult to come by. When "exotic"
instances are cited, it is usually for so broad a proposition as that every

society has an incest taboo or that "families" exist everywhere—neither of which, incidentally, is quite true. The difficulties posed by particularly challenging examples are either dismissed as deviants (rather than statistical oddities) or, worse yet, as an invitation to rescue human nature or the human mind from the clutches of a misunderstood relativism "by placing morality beyond culture and knowledge beyond both" (Geertz 2000, 65).

Others, however, have sought "natural" principles not in religious or philosophical speculation and belief but in those "laws of nature" they see as manifest in human sociality. In doing so they rely on ideas of the marketplace, sociobiology, or a mixture of the two. Thus Richard Posner can argue that, in a kind of free market of emotions, if the quest for companionate relationship cannot be found in heterosexual ties it will be found elsewhere, and while the promptings of biology are not essential to the explanation of such relationships, at "later stages in the evolution of sexual morality" the marketplace—through employment opportunities outside the household and the diminished advantages of marriage for economic well-being—adequately accounts for shifts in sexual practice and morality (Posner 1992, chap. 4). Notwithstanding the disclaimers, the connection to sociobiology exists both in the inherent evolutionism of this account and in the claimed biological basis for the foundations of human sexuality. This approach (again with ritualistic disclaimers of biological determinism) is made more explicit, for example, by Richard Epstein, who asserts that "men and women are more comfortable in playing the roles that are congenial to their biological roles, and will find themselves uneasy with powerful social [or legal] conventions that dictate a parity in social roles in courtship, marriage, and parenting."[3] Similarly, the assertion that women are more "cooperative" than men (or even just perceived to be so) is taken to mean that women's need for relationship often leads them to settle for less than is acceptable to men, who can more readily treat particular relationships like any other "inelastic" good they could do without (Rose 1994, 233–63).

Comparisons to other cultures enter these discussions in a characteristically limited and selective manner. Not only are instances of contrary power relations among men and women (or among various racial and ethnic groups) broadly ignored, but, as we shall see, certain fundamental premises of anthropology are reduced to simplistic assertions—for example, that the causal role of rational decision making always follows along the lines first discerned in Western thought. The occasional nod at the "exotic" is little more than that—a less than serious attempt to come to terms with alternative ways of constructing experience and the theoretically disruptive implications they pose. Thus market rationality is regarded as a unitary phenomenon, the implications of socially constructed versus biologically grounded practices are left uninvestigated, and no larger social theory is produced in these purportedly "theoretical" writings. Whether it is judges groping (with understandable difficulty) for some social science grounding or academic lawyers (with far less understandable difficulty) ignoring inconvenient examples, the result is a kind of potholing of anthropological information rather than a concerted attempt to come to grips with it. To see just how this plays out, let us consider several specific instances: the question of incest, the claims about infant-parent bonding, and the challenge posed to the universality of marriage and kinship by the example of the Na of China.

Theories of incest come in several basic flavors: "the children will be weird" (associated with various genetic and eugenic theorists); "familiarity breeds contempt" (associated with Edward Westermarck and, rather differently, Sigmund Freud); "marry out or die out" (associated with Claude Lévi-Strauss, among other alliance theorists); and "I am my own grandfather" (associated with those who see social structure as requiring a set of discrete roles). Each has its particular varieties and attachments to grander theories (evolutionism, functionalism, structuralism), and each has served as a basis for modern courts and legal scholars to justify both general and specific limitations on the right to marry.[4] The more biologically based explanations still find favor with the sociobiologists who read the anthropological studies much more restrictively than do most anthropologists.[5] That thirty-eight states prohibit marriage to first cousins whereas the rest do not, that recent studies demonstrate that first-cousin marriage is no more likely to yield deleterious results than other alliances, and that until the nineteenth century marriage to a wife's sister (even if the wife herself was dead) was regarded as incestuous should suggest the contingent and malleable nature of the incest taboo even within our own culture.[6] Although some boundary does apply in almost every culture, no one theory seems to account for all instances. Thus one of the most intriguing variants on the role distinctiveness argument is that of Margaret Mead, who suggested that there must be some zone in which actions that might otherwise carry sexual overtones—various states of undress, caressing, and so forth—would carry only implications of nonsexual intimacy. But even this theory can hardly yield answers as to whether that bounded zone must necessarily be correlated with residence, affinity, or age.[7]

In recent years, social scientists have also demonstrated that many ostensibly objective theories are, in fact, projections of (or at least deeply suffused by) their proponents' own cultural assumptions. An example that is particularly pertinent to the present discussion is that of mother-infant "bonding." This theory claims that an infant needs to "bond" immediately with its mother and that if the process is successful much subsequent psychological harm to the child may be avoided. But as Diane Eyer has demonstrated, this "theory" grew out of a single highly suspect article published in 1972, it coincided with women who were moving out into careers feeling guilty about not being constant caregivers to their children, and it thus constituted an explanation and course of action that had great credibility given the psychological and economic factors of the time. (Incidentally, men could actually purchase a "nursing bra" into which two baby bottles could be fit so that they could bond with the child as well!) The theory turns out to be complete scientific nonsense but to have made eminently good sense in the cultural moment in which it was placed. Once again, as in so many other domains, what was claimed in the name of social science turns out to be a feature whose own circumstances explain its attractiveness.[8]

Indeed, anthropological information, among other sources, has long confounded ideas of sexuality itself. Instances of cultures that construe male sexual identity as being granted first through a homosexual rite, or that conceptualize multiple genders each with its attendant social roles are brought home to us when, as a result of our own medical knowledge or procedures, the very gender of an individual becomes open to question.[9] The law must now decide if a postoperative transsexual is validly married (depending, perhaps, on whether the operation occurred before or after the wedding), or whether a prisoner has a valid claim against officials who do not assign him (her) to a prison environment consonant with his (her) claimed gender.[10] Once again, scholars and courts may cite anthropological instances, but they usually do so as idiosyncratic instances rather than drawing any broader practical or theoretical conclusions on the basis of which to construct a more solidly based idea of how and why we choose to conceive of gender as we do.

Anthropologists were themselves quite exercised for a time over issues of *universality*, and such subjects as marriage and the family could hardly escape such concern. And so assertions are made about the family citing various anthropological examples. To the question, Is marriage universal? examples would be cited such as the Nayar of coastal India. There, a woman is ritually "tied" to a man of equal or higher caste, but her only duty is to mourn him on his death. She is free to have sexual liaisons with any appropriate caste male, though some individual must step forward to assert himself as a possible progenitor. Kathleen Gough argued that this is marriage inasmuch as the ritual tie and acknowledgment constitute validations of permissible sexuality, legitimacy of birth, and even rights of exclusive sexual access in that men of only certain castes are allowable lovers.[11] But if "marriage" may involve no intimate contact between spouses, why, a number of anthropologists have argued, should we not abandon attempts at defining marriage altogether? Riviere thus wrote: "I am left in the position of claiming that if we are not to condemn ourselves for ever to the tautologies of functionalist explanations we must come to realize that marriage as an isolable phenomenon of study is a misleading illusion" (Riviere 1971, 57–74). Similarly, Needham argued: "So 'marriage,' too, is an odd-job word: very handy in all sorts of descriptive sentences, but worse than misleading in comparison and of no real use at all in analysis" (Needham 1971, 7–8). However, as even these two commentators note, while no strict definition of marriage may be possible, the anthropological record and changing family patterns continue to raise questions that, while failing to produce universals, nevertheless call for comparative analysis. Thus while the Nayar may have seemed to press the limits of what Westerners understand by marriage, the recently described Na of China would appear to press them to the null point.

The Na, a tribal people of Tibetan-like Buddhists living in southern China, recognize no paternity, allow women to receive sexual visits from any man not part of their household (sex within that domain being unthinkable incest), do not form solidary groups based on descent or alliance, and demonstrate no jealousy in relation to "visits" by a woman's other lovers. No words exist in their language for "promiscuity," "bastard," or "infidelity"; brothers and sisters live together all their lives with some of their maternal kin; and since paternity is not socially recognized, a man may on occasion even wind up sleeping with his own daughter. The account of the Na by the French-trained anthropologist Cai Hua comes with endorsements from Lévi-Strauss and others and has been very favorably reviewed by leading anthropologists.[12] The example of the Na, therefore, suggests that it is sexuality rather than genealogical ordering on which this society is constructed, and that the "naturalness," to say nothing of the universality, of family and descent are once again in play. Indeed, as we shall see later, the question arises whether the Na are truly unusual or whether Western societies are themselves becoming like the Na in certain crucial ways. The Na thus pose a new test for anthropological comparison —and a challenge to generalizations about kinship generally. They do so, among other ways, by challenging some of the working notions that relate to the functions of families in general.

Family Functions

In 1950 a group of social scientists associated with Harvard's short-lived social relations department published an article entitled "The Functional Prerequisites of a Society."[13] In it they listed, among others, the need for "shared cognitive orientations," a "shared articulated set of goals," the regulation of both means and affective expression, and the effective recruitment of members who would then be properly socialized to the standards of the group. One problem, however, was that they were unable to show any relationship between form and function. Thus while it seems reasonable to suggest that some human endeavors must benefit from cooperation or that children need to be fed, there is no demonstrable correlation between these endeavors and the ways in which they may be accomplished. Form not only does not follow function, but multifarious forms challenge the concept of function itself. If children can be raised in a separate children's house or if paternity is irrelevant in a given society, it is difficult to maintain a strict list of societal requirements. The entire enterprise thus fell into disfavor for much the same reason that family law has become so problematic in Western countries—because the multitude of forms has overwhelmed former certainty about function.

The alterations that have occurred in Europe and the United States clearly demonstrate how much form has outstripped function. In the last quarter of the twentieth century roughly a quarter of all pregnancies in America were aborted, half of the marriages ended in divorce, and three-quarters of African American children were raised without a resident father.[14] At present in the United States, 79 percent of children spend some time in day care (39 percent spending more than thirty hours per week).[15] The rate of births to unwed parents in Europe now ranges from 49 percent in Norway, 38 percent in Britain, and 41 percent in France, to 62 percent in Iceland and even 31 percent in Catholic Ireland (Lyall 2002). Most parents still marry at some point in time, but since cohabiting and married couples may differ in their economic attitudes and knowledge of public policy, it may be, as one commentator on the Swedish example suggests, that "[t]he formal similarity between consensual unions and marriage does not necessarily imply that the 'social contract' between the partners is the same" (Bjornberg 2001, 359). Governmental programs have changed along with these familial alterations: Britain has abandoned most policies that favor the traditional family form, Swedish income taxes are neutral on all matters of civil status, and even rights of succession are beginning to effectively alter as the distinction between children born in or out of wedlock has evaporated. Such profound alterations are hardly unique in the West: studies of family history suggest that children in early modern Europe were often raised outside of their natal homes, that marriage became a concern of the state only in the sixteenth-century (and indeed a sacrament only in the early Middle Ages), and that nineteenth-century Americans found many ways around the difficulty of obtaining a divorce—thus reinforcing H. L. Mencken's famous quip that in America "adultery is democratized marriage."[16]

Notwithstanding increased awareness of these contemporary and historic alterations in family forms, many scholars and policymakers remain attached to a functionalist conception of marriage and the family, whatever their views on the proper role of the state in such matters. Martha Fineman calls for the abolition of marriage as a legal category (Fineman 1995, this volume) but demonstrates her functionalist leanings when she also rhetorically asks: "If the terms of the marital contract are altered, should we not reflect on whether the functional role that the family plays within society must, of necessity, also be altered?" (Fineman 1998, 183–95). Others are more explicit in the functions they expect marriage and the family to perform. In supporting no-fault divorce legislation, the California Supreme Court in 1952 first outlined the functions of the family and then held that when those functions were no longer being performed, the parties should be able to terminate the relationship.[17] On the opposite end of the sociopolitical spectrum, the 16 million–strong Southern Baptist Convention in 1998 specified the functions each spouse must play in a marriage when it changed its statement of beliefs to read: "[A husband] has the God-given responsibility to provide for, to protect and to lead his family. A wife is to submit graciously to the servant leadership of her husband even as the church willingly submits to the headship of Christ" (Niebuhr 1998).

But if many of the purported functions of marriage and the family can be performed without publicly institutionalized regularization, it is difficult to know what "functions" are being assumed.[18] This is true even in the domain of child welfare, since it is by no means clear that one or another family form best serves a child's needs. In their ongoing consideration of same-sex marriage, the Hawaiian courts, for example, have held that the optimal development of children has not been proved to be adversely affected by rearing in a same-sex household.[19] Similarly, studies can be cited on either side—quite often as a matter of what I would call "the higher personal politics," rather than as part of a quest for greater truth—to support or attack the proposition that divorce has adverse consequences for children.[20] And if there is support for the recent, though quite controversial, studies by Judith Rich Harris, who argues that peers are far more important than parents to a child's psychological development, the examples of other societies—from the children's houses of the kibbutz to the intense day care situations found in some parts of Italy—may yet affect the entire discourse of functioning families and child welfare (Gladwell 1998).

To some extent, of course, all social scientists (and legal scholars) are functionalists: we see usefulness and connection even when we may append other theories (Marxist, structuralist, evolutionary, economistic) to the functional foundation. The irony is that much of the debate about the abolition of marriage is being carried on in terms of functionalism even though functionalism is rife with limitations. Functionalism has always had great difficulty conceptualizing change or, since everything is said to contribute to the working of the whole, establishing criteria for the "dysfunctional."[21] Indeed, as the variety of forms expands, in both our anthropological awareness and our own experiences, it becomes ever more difficult to assume universal propositions about social functioning at all. So it is striking to see the terminology of functionalism remaining so central to the abolition of marriage debates. Thus when courts, like those in Canada and Massachusetts, have held that it is unconstitutional to impose differences on same-sexed, as opposed to opposite-sexed, couples, it is noteworthy that the courts have relied on ideas of the ways in which nonmarital relations are functionally like those receiving state sanction, even though courts commonly renounce any single functional model.[22] The result is a kind of approach to vagueness: neither courts nor commentators can quite give up regarding marriage as "doing something" for people and society at large, yet as they expand the range of "equivalent" forms, they can no longer specify with clarity what those functions are.

One way to finesse the issue is to try to remove sexuality from the equation altogether. For example, it has been argued that it is inappropriate to consider sexuality when deciding the role of the state in relationships, since the only legitimate interests of the state should go to the well-being of individual children or partners. The comparison to the Na is intriguing, for it could be said that we are becoming more like the Na than like our earlier selves—rendering sexuality central but without specifiably distinctive spousal implications. Indeed, the anthropological literature could be used to suggest that functionalism is either in the eye of the beholder or bound to a given culture, and that claims to naturalness, necessity, or universality are claims for legitimacy of one's position, not claims to scientific validation.[23] However, we need to consider one other matter, that of legitimacy itself, before we can explore the ways in which the anthropological approach to culture may be able to address the relation of structure and function in marriage and the family.

Creating Legitimacy

What is it one seeks in asking outside persons or institutions to ratify one's conjugal or familial relationship? Obviously that answer varies with each culture, and any universal answer falls into the same trap of functionalism or generalization that always beckons. But if, in the American context, one poses the question in this way, both the contributions and the limitations of anthropology to the discussion can be explored.

The central question in legitimacy is: Why should I do what someone else says, or at least seek their approval for my own actions? But what we seek to legitimize is complex. It may be recognition that we are members of the group or that we have done things the "right" way. It may be that we have reached a given stage in life and are allowed to possess and feel the things that society has assigned to such a position or role. It may be that we are now licensed to engage in acts previously denied us. Legitimization may be a bald-faced statement that whatever others may do, this is who *we* are. Indeed, legitimacy may be the assignment of a dangerous capability that must nevertheless be contained if society itself is to be replicated. Or it may simply be a grant of power that we seek, as Verlaine said, with no particular goal in mind but simply because we do not know to what uses we may have to put it.

Specific examples of each of these factors can be found in our own, as in any society's, history. Thus, in the West marriage moved only in recent centuries from the concern of religion to that of the state as the state itself sought to have its citizens depend on and identify their well-being with the burgeoning central government. Marriage may even have legitimized extramarital relations, so long as they were discreet and the needs of social replication—by class, by race, by symbolic appropriation—were fulfilled. For others, marriage may have come to mean the relief of no longer having to compete for a mate in a marketplace of relations. Indeed, marriage may be less about the relationships of individuals or groups than about legitimization itself—about the capacity of government or religion to tell us what we may do. As a consequence, for revolutionaries—in Britain in the seventeenth century, in Russia at the time of the Bolshevik revolution, in the United States in the 1960s—sex, marriage, and family form could serve as vehicles for protest against the claims of the state.[24] To alter the terms of the relationships may, therefore, be to call into question legitimacy itself.

If, as we shall see, anthropology suggests that every domain of a sociocultural system has some bearing on every other, then changes, or proposed changes, in the legal status of marriage and the family would be expected to have systemic effects. Some of these effects are more easily missed than others if one did not assume from the outset—based on a wide range of comparative ethnographic instances—that such connections invariably do exist. If, then, we were, for example, to take up the suggestion that marriage be returned to the domain of religion, or be rendered an entirely contractual matter, with the state playing only the role of enforcing private agreements and deferring all its own objectives to the realm of individual support (rather than trying to get the family to do its work for it) (Fineman, this volume; Bernstein, this volume), one might ask the relevant anthropological question in either of two ways: What supportive changes elsewhere in the sociocultural system will affect the course and success of the outcome? Or: What systemic alterations can one look for that might not at first seem to be connected to these changes but, given comparative studies, do indeed appear likely to be implicated?[25] Some of these connections are predominantly legal in origin, others more broadly cultural.

Martha Fineman, for example, suggests that "ameliorating doctrines would fill the void left by the abolition of family law. In fact, it seems apparent to me that a lot more regulation (protection) would occur once the large category of interactions in families were removed from behind the veil of privacy that now shields them" (Fineman, this volume, 58). But the very idea of privacy may be affected in the process, and with it notions of responsibility, the religious images that support ideas of the family, and even concepts of time—as stages of life or development are reconceptualized. Similarly, if one moves to a wholly contractual system numerous questions arise: Will the "convenant marriage" contracts now permitted in several states (and under consideration by many others), which allow parties to agree to more limitations on exiting their marriages than exist under current state laws, affect personal identity and ideas of democracy as individuals have different relationships to the state and children identify their parents' relationships differently?[26] Will use of the Uniform Premarital Agreement Act, particularly its provision allowing agreements about the behavior of each party, affect ideas of free will, choice, the American romance of romance, and the image we have of our inalienable right to the pursuit of happiness?[27] If marriages are fraught with contractual elements, will they really be seen as binding contracts, for which few changes in circumstance would constitute grounds for revision, or will they be seen as moral agreements, metaphors of intent, or similar to international treaties from which parties may exit when it is in their "interest" to do so (Scott and Scott 1998)? And if the effects are moral rather than legally enforceable, what effects will this have on images of the self and the arrangements to which marriage has itself become analogized? Indeed, the use of such contracts highlights the problematic nature of the state itself. For as Judith Butler (2002) argues, if the state uses the family as a domain for replicating the composition and structure of national distinctiveness, does shifting away, say, from the image of the family as grounded on heterosexual kinship affect such other factors as the place of immigration in the symbolic image of the nation, or the claim that state policy is not based on nationalism but on some ineffable natural principles?

Even if one does not agree with the proposition that society may, through the institutions of the state, withhold its imprimatur from certain relationships, there is little doubt that "informal" mechanisms—from metaphoric shifts to revised views of the person—will be affected by the contest over state validation. As legitimacy and privacy are altered, so, too, will be all those other cultural elements connected with them. And like other such instances of significant social and cultural change, the uses to which anthropological information is put, and the repercussions for theoretical development within the discipline itself, will also be profound. How, if at all, to attend these impending alterations is also worthy of brief consideration.

What Is to Be Done—Anthropologically?

Marital Status (circle one):
Married. Single. Not sure.
    —magazine questionnaire

"Not sure" may seem the safe answer all around. Far from being a predictive science, anthropology has enough difficulty stating what's what at any given moment. Of course, prediction and certainty are not the criteria for judging disciplinary insight, nor is science the singular, invariant entity our mythologies often make it out to be.[28] Nevertheless, it may be well to match up the occasional uses to which anthropology is put by those who debate the issues surrounding the abolition of marriage with the more realistic claims with which anthropologists (at least those with whom the present author identifies) may be tagged. Here, it is worthwhile asserting how it is that anthropologists like myself conceive of culture and how, working from such an approach, we may be able to cast more useful light on the subject of marriage, family, and the state.

Put very simply: Human beings are unique for their capacity to create the categories of their own experience. Indeed, we achieved this capability before we acquired our present speciation. The existence of this capacity for culture, while hardly rendering us nonbiological entities, means that instinct has been replaced by culture, and that, as we have gone about creating and re-creating our own experience, we have had to adapt to our own adaptations. The universe of meanings, no less than of relationships, the conceptualizations of our surroundings, no less than the ways we organize our social relations in terms of our cosmological understandings, are factors of our own design, and as those designs have changed, so have the ways we envision and organize ourselves for these changing experiences. The range of variation seen in human social and cultural forms is not a simple function of biological or environmental necessity or permissible leeway; it is the direct expression of that very ability evolution has yielded by which we fashion our own fabric of meaning. Therefore, one cannot take instances out of their contexts without doing them great violence, for what is central to our human identity is an inherent capacity rather than specific solutions required by nature.

There is a Yiddish saying: "For example is no proof." Nowhere is this more true than in the uses of anthropological findings. To take, say, an individual example of marital arrangements or familial forms and use it to prove (or disprove) a universal proposition about all marriages or all families misses the category of which these practices are an instance. For it is not some particular view of marriage or family that these instances can establish but the still more general idea that what is being demonstrated is a capability, indeed a mode of that capability's expression. To say that the Na prove marriage can be dispensed with or that the kibbutz proves that children do not need parents misses the anthropological point: what each instance demonstrates is that the nested webs of relationship, organization, concepts, and histories must be unpacked so that the "sense" they make becomes a demonstration of the sense-making of culture as the quintessentially human capacity.

Toward this end, as we have seen, anthropologists look for the reverberations across and among diverse domains of a culture precisely because it is this replication that gives a set of cultural notions its greatest power— the power to appear, to those who conceive of their lives in its terms, as natural. Whether this is because one cannot, so to speak, constantly reinvent the wheel or because this capacity serves to replicate society with enormous success, the evidence all suggests that, however contested and inexact, however open-textured or ambivalent, cultures achieve their integrity through reinforcement across domains. And that means that what anthropology can contribute most is sensitivity, through diversified examples, of how the processes of replication and integration, in all their variations of mode and result, may work for this most distinctive of species.

To follow such an approach is certainly not to pursue mindless relativism. Critics consistently misunderstand anthropologists in this regard. We do not equate all cultures on some moral scale: to the contrary we "suspend disbelief" about all specific practices in order to investigate the ways in which, to the people themselves, their ideas and relationships form some ordered sense by being suffused through multiple domains of their lives. Nor does anthropology deny that there may indeed be some "truths" out there that comparison can highlight. But what such a theoretical and investigative stance does imply is that if human beings are the producers of their own comprehensions, then we cannot prejudge the results by limiting truth claims to our own values or lose sight of the crucial human propulsion to generate categories and link them across seemingly separate domains. Claims for sociobiological determinism thus miss the distinctively biological nature of culture—that the capacity for culture arose through biological forces and may well remain subject to biological aspects, but that at every point it is the ability to conceptualize our own situations that is dominant. Thus claims of natural law are like any other cultural product: they are concepts that, by proliferating through and linking diverse aspects of one's culture, take on the air of being beyond human construct. We are not, therefore, ever dealing with natural law but with law naturalized—a process that is no less true for a legal concept than for any other cultural artifact.[29]

To move from the nature of human culture to the specifics of marriage and family is not, in actuality, so great a leap. If one "abolishes" marriage (in the sense of removing the state, or making marriage contractual, or returning it to religion), it will be the reverberations across diverse realms of cultural life that will be called into play. Metaphors, those most critical of means by which we make connections among domains, will play out in ways whose implications will be vast yet unpredictable; justifications, whether through the capturing of the institutions of legitimacy or resource allocation, will affect such seemingly "irrelevant" aspects of life as concepts of time and space; reformulations of the state's role in family support will be tied up with changes that occur in the concept of the person and the sense of self-worth. It is not that "nature" will always reassert itself: it is that culture works by appearing to its adherents as the proof and product of naturalization. It is not, as the French seem to believe, that the national assembly must be half female because nature has divided us in twain: it is that naturalizing the state in these terms constitutes a reaction to fears of multiculturalism, a sense of national identity slipping away. New marital covenants or contracts will most likely yield a new functionalism, as people assume that the purposes of these arrangements fulfill ends beyond themselves. And as much as comparison will once again demonstrate the indubitable fact that each solution is a construct of human endeavor, the power of culture to make each approach appear imminent will almost certainly lead even those who should know better to use anthropology selectively to "prove" that they are merely describing a human necessity rather than a momentary human solution.

Universal donor, perhaps; universal source for poaching, almost certainly. The vital lesson of anthropology—connections—carries implications that are easily dismissed as standardless relativism, inapposite practices from distant climes and peoples, or alternative ways of being that we should adopt piecemeal or reject wholesale as less than truly human. But if we think systemically, about the ways alternatives both integrate with elements of their overall constructs and reveal their capabilities and failings in specific situations, we may get at the full range of human experiences and what they can teach us about marriage, the family, and the uses of anthropology. The "answer" to the debate over the abolition of marriage —like many other issues in law and social policy—does not lie in some arcane example proving or disproving a universal proposition, but in the comprehension of how, in each society, linkages are configured. Variation being as central to culture as it is to biology, only the most responsible use of comparative examples will help us to understand the potential implications of our own actions.

NOTES

1. M. A. Glendon, *The Transformation of Family Law: State, Law, and Family in the United States and Western Europe* (Chicago: University of Chicago Press, 1989), 146, cited in J. Witte Jr., *An Apt and Cheerful Conversation on Marriage.* Sixth Distinguished Faculty Lecture, Emory University, 2001, 22.

2. Edward O. Wilson, the dean of sociobiologists, asserts that genes "prescribe" the hereditary regularities in physical and mental development (epigenetic rules) that "animate and channel the acquisition of culture," which, in turn "helps to determine which of the prescribing genes" survive and multiply such that these successful genes "alter" the epigenetic rules that "change the direction and effectiveness of the channels of cultural acquisition." E. O. Wilson, *Consilience: The Unity of Knowledge* (New York: Vintage Books, 1998), 171. For a similar denial of the role of culture, taken from the vantage of environmental determinism (and citing only those writers in cultural evolutionism who have, in fact, long since rejected their earlier theories, see J. Diamond, *Guns, Germs, and Steel: The Fates of Human Societies* (New York: Norton, 1997).

3. R. Epstein, "Two Challenges for Feminist Thought," *Harvard Journal of Law and Public Policy* 18 (1995): 336. The bracketed addition is borrowed from W. N. Eskridge Jr. and N. D. Hunter, *Sexuality, Gender, and the Law: 1998 Supplement* (Westbury, N.Y.: Foundation Press, 1998), 40.

4. "The crime [of incest] is also punished to promote and protect family harmony, to protect children from the abuse of parental authority, and because society cannot function in an orderly manner when age distinctions, generations, sentiments and roles in families are in conflict." *State v. Marvin K. Kaiser,* 34 Wash. App. 559, 663 P.2d 839 (Wash. Ct. of App. 1983), cited in W. N. Eskridge Jr. and N. D. Hunter, *Sexuality, Gender and the Law* (Westbury, N.Y.: Foundation Press, 1997), 276.

5. Thus, Wilson (*Consilience,* 190–91) cites the study by Arthur Wolf of Taiwanese girls who resisted marriage to the boy they were contracted to marry if

they were under thirty months of age when they were first brought into the household of their future spouse, and the studies of Israeli kibbutzim in which boys and girls raised in the communal "children's house" regarded one another as being like siblings and very rarely married someone with whom they were so raised. Wilson takes this as proof of the Westermarck hypothesis that individuals spurn as mates those with whom they were raised in early life. But there is no proof that this is not caused by cultural constraints rather than any natural repugnancy. See A. P. Wolf, *Sexual Attraction and Childhood Association: A Chinese Brief for Edward Westermarck* (Stanford, Calif.: Stanford University Press, 1995); and M. E. Spiro, *Childhood in the Kibbutz* (Cambridge, Mass.: Harvard University Press, 1958).

6. Eleven states and the District of Columbia prohibit stepsibling marriage; Alaska and Louisiana prohibit marriage within four degrees of relatedness; and Utah prohibits marriage within five degrees of affinity. See Eskridge and Hunter, *Sexuality, Gender and the Law.* On recent discoveries about the genetics of first-cousin marriage, see D. Grady, "Few Risks Seen to the Children of First Cousins," *New York Times,* April 4, 2002; On sister-in-law marriage, see J. B. Twitchell, *Forbidden Partners: The Incest Taboo in Modern Culture* (New York: Columbia University Press, 1987); F. Héritier, *Two Sisters and Their Mother: The Anthropology of Incest* (New York: Zone Books, 1999). Note, too, the final line in some versions of the song "My Darling Clementine," which goes: "So I kissed her little sister / and forgot my Clementine."

7. See M. Mead, "Anomalies in American Post-divorce Relationships," in *Divorce and After,* ed. P. Bohannan (Garden City, N.Y.: Doubleday, 1970), 97–112.

8. D. Eyer, *Mother-Infant Bonding: A Scientific Fiction* (New Haven, Conn.: Yale University Press, 1992). Other forms of bonding taken as commonsensical may also be rendered questionable in the light of historical and comparative contexts. Thus courts commonly state that persons other than parents may have rights of custody or visitation based on whether they have established psychological bonds to the child. J. Goldstein, A. Freud, and A. J. Solnit, *Beyond the Best Interests of the Child* (New York: Free Press, 1973). See also *J.A.L. v. E.P.H.,* 682 A.2d 1314 (Pa. Super. 1996), in Eskridge and Hunter, *Sexuality, Gender, and the Law: 1998 Supplement,* 118 ("[W]hile it is presumed that a child's best interest is served by maintaining the family's privacy and autonomy, that presumption must give way where the child has established strong psychological bonds with a person who, although not a biological parent, has lived with the child and provided care, nurture, and affection, assuming in the child's eye a stature like that of a parent.") Would a babysitter qualify? Indeed, what support is there for the theory itself? Goldstein et al. suggest that the primary psychological parent should be able to cut the other parent off from all visitation, an approach courts first accepted and then gradually rejected in favor of a return to joint custody. Goldstein, Freud, and Solnit, *Beyond the Best Interests of the Child.*

9. See the anthropological sources and arguments as discussed for law students in Eskridge and Hunter, *Sexuality, Gender and the Law,* 209–11.

10. Cf. *M.T. v. J.T.,* 140 N.J. Super. 77, 355 A.2d 204, cert. denied, 71 N.J. 345, 364 A.2d 1076 (N.J. App. Div. 1976) (individual who has made his body conform to his psychological self has changed gender for purposes of marriage), with *In re Elaine Frances Ladrach,* 32 Ohio Misc. 2d 6, 513 N.E. 2d 828 (Probate Ct. for Stark Cty., Ohio 1987) (postoperative transsexual not granted marriage license). Other cases have, for example, addressed whether a transsexual should lose his rights as an adopting parent owing to the change in gender. D. Canedy, "Sea Change Complicates Battle over Child Custody," *New York Times.* In *Murray v. United States Bureau of Prisons, et al.,* 106 F.3d 401 (unpublished) (Table) (6th Cir. 1997), cited in Eskridge and Hunter, *Sexuality, Gender, and the Law: 1998 Supplement,* 153–55, the court rather mysteriously raises no question about the actual gender identity of a prisoner who has had breast implants, is required to wear a brassiere in the all-male prison, and has been castrated, but who, says the court, "remains anatomically male."

11. E. K. Gough, "The Nayars and the Definition of Marriage," *Journal of the Royal Anthropological Institute* 89 (1959): 23–34; and C. J. Fuller, *The Nayars Today* (London: Routledge and Kegan Paul, 1976). Compare the definition of marriage given in Royal Anthropological Institute, *Notes and Queries on Anthropology* (London: Routledge and Kegan Paul, 1951), 110 ("a union between a man and a woman such that children born to the woman are the recognized legitimate offspring of both partners") with the critique of that definition in E. Leach. "Polyandry, Inheritance and the Definition of Marriage," *Man* 55 (1955): 182–86. For additional comparisons, see G. A. Marshall, "Marriage: Comparative Analysis," in *International Encyclopedia of the Social Sciences,* ed. D. L. Sills (New York: Macmillan and Free Press, 1968), 10:8–19; A. Barnard, "Rules and Prohibitions: The Form and Content of Human Kinship," in *Companion Encyclopedia of Anthropology,* ed. T. Ingold (London: Routledge, 1994), 783–812.

12. C. Hua, *A Society without Fathers or Husbands: The Na of China* (New York: Zone Books, 2001). See also the review by C. Geertz, "The Visit [review of Cai Hua, A Society without Fathers or Husbands: The Na of China]," *New York Review of Books,* October 18, 2001, 27–30. Geertz expresses concern, however, that Hua does not give a fuller description of how these sexual and procreative customs relate to a broader range of Na cultural features. One might also ask why the Na are so secretive about these sexual visits if they see no reason to be concerned about their legitimacy or effects on other social relationships.

13. D. F. Aberle, A. K. Cohen, A. K. Davis, M. J. Levy Jr., and F. X. Sutton, "The Functional Prerequisites of a Society," *Ethics* 60 (1950): 100–111. For a more recent —and, despite its lengthy enumeration, far more vague—set of universals, see S. Pinker, *The Blank Slate: The Modern Denial of Human Nature* (London: Penguin/Allen Lane, 2002).

14. Cited in Witte, *An Apt and Cheerful Conversation on Marriage*, 2. The divorce rate has actually been declining, from 5 per thousand in 1985 to 4.7 in 1990 to 4.1 in 1995. J. H. DiFonzo, "Customized Marriage," *Indiana Law Journal* 75 (2000): 877–78.

15. Kathleen McCartney (Harvard University), Cambridge Forum, National Public Radio broadcast of July 3, 2002. McCartney's study of more than 1,350 children shows no adverse consequences to such care when the child also has good parental attention. K. McCartney, ed., *Child Care and Maternal Employment: A Social Ecology Approach* (San Francisco: Jossey-Bass, 1990).

16. On the early modern period, see L. Stone, *Family, Sex and Marriage in England, 1500–1800* (New York: Harper and Row, 1977); E. A. Wrigley, *English Population History from Family Reconstitution, 1580–1837* (Cambridge: Cambridge University Press, 1997); on America, see H. Hartog, *Man and Wife in America* (Cambridge, Mass.: Harvard University Press, 2000). See also N. F. Cott, *Public Vows: A History of Marriage and the Nation* (Cambridge, Mass.: Harvard University Press, 2000); D. D. Rougement, *Love in the Western World* (New York: Pantheon, 1956).

17. "The family is the basic unit of our society, the center of the personal affections that ennoble and enrich human life. It channels biological drives that might otherwise become socially destructive; it ensures the care and education of children in a stable environment; it establishes continuity from one generation to another; it nurtures and develops the individual initiative that distinguishes a free people. Since the family is the core of our society, the law seeks to foster and preserve marriages. But when a marriage has failed and the family has ceased to be a unit, the purposes of family life are no longer served and divorce will be permitted." *DeBurgh v. DeBurgh*, 250 P.2d 598 (Cal. 1952), quoted in DiFonzo, "Customized Marriage," 897.

18. See generally E. Clive, "Marriage: An Unnecessary Legal Concept?" in *A Reader on Family Law*, ed. J. Eekelaar and M. Maclean (Oxford: Oxford University Press, 1994), 175–91.

19. *Ninia Baehr, et al. v. Milke*, 1996 WL 694235 (Hawaii Cir. Ct., 1st Cir. 1996), cited in Eskridge and Hunter, *Sexuality, Gender, and the Law: 1998 Supplement*, 111.

20. Compare the citations and discussions of the work of Judith Wallerstein and others, who claim to have demonstrated the ill effects on children of divorce, cited in DiFonzo, "Customized Marriage," 925–26, with E. M. Hetherington, *For Better, for Worse: Divorce Reconsidered* (New York: Norton, 2002), who argues that any ill effects are not long-lasting. The politics of the former position are evident in the work of J. Q. Wilson, *The Marriage Problem: How Our Culture Weakens Families* (New York: HarperCollins, 2002). After criticizing him for his failure to cite Hetherington's work, a reviewer of Wilson's book notes: "Why does he dabble in tinhorn biology to claim that men are better at climbing the corporate ladder and more likely to work longer hours because he-man aggressiveness was once an

evolutionary advantage? Or declare that a mother wonders whom the baby resembles, while a father 'suspects that the infant looks like—well, a baby?'" P. Cohen, "From 'I Do' to 'I Don't': Review of James Q. Wilson, The Marriage Problem." *New York Times Book Review,* March 24, 2002, 16.

21. On the question of functionalism in social theory and comparative law, see L. Rosen, "Beyond Compare," in *Comparative Legal Studies: Traditions and Transitions,* ed. P. Legrand and R. Mundy, 493–510. (Cambridge: Cambridge University Press, 2002).

22. See generally, B. Cossman and B. Ryder, "What Is Marriage-Like Like? The Irrelevance of Conjugality," *Revue Canadienne de Droit Familial* 18 (2001): 269–326. As the authors quip, apropos the use of a baseline of the idealized marital relationship: "Indeed, it is tempting to speculate how many marriages would fail to qualify as 'marriage-like' if they were subjected to similar scrutiny" (288).

23. As Clifford Geertz has put it: "If you want a *good* rule of thumb generalization from anthropology, I would suggest the following: Any sentence that begins, 'All societies have . . .' is either baseless or banal." C. Geertz, *Available Light: Anthropological Reflections on Philosophical Topics* (Princeton, N.J.: Princeton University Press, 2000), 135.

24. See C. Hill, *The World Turned Upside Down: Radical Ideas during the English Revolution* (London: Temple Smith, 1972); and G. Massell, *The Surrogate Proletariat: Moslem Women and Revolutionary Strategies in Soviet Central Asia* (Princeton, N.J.: Princeton University Press, 1974).

25. For the argument in favor of returning marriage to religion, see Cossman and Ryder (cited in n. 22). On converting marriage to a largely contractual matter, see DiFonzo, "Customized Marriage," 934–45.

26. See generally, DiFonzo, "Customized Marriage," 934–37. See also the Web site of the Institute for American Values (www.americanvalues.org), a conservative action group, for information on faith-based support for marriage and agreements to stay married.

27. See generally, DiFonzo, "Customized Marriage," 954–59. The Pennsylvania Supreme Court has even refused to engage any longer in the "business of policing the reasonableness of premarital bargains." Recent Developments, 104 *Harvard Law Review* 1399, 1400 (1991), cited in DiFonzo, "Customized Marriage," 938.

28. See, e.g., the discussion in C. Geertz, *Available Light: Anthropological Reflections on Philosophical Topics* (Princeton, N.J.: Princeton University Press, 2000), 155: "Sciences, physical, biological, human, or whatever, change not only in their content or their social impact (though they do, of course, do that, and massively), but in their character as a form of life, a way of being in the world, a meaningful system of human action, a particular story about how things stand. Like all such ways, forms, systems, stories—still life, say, or criminal law—they are constructed in time (and, despite their reach for universality, to an important degree in space

as well), and thus any image of them that remains stable over their entire course and across the whole range of activities and concerns is bound to turn into an obscuring myth."

29. Alan Dershowitz says: "'Natural law' is little more than a matter of personal opinion or belief dressed up as the objective law of nature or God. One judge's notion of what is natural is another's sense of what is unnatural." A. M. Dershowitz, *Shouting Fire: Civil Liberties in a Turbulent Age* (Boston: Little, Brown, 2002). Justice Scalia has gone so far as to assert that democracy obscures God's law and the natural law presuppositions it embraces: "The reaction of people of faith to this tendency of democracy to obscure the divine authority behind government should not be resignation to it, but the resolution to combat it as effectively as possible." Quoted in S. Wilentz, "From Justice Scalia, a Chilling Vision of Religious Authority in America," *New York Times*, July 8, 2002.

REFERENCES

Aberle, D. F., A. K. Cohen, A. K. Davis, M. J. Levy Jr., and F. X. Sutton. 1950. "The Functional Prerequisites of a Society." *Ethics* 60:100–111.

Barnard, A. 1994. "Rules and Prohibitions: The Form and Content of Human Kinship." In *Companion Encyclopedia of Anthropology*, ed. T. Ingold, 783–812. London: Routledge.

Bjornberg, U. 2001. "Cohabitation and Marriage in Sweden: Does Family Form Matter?" *International Journal of Law, Policy and the Family* 15:350–62.

Butler, J. 2002. "Is Kinship Always Already Heterosexual?" Unpublished ms.

Canedy, D. 2002. "Sea Change Complicates Battle over Child Custody." *New York Times*, February 18.

Clive, E. 1994. "Marriage: An Unnecessary Legal Concept?" In *A Reader on Family Law*, ed. J. Eekelaar and M. Maclean, 175–91. Oxford: Oxford University Press.

Cohen, P. 2002. "From 'I Do' to 'I Don't': Review of James Q. Wilson, The Marriage Problem." *New York Times Book Review*, March 24.

Cossman, B., and B. Ryder. 2001. "What Is Marriage-Like Like? The Irrelevance of Conjugality." *Revue Canadienne de Droit Familial* 18:269–326.

Cott, N. F. 2000. *Public Vows: A History of Marriage and the Nation.* Cambridge, Mass.: Harvard University Press.

Dershowitz, A. M. 2002. *Shouting Fire: Civil Liberties in a Turbulent Age.* Boston: Little, Brown.

Diamond, J. 1997. *Guns, Germs, and Steel: The Fates of Human Societies.* New York: Norton.

DiFonzo, J. H. 2000. "Customized Marriage." *Indiana Law Journal* 75:875–962.

Epstein, R. 1995. "Two Challenges for Feminist Thought." *Harvard Journal of Law and Public Policy* 18:331–47.

Eskridge, W. N., Jr., and N. D. Hunter. 1997. *Sexuality, Gender and the Law.* Westbury, N.Y.: Foundation Press.

———. 1998. *Sexuality, Gender, and the Law: 1998 Supplement.* New York: Foundation Press.

Eyer, D. 1992. *Mother-Infant Bonding: A Scientific Fiction.* New Haven, Conn.: Yale University Press.

Fineman, M. A. 1995. *The Neutered Mother, the Sexual Family, and Other Twentieth Century Tragedies.* New York: Routledge.

———. 1998. "Contract, Marriage and Background Rules." In *Analyzing Law: New Essays in Legal Theory,* ed. B. Bix, 183–95. Oxford: Clarendon Press.

Fuller, C. J. 1976. *The Nayars Today.* London: Routledge and Kegan Paul.

Geertz, C. 2000. *Available Light: Anthropological Reflections on Philosophical Topics.* Princeton, N.J.: Princeton University Press.

———. 2001. "The Visit [review of Cai Hua, A Society without Fathers or Husbands: The Na of China]." *New York Review of Books,* October 18, 27–30.

Gladwell, M. 1998. "Do Parents Matter?" *New Yorker,* August 17, 54–64.

Glendon, M. A. 1989. *The Transformation of Family Law: State, Law, and Family in the United States and Western Europe.* Chicago: University of Chicago Press.

Goldstein, J., A. Freud, and A. J. Solnit. 1973. *Beyond the Best Interests of the Child.* New York: Free Press.

Gough, E. K. 1959. "The Nayars and the Definition of Marriage." *Journal of the Royal Anthropological Institute* 89:23–34.

Grady, D. 2002. "Few Risks Seen to the Children of First Cousins." *New York Times,* April 4.

Hartog, H. 2000. *Man and Wife in America.* Cambridge, Mass.: Harvard University Press.

Héritier, F. 1999. *Two Sisters and Their Mother: The Anthropology of Incest.* New York: Zone Books.

Hetherington, E. M. 2002. *For Better, for Worse: Divorce Reconsidered.* New York: Norton.

Hill, C. 1972. *The World Turned Upside Down: Radical Ideas during the English Revolution.* London: Temple Smith.

Hua, C. 2001. *A Society without Fathers or Husbands: The Na of China.* New York: Zone Books.

Leach, E. 1955. "Polyandry, Inheritance and the Definition of Marriage." *Man* 55: 182–86.

Lyall, S. 2002. "For Europeans, Love, Yes; Marriage, Maybe." *New York Times,* March 24.

Marshall, G. A. 1968. "Marriage: Comparative Analysis." In *International Encyclopedia of the Social Sciences,* ed. D. L. Sills, 10:8–19. New York: Macmillan and Free Press.

Massell, G. 1974. *The Surrogate Proletariat: Moslem Women and Revolutionary Strategies in Soviet Central Asia.* Princeton, N.J.: Princeton University Press.

McCartney, K., ed. 1990. *Child Care and Maternal Employment: A Social Ecology Approach.* San Francisco: Jossey-Bass.

Mead, M. 1970. "Anomalies in American Post-divorce Relationships." In *Divorce and After,* ed. P. Bohannan, 97–112. Garden City, N.Y.: Doubleday.

Needham, R. 1971. "Remarks on the Analysis of Kinship and Marriage." In *Rethinking Kinship and Marriage,* ed. R. Needham, 1–34. London: Tavistock.

Niebuhr, G. 1998. "Southern Baptists Declare Wife Should 'Submit' to Her Husband." *New York Times,* June 10.

Pinker, S. 2002. *The Blank Slate: The Modern Denial of Human Nature.* London: Penguin/Allen Lane.

Posner, R. 1992. *Sex and Reason.* Cambridge, Mass.: Harvard University Press.

Riviere, P. 1971. "Marriage: A Reassessment." In *Rethinking Kinship and Marriage,* ed. R. Needham, 57–74. London: Tavistock.

Rose, C. M. 1994. *Property and Persuasion: Essays on the History, Theory, and Rhetoric of Ownership.* Boulder, Colo.: Westview Press.

Rosen, L. 2002. "Beyond Compare." In *Comparative Legal Studies: Traditions and Transitions,* ed. P. Legrand and R. Mundy. Cambridge: Cambridge University Press.

Rougement, D. D. 1956. *Love in the Western World.* New York: Pantheon.

Royal Anthropological Institute. 1951. *Notes and Queries on Anthropology,* 110. London: Routledge and Kegan Paul.

Scott, E. S., and R. E. Scott. 1998. "Marriage as Relational Contract." *Virginia Law Review* 84:1225–334.

Spiro, M. E. 1958. *Childhood in the Kibbutz.* Cambridge, Mass.: Harvard University Press.

Stone, L. 1977. *Family, Sex and Marriage in England, 1500–1800.* New York: Harper and Row.

Twitchell, J. B. 1987. *Forbidden Partners: The Incest Taboo in Modern Culture.* New York: Columbia University Press.

Wilentz, S. 2002. "From Justice Scalia, a Chilling Vision of Religious Authority in America." *New York Times,* July 8.

Wilson, E. O. 1998. *Consilience: The Unity of Knowledge.* New York: Vintage Books.

Wilson, J. Q. 2002. *The Marriage Problem: How Our Culture Weakens Families.* New York: HarperCollins.

Witte, J., Jr. 2001. *An Apt and Cheerful Conversation on Marriage.* Sixth Distinguished Faculty Lecture, Emory University.

Wolf, A. P. 1995. *Sexual Attraction and Childhood Association: A Chinese Brief for Edward Westermarck.* Stanford, Calif,: Stanford University Press.

Wrigley, E. A. 1997. *English Population History from Family Reconstitution, 1580–1837.* Cambridge: Cambridge University Press.

Chapter 5

Marriage as a "Badge and Incident" of Democratic Freedom

Peggy Cooper Davis

This chapter lies in the company of deeply thoughtful critiques of marriage. I begin somewhat defensively, narrowing my focus and claims so as to make of myself a smaller target. My focus is African Americans' embrace of family, both during slavery and immediately after Emancipation. More precisely, I consider two related phenomena: the profound but legally unrecognized intimate relationships through which enslaved people made social meaning during slavery, and the simultaneously political and personal marriages by which people who had won freedom seized the opportunity to make meaning in more recognized and public ways. I read the family affiliations of enslaved people as acts of resistance against laws and customs that supported slaveholding by defining people as property rather than as progeny and by denying them moral and affiliational choice. In the cauldron of antislavery struggle, these acts of resistance, and the forced separations, restrictions on time and mobility, coerced partnerings, and retaliatory violence by which they were often punished or frustrated, combined to produce an understanding of family rights as essential to democratic citizenship and human freedom. When the antislavery struggle was won, marriage, now more richly understood, became a badge of free citizenship and a means of enacting it. These are the claims that I will set out in the two sections that follow.

Here's what I won't do. Although I will tell a story of emancipated people embracing rather traditional forms of marriage, I will not endorse—or critique in any detail—the forms that marriage has taken in the United States. I will not touch here on the pressures on African American, and other American, people to conform to a patriarchal, monogamous, and heterosexual "norm." I will not explore the interesting questions of how African American marriages were affected by African polygamous traditions, the economic status of black women, an understanding of homophobia as something akin to racism, or a homophobic reaction to a slave system that inhibited the realization of traditional "manhood" or of "true womanhood." Nor will I endorse—or critique in any detail—cultural pressures to form families. I will not ask—or tell—whether sexual jealousy is an evil, or the root of other evils, or whether communal or solitary living is healthier, more noble, or more beautiful than coupling.

Although I acknowledge that antislavery families were influenced by the heterosexual and monogamous biases that were enforced in the cultural milieu of nineteenth-century America, I will argue that their struggle and motivation were more liberating than deferential, as often egalitarian as patriarchal. Antislavery activists and thinkers did not simply embrace the right to conform to a particular marriage form. Rather, they embraced, and guaranteed in the reconstructed Constitution, the equal rights of men and women of all races *to choose* their intimate affiliations, to have them officially recognized, and, through them, to have a part in the design of the social fabric. As I will explain, this history suggests that the right to choose to participate in the culture through marriage should be protected. But the history—which valorizes action to challenge and improve upon traditional institutions as much as it valorizes participation in mainstream institutions—does not tell us whether, in a world in which a greater variety of marriage forms could be officially recognized, it would be nobler to marry or to forge a new way of constructing lives and affiliations.

Family Deprivation as a Badge and Incident of Slavery

Scholars of slavery tell us that denial of family bonds is a hallmark of slave status: "[T]he slave was always a deracinated outsider—an outsider first in the sense that he originated from outside the society into which he was introduced as a slave, second in the sense that *he was denied the most elementary of social bonds, kinship*" (Finley 1980, 75; emphasis added). Slavery in the United States was not exceptional in this respect. Enslaved people were not only outsiders in the sense that they had come from another continent and a set of cultures unfamiliar to the slaveholding class. They were shut out of mainstream civic life by being designated property rather than progeny and progenitors.

United States slavery began, of course, with family separation, as men, women, and children were purchased or kidnapped from families and communities, and transported among strangers to America and slavery. The first-generation American slave carried memories of lost families. Most of those memories survived only in the oral traditions of enslaved people, but some were recorded. After the successful mutiny by the slave cargo of the *Amistad,* for example, interviews with the men and women who had seized their freedom documented their familial losses: Singgbe had been taken from a father, a wife, and three children; Gilabaru from a wife; Burna from a wife, child, father, three sisters, and a brother; Sessi from three brothers, two sisters, a wife, and three children; Ndamma, from a mother, brother, and sister; Kinna from his parents, grandparents, four brothers, and a sister; Ngahoni, from a wife and child; Fakinna from a father, wife, and two children; Burna from a mother, four sisters, and two brothers; and Kagne from her parents, four brothers, and four sisters (Gutman 1976, 329–30).

The violation of family was repeated on American soil in each succeeding generation of slaves. United States slavery's denial of parental ties touched each enslaved person at the moment of birth, imposing a social construction by which he or she would be defined as a commodity rather than as the child of a family, community, and nation. The *Narrative of the Life of William W. Brown* opens with a description of that process: "I was born in Lexington, Ky. The man who stole me as soon as I was born, recorded the births of all the infants which he claimed to be born his property, in a book which he kept for that purpose. My mother's name was Elizabeth" (Brown 1969, 13). Because Elizabeth Brown was his slave, the man who "stole" William Brown was entitled under the law to claim each of her children as his property. A more detached observer, the Treasury Department special agent for the South Carolina Sea Islands, made the point less dramatically in a report to the secretary of the Treasury: "The children have been regarded as belonging to the plantation rather than to a family, and the parents . . . in their condition can never have but a feeble hold on their offspring" (reprinted in Berlin et al. 1990, 205). When an infant was designated slave, it was—to borrow Brown's term and his sense of natural right—stolen from parental care and claimed, like its mother and, perhaps, like its father,[1] as a commodity. In parental care and control, the child is dependent upon the discretion and goodwill of one, two, or several adults with whom it has bonds of biology or of chosen familial commitment and, in all but the most extraordinary cases, bonds of affection. As commodity, the child is subject at every stage to disruption of those bonds. It was this legal and social construction of the slave as commodity rather than as the child of parents, community, and nation that the historian M. I. Finley referred to when, quoting Plautus's *Captiva*, he examined the slave's profound social isolation. At a time when the father was the head and emblem of the family, Finley asked, "What father, when he is a slave?" (1980, 75).

According to the slaveholder's logic, the slave's status as commodity rather than progeny made marriage among slaves an incoherence, and a threat to the right to possess and discipline human property. The laws of every slaveholding state made it impossible for a slave to enter a legally binding marriage, and they permitted the separation, by sale or otherwise, of slaves who considered themselves husband and wife. Thomas R. R. Cobb, a defender of slavery and author of a comprehensive treatise on its laws, who confessed a bias "by . . . birth and education in [the] slave-holding State [of Georgia]" (1858, 1), described the impossibility of legal marriage between slaves and assessed the security of de facto, or "contubernial," unions between slaves: by his account, an enslaved person was unable to contract, and therefore unable to enter a contract of marriage. That being the case, none of the consequences of official family formation followed. Issue of the marriage had "no inheritable blood." Cobb speculated that separations of enslaved families was rare but added that it was, and must be, permissible. As he put it, "[T]o fasten upon a master of a female slave, a vicious, corrupting negro, sowing discord, and dissatisfaction among all his slaves; or else a thief, or a cutthroat, and to provide no relief against such a nuisance would be to make the holding of slaves a curse to the master" (1858, 245–46).

The abolitionist legal scholar William Goodell read the letter of the law no differently, although he would undoubtedly have quarreled with Cobb concerning the frequency with which slave families were separated by force of their masters' will or by failure of their masters' enterprises. Goodell reported, "A slave cannot even contract matrimony; the association which takes place among slaves, and is *called* marriage, being properly designated by the word *contubernium*, a relation which has no sanctity, and to which no civil rights are attached" (1853, 91).

The practice of forming life partnerships was not, of course, obliterated for want of legal sanction. Enslaved people celebrated matrimony and lived marriages as best they could. Within what critical race theory scholar Charles Lawrence calls home places, slaves forged opportunities for moral and intellectual self-definition. Parents and de facto spouses ran the risks of separation and closed their eyes to the obstacles slavery placed in the way of nurturing; bonded with their children, husbands and wives; and created families unacknowledged and unprotected by law. Men like Westly Jackson, remembered in the words of his daughter, held "deep affection" for his kin, having "no other link to fasten him to the human family but his fervent love for those who were bound to him by love and sympathy" (Gates 1988, 6). The American slave Henry Bibb described the process by which he and his "wife" were married: "Clasping each other by the hand, pledging our sacred honor that we would be true, we called on high heaven to witness the rectitude of our purpose. There was nothing that could be more binding upon us as slaves than this; for marriage among American slaves, is disregarded by the laws of this country" (1969, 38). A former slave interviewed in the 1930s described the process more simply: "When they got married on the places, mostly they just jumped over a broom and that made 'em married. Sometimes one of the white folks read a little out of the Scriptures to 'em, and they felt more married" (Botkin 1989, 86).[2]

Bibb's marriage was disrupted when he was sold to a distant master, and it ended years later when he learned that his wife was the mistress of a slave owner and mother of several of the slave owner's children. By Bibb's account, the marriage ended not with legal annulment but with the surrender of his resolve, for, in his terms: "The relation once subsisting between us, to which I clung, hoping against hope, for years, after we were torn asunder, not having been sanctioned by any loyal power, [could not] be cancelled by a legal process" (Bibb 1969, 192).

Stories like that of Henry Bibb were common and notorious in the mid–nineteenth century. Gutman's comprehensive analysis of the slave family probes "[t]he best available evidence—that reported by [nine thousand] Mississippi and northern Louisiana ex-slaves" to Union army clergy registering marriages—"to establish that about one in six (or seven) slave marriages were ended by force or sale" (1976, 318). In response to this fact of slave life, the bondsman J. W. Loguen said, when asked whether he was "married": "I determined long ago never to marry until I was free. Slavery shall never own a wife or child of mine" (White 1985, 147, quoting Loguen 1859, 223). His comment expresses both the shame engendered in a nineteenth-century man who could not guard against the abuse or seduction of his wife, and the slave's ever-present fear that what Frederick Douglass called the "unnatural power" of slave law would, with one "word of the appraisers, against all preferences and prayers, . . . sunder all the ties of friendship and affection, even to separating husbands and wives, parents and children" (1962, 95–96).

The historian Gerda Lerner reports that "Moses Grandy, suspecting nothing, was standing in the street when the slave coffle passed with his wife in chain" (1972, 8). Grandy's biography tells the rest of the story:

> Mr. Rogerson was with them on his horse, armed with pistols. I said to him, "For God's sake, have you bought my wife?" He said he had; when I asked him what she had done, he said she had done nothing, but that her master wanted money. He drew out a pistol and said that if I went near the wagon on which she was, he would shoot me. I asked for leave to shake hands with her which he refused, but said I might stand at a distance and talk with her. My heart was so full that I could say very little. . . . I have never seen or heard from her from that day to this. I loved her as I love my life. (Lerner 1972, 8–9, quoting Grandy 1844)

Frederick Douglass described the sale of a husband in these terms: "His going . . . was like a living man going into a tomb, who, with open eyes, sees himself buried out of sight and hearing of wife, children and friends of kindred tie" (Douglass 1969, 177). Some couples preferred literal death to this kind of separation. A former slave reported that her grandmother killed herself when she discovered that her husband had been sold. A 1746 edition of the *Boston Evening-Post* told of a couple who made a suicide pact upon learning that the woman was to be sold "into the Country" (Gutman 1976, 349). Others faced the perils of escape to avoid sale and separation (Gates 1988).

The effects of slavery on the African American family were paramount concerns of abolitionists. Goodell's treatise was published by the American and Foreign Anti-Slavery Society to "test the moral character of American slaveholding" by exhibiting the American Slave Code (1853, 17). It made the provisions of that code vivid with anecdotal accounts of slave families separated by sale and distanced by the demands of servitude. Accounts of family separations were buttressed by advertisements from Southern newspapers offering rewards for the capture or killing of slaves reported to have run away to join family members (115–21). Harriet Beecher Stowe wrote in 1853 that "[t]he worst abuse of the system of slavery is its outrage upon the family and . . . it is one which is more notorious and undeniable than any other" (1853, 133).[3] An 1837 essay on the family in the *Liberator* declared, "[T]he most appalling feature of our slave system is, the annihilation of the family institution" (Wells 1837, 192). Samuel Ward, an antislavery activist and former slave, embedded a condemnation of the slave system's treatment of the fundamental human right to marry in a bitterly ironic account of the flogging of his father and the response, and subsequent punishment, of his mother. His story captures nicely how denial of family was central to the subordination of human will that slavery required:

[My father] received a severe flogging, which left his back in . . . [a] wretched . . . state. . . . This sort of treatment of her husband not being relished by my mother, who felt about the maltreatment of her husband as any Christian woman ought to feel, she put forth her sentiments, in pretty strong language. This was insolent. Insolence in a negress could not be endured—it would breed more and greater mischief of a like kind; then what would become of wholesome discipline? Besides, if so trifling a thing as the *mere marriage relation* were to interfere with the supreme proprietor's right of a master over his slave, next we should hear that slavery must give way before marriage! Moreover, if a negress may be allowed free speech, touching the flogging of a negro, simply because that negro happened to be her husband, how long would it be before some such claim would be urged in behalf of some other member of a negro family, in unpleasant circumstances? Would this be endurable, in a republican civilized community, A.D. 1819? By no means. It would sap the very foundation of slavery—it would be like "the letting out of water": for let the principle be once established that the negress Anne Ward may speak as she pleases about the flagellation of her husband, the negro William Ward, as a matter of right, and like some alarming and death-dealing infection it would spread from plantation to plantation, until property in husbands and wives would not be worth the having. No, no: marriage must succumb to slavery, slavery must reign supreme over every right and every institution however venerable or sacred; *ergo*, this free-speaking Anne Ward must be made to feel the greater rigours of the domestic institution. Should she be flogged? that was questionable. . . . Well, then, they could sell her, and sell her they would. (1968, 15)

Memories such as these, and the inspiration provided by families that continued to form in the face of insult and risk, led antislavery Americans, black and white, to posit a necessary relationship between family and democratic freedom.

Family as a Badge and Incident of Freedom

The antislavery critique of slavery's denial of family was more than a sentimental reaction to the drama of wounded pride, frustrated love, and wrenching separations. It was grounded in an analysis of the human condition as a moral quest for affiliation and self-assertion, an analysis that led to the conclusion that slavery is wrong because it unacceptably compromises moral and affiliational behavior. Abolitionists undergirded their position with the natural law argument that rights of marriage and family are necessary to the fulfillment of religious and moral duty and therefore inalienable. To be recognized as human is to be recognized as morally autonomous, and moral as well as religious autonomy require *family* autonomy. Antislavery rhetoric reflected as much, demanding human rights and recognition of marriage in the same breath: "The slaves must be immediately recognized as human beings by the laws, their persons and their rights must be protected. Provisions must be made to establish marriage between them" (S.F.D. 1827).

The widespread commitment among antislavery Americans to protect rights to marry and to form and maintain families was sufficiently deep and appropriately placed to affect the meaning of the Reconstruction amendments. Indeed, it was expressed in Congress as a motivating factor in crafting the Thirteenth and Fourteenth Amendments. Many of those expressions touched specifically upon the right to marry. The inability of slaves to form and maintain marital bonds and the inalienability of their right to do so were recurring topics in the debates of the Reconstruction Congress. Speaker after speaker pronounced marriage rights fundamental and resolved that freedom in the United States would entail the right to marry:

> The slave could sustain none of those relations which give life all its charms. He could not say my wife, my child, my body. It is for God to say whether he could say my soul. The law pronounced him a chattel, and these are not the rights or attributes of chattels.[4]
>
> [I]n none of the slave States . . . is . . . [the marriage] relation tolerated in opposition to the will of the slave-owner; and . . . in many of them . . . it . . . [is] prohibited absolutely by their statute laws. This, I take it then, is the matured, ripened opinion of the people of those States. In their opinion the prohibition of the conjugal relation is a necessary incident of slavery. . . .
>
> The existence of this institution therefore requires the existence of a law

that annuls the law of God establishing the relation of man and wife, which is taught by the churches to be a sacrament as holy in its nature and its designs as the eucharist itself.[5]

What vested rights [are] so high or so sacred as a man's right to himself, to his wife and children, to his liberty, and to the fruits of his own industry? Did not our fathers declare that those rights were inalienable? And if a man cannot himself alienate those rights, how can another man alienate them without being himself a robber of the vested rights of his brother-man?[6]

Slavery cannot know a home. Where the wife is the property of the husband's master, and may be used at will; . . . where man and woman, after twenty years of faithful service from the time when the priest with the owner's sanction by mock ceremonies pretended to unite them, are parted and sold at that owner's will, there can be no such thing as home. Sir, no act of ours can fitly enforce their freedom that does not contemplate for them the security of home.[7]

[W]hen this [thirteenth] amendment to the Constitution shall be consummated . . . the sharp cry of the agonizing hearts of severed families will cease to vex the weary ear of the nation. . . . Then the sacred rights of human nature, the hallowed family relations of husband and wife, parent and child, will be protected by the guardian spirit of that law which makes sacred alike the proud homes and lowly cabins of freedom.[8]

The ideology that motivated these statements—and, in turn, motivated the Thirteenth and Fourteenth Amendments—becomes a principle of democratic theory when it is seen in terms of the dialectic of constraint and choice that balances social stability against an openness to individual choice and social change. Let me explain first the dialectic and then the relationship between the dialectic and the democratic lessons of antislavery.

We humans are social beings. This rather simple fact has far-reaching implications. Jerome Bruner's transactional model of the mind reflects a consciousness that is as old as human discourse, but felt with special keenness in the wake of the cognitive revolution. Human meaning is actualized when it becomes, as Bruner puts it, "public and communal rather than private and autistic" (1990, 33). The self is inevitably defined in its interpersonal and social manifestations—in its relationships to others. At the same time, however, the human self is actualized through cultural forms —forms of language, of discourse, of logic, of narrative, and of response to patterned stimuli. There is a dialectic between the individual self and the community: on the one hand, individual development is constrained by the community's shared cultural forms. We are all products of our cultures and inclined to share culturally determined predispositions. But on the other hand, cultural forms are the sum of, and are incrementally altered by, individual acts of meaning. Each of us is a unique manifestation of slightly different cultural influences and capable of effecting some degree of change in cultural norms.

Most of what a culture does to structure or constrain individual choice is informal, subliminal, and outside the reach of constitutional protection. It is manifested by the very nature of the culture's markets, customs, scripts, words, and stories. Still, explicit and official constraints on individual choice are significant. The state controls private behavior with blunt effectiveness. Moreover, intrusiveness or restraint in the official control of private behavior is an important marker of a society's character. As the dialectic between individual choice and cultural form plays out in a culture, official restraints upon private choice make the social environment more stable, predictable, and controlled. Protection of civil liberty, on the other hand, makes the social environment more open, responsive, and dynamic. Extremes in either direction are problematic. Without social controls, government cannot protect its subjects against internal or external harms or mobilize resources for the common good. Moreover, a measure of stability and predictability may be necessary as a nucleus for the sense of oneness that makes the social contract viable. But excessive social controls prove intolerable as government becomes unresponsive to the needs and values of its different subjects and unduly inhibiting of their efforts to make meaning. And rights of moral autonomy and self-definition seem necessary to the realization of human potential. Rational, morally conscious beings seem to require a place in the social dialectic, and a balance between its competing forces, such that community and cultural constraints do not freeze individual acts of meaning or foreclose incremental, bottom-up social change.

The experience of slavery and the lessons of antislavery enliven the justifications for structuring the social dialectic so that official constraints do not overwhelm opportunities for personal choice. Subjects in a rigidly totalitarian state are frozen in the social dialectic that I have described— unable to effect change or express individuality. The image of the totalitarian subject gives life to arguments for individual autonomy and choice by forcing us to contemplate their lack. The experience of slavery had the same effect on the people of the United States. Sociologist Orlando Patterson argues that people in Western societies "came to value freedom [and] to construct it as a powerful shared vision of life, as a result of their experience of, and response to, slavery." As Patterson points out, "What was distinctive in the New [World] was, first of all, its claim to freedom and, second, the presence of the unfree within the heart of the democratic experiment—the critical absence of democracy, its echo, shadow, and silent force in the political and intellectual activity of some not-Americans" (1991, xiii). The presence of the unfree was a profound argument for recognition of human autonomy.

Enslaved people were positioned *outside* the dialectic of cultural constraint and change. They were constrained, of course, but they were constrained as cultural outsiders. They were not expected to observe the cultural forms of the dominant culture; they were expected to observe cultural forms imposed upon their caste and the private "law" of their masters. And, perhaps most important, there was in the slaveholder's legal and cultural scheme *no* room for the individual agency of enslaved people to reshape either the dominant culture or the public codes governing the slave caste. This was the nature of what Patterson calls social death.

The story of antislavery is a story about the starkness of social death and the kind of freedom that confers social agency. It is about the political as well as the personal. On a personal level, enslaved people were haunted by the knowledge that they might, on any day, look up to see a partner or parent or child being shackled and taken away for service to a distant master. Children lacked the comfort of adequate parental attention and the security of knowing that their parents spoke and acted from a position of social authority. Adults endured the indignity of sexual exploitation. Parents endured the frustration of being unable to nurture, protect, or direct their children.

But quite apart from the personal costs of enslavement, enslaved people were denied legal and social recognition as individual members of civil society, as partners, or as families. They could not combine property as partners in life or bequeath it in death. If, as partners, they made commitments of monogamy, the law and the larger culture gave those commitments no formalized (and little de facto) reinforcement. If they made commitments of mutual support, the law and the larger culture could choose to ignore them. They could not provide a home for children that the law and the larger culture would regard as "legitimate" and acknowledge as the appropriate primary site for the children's socialization.

At the same time, enslaved people had only a very limited ability to affect the character of the larger culture in which they lived. The quality and character of enslaved people's lives had little impact on institutional definitions of the family. The law's understandings of obligations of support, loyalty, and common enterprise within marriage and of the privileges and responsibilities of parenting were developed in response to the experiences and situations of free people. Enslaved people were precluded not only from claiming the protections of laws governing marriage and parenting but also from arguing the applicability or inapplicability of those laws to their situations, and from challenging their terms in formal exercises of civil freedom.

Enslaved people and other antislavery advocates responded to the civil death that slavery inflicted with demands for universal civil freedom that encompassed the right to form a legitimate and socially recognized family. The right of family formation was necessary to fulfillment of moral and religious obligations and necessary to self-realization through lasting affiliations. When, in the midst of the Civil War, enslaved people began to claim the right to have their marriages recognized, they claimed that right as a component of the broader right to unseat the color caste system and to be established as a people. A soldier equated recognition of his family and acknowledgment of his humanity. Another said that legalized marriage was at the foundation of all rights. Another demanded that the children who were his flesh and blood be surrendered by a former master so that they could be educated and socialized to the values of their birth parents. Marriage was seen as a step in the direction of responsibility and honorable citizenship. The stability of family life was a badge of freedom.[9]

The Reconstruction amendments were a culmination of struggle not only to assure that no person's labor was owned but also to assure that each person was autonomous and self-defining—free to act within and upon the culture. Slaves demanded freedom to make meaning by taking chosen, rather than dictated, paths. Antislavery ideology demanded universal freedom such that every citizen would have a role in the collective that could be chosen, rather than prescribed. Democracy seen through the experiences of slavery and antislavery contemplates what Du Bois called "domination of political life by the intelligent decision of free and self-sustaining [people]" (Du Bois 1976, 29).

There are seeds of an autonomy principle in the Supreme Court's family rights cases. When *Meyer v. Nebraska*[10] established parents' right to control the education of their children, the Court alluded to principles touching the relation between individual and state that caused the people of the United States to reject the Platonic notion of creating ideal citizens through official control of marriage and parenting. When, in *Pierce v. Society of Sisters,*[11] the Court again addressed parental rights over the education of their children, it identified a fundamental theory of liberty according to which the child must not be the creature of the state and subject to its standardizing practices. Justice Harlan's dissent in *Poe v. Ullman,* an early and inconclusive case concerning contraception control, also makes a cautionary reference to the prospect of state standardization of child rearing and, in terms that have been repeated in many subsequent opinions of the Court, argues that the due process clause requires the Court to strike a balance between order and liberty that is appropriate to a nation "built upon postulates of respect for the liberty of the individual."[12] Justice Douglas, also writing in *Poe v. Ullman,* echoed *Pierce*'s caution against state standardization when he argued that the United States' constitutional scheme is antitotalitarian (522). The centrist justices who cast decisive votes in *Planned Parenthood v. Casey,*[13] affirming the right of abortion choice, came closest to offering a rationalizing principle for vigilant protection of individual autonomy when they added to the concern over state standardization or totalitarian control an articulation of the effect that control of this kind has on individual human lives. The *Casey* centrists said: "At the heart of liberty is the right to define one's own concept of existence, of meaning, of the universe, and of the mystery of human life. Beliefs about these matters could not define the attributes of personhood were they formed under compulsion of the State" (851). In these words, the centrist justices begin to capture the meaning of the antislavery claim that it is the right of all people "to organize their lives in accordance with their own sense of propriety [and] establish their families as independent units" (Berlin et al. 1985, 48). They were therefore able to safeguard what antislavery activists called "rights of conscience" vouchsafed to all who "occupy space . . . in the moral world . . . as rational beings" (Aptheker 1969, 8–9). But the centrists did not ground their words in the history and traditions of constitutional Reconstruction. Nor did they identify an alternative basis for interpreting the Fourteenth Amendment and its protection of liberty in terms of human rights of conscience and self-definition. This failure made *Casey*'s autonomy principle less illuminating than it might be, and more assailable than it deserves to be.

In 2003, *Casey*'s autonomy principle was applied to reverse *Bowers v. Hardwick*,[14] the 1986 case in which the Supreme Court, in terms gratuitously hostile to gay and lesbian people, held that the Constitution did not protect against criminal prosecution of homosexual intimacy. In the 2003 case *Lawrence v. Texas*,[15] the Court acknowledged the undemocratic cruelty of *Bowers* and embraced *Casey*'s understanding of "the respect the Constitution demands for the autonomy of the person" in making "personal decisions relating to marriage, procreation, contraception, family relationships, child rearing and education."[16] The Court understood that nothing but majoritarian moral preference sustained laws prohibiting homosexual intimacy, and it held that majoritarian moral preference was too flimsy a basis for making criminals of homosexual lovers.

Still, despite the Court's commitment to *Casey*'s autonomy principle, and despite its recognition that majoritarian morality is an insufficient justification for constraining intimate and life-defining choices, the Court noted pointedly that its decision did not address "[w]hether the government must give formal recognition to any relationship that homosexual persons seek to enter."[17] And dissenting justices made clear that they counted the *Casey* autonomy principle as nothing more than "sweet mystery of life" verbiage, without value as precedent.[18]

Return for a moment to the narrow promise made at the outset of this chapter. I said that I would not address the extent to which African American and other antislavery people accepted or approved limitations on marriage forms, but I promised to show how the critique of slavery yielded arguments for rights of choice in intimate affiliations. I end by testing the human rights ideologies of antislavery against the legal practice of recognizing only heterosexual marriage. Lord Devlin (1965) was right when he asserted, in defense of Great Britain's Royal Commission *Report on Homosexual Offenses and Prostitution* that a society would change, in unpredictable ways, if it went from legal prohibition to legal tolerance of homosexual intimacy. His reasoning with respect to the prohibition of homosexual intimacy applies as well to the denial of the right to marry. In a world in which homosexual marriage was permitted, social norms would cease to be officially frozen with respect to the gender of sexual intimates or life partners. Social norms might, and might not, change with respect to a host of related matters such as the perceived link between procreation and life satisfaction or the proper allocation of roles and responsibilities within a household. The society might, or might not, continue to be predominantly heterosexual. The definition of the community would be more open to influence by homosexual people. Homosexual people in a climate of prohibition can be fairly described as people subjected to civil disabilities akin to the civil death of the enslaved. The ramifications of those civil disabilities are both personal and political. On a more personal level, homosexual couples are haunted by the fear that their bedrooms will be raided and they will be arrested, prosecuted, and punished for their intimate expressions. But whether or not they are prosecuted, homosexual couples are denied legal and social recognition as partners or as families. They can, with some difficulty, combine property in life and bequeath it in death. But if they make commitments of monogamy, the law and the larger culture give those commitments no formalized (and little de facto) reinforcement. If they make commitments of mutual support, the law and the larger culture can choose to ignore them. Homosexual couples cannot provide a home for children that the law and the larger culture will predictably regard as "legitimate" and acknowledge as the appropriate primary site for the children's socialization.

What would we say about homosexual marriage if we grounded the *Casey* autonomy principle in the history of the Fourteenth Amendment? If the liberty protections of the second Reconstruction amendment were interpreted in light of the ideals and traditions of antislavery? Denial of the right to marry would have to be justified by state interests that are sufficiently compelling to outweigh the claims of a substantial segment of the United States' population to the autonomy, choice, and civil agency that proponents of the Fourteenth Amendment struggled to guarantee. And we would have to count it against the state seeking to deny homosexual marriage if the proffered justification were nothing more than the community's wish to control its identity by constricting the moral agency that it is due process liberty's function to protect.

NOTES

1. Slave status was legally derived from the mother. The father was often a slave and was often not. In the case of William Brown, the father was "a relative of . . . [the] master, and connected with some of the first families of Kentucky" (Brown 1969, 1).

2. For a description of slave marriage rituals and suggestions concerning their origins, see Gutman 1976, 273–81.

3. Stowe writes in response to charges that family separations depicted in *Uncle Tom's Cabin* were unrealistic or atypical. Her evidence of the prevalence of slave family disruption includes eyewitness accounts of family separations resulting from slave auctions (137), and advertisements for the sale of slaves in South Carolina (134–36, 138–42).

4. Representative Creswell, *Congressional Globe*, 38th Cong., 2nd sess., 1865.

5. Senator Harlan, *Congressional Globe*, 38th Cong., 1st sess., 1439, 1864.

6. Representative Farnsworth, *Congressional Globe*, 38th Cong., 2nd sess., 200, 1865.

7. Senator Eliot, speaking with respect to the homestead provisions of the Freedmen's Bureau Bill, *Congressional Globe*, 39th Cong., 1st sess., 2778, 1866.

8. Senator Wilson, *Congressional Globe*, 38th Cong., 1st sess., 1479, 1864.

9. For a fuller account of these responses, see Cooper Davis 1997, 36, 111–12.

10. *Meyer v. Nebraska*, 262 U.S. 390, 401–2 (1923).

11. *Pierce v. Society of Sisters*, 268 U.S. 510, 534 (1925).

12. *Poe v. Ullman*, 367 U.S. 497, 542 (1961).

13. *Planned Parenthood v. Casey*, 505 U.S. 833, 851 (1992).

14. *Bowers v. Hardwick*, 478 U.S. 186 (1986).

15. *Lawrence v. Texas*, 539 U.S. 558 (2003).

16. Id. at 574.

17. Id. at 578.

18. Id. at 586, dissenting opinion of Justice Scalia.

REFERENCES

Apthecker, H. 1969. *A Documentary History of the Negro People in the United States.* New York: Citadel Press. Reprinted from Petition to the Governor, the Council and House of Representatives of Massachusetts, 25 May 1774.

Berlin, I., B. J. Fields, T. Glymph, J. P. Reidy, and L. S. Rowland, eds. 1985. *The Destruction of Slavery.* New York: Cambridge University Press.

Berlin, I., T. Glymph, S. F. Miller, J. P. Reidy, L. S. Rowland, and J. Saville, eds. 1990. *The Wartime Genesis of Free Labor: The Lower South.* Cambridge: Cambridge University Press. Reprinted from Port Royal, S.C. Report, 1862.

Bibb, H. 1969. *Narrative of the Life and Adventures of Henry Bibb, an American Slave.* 1850. New York: Negro Universities Press.

Botkin, B. A. 1989. *Lay My Burden Down: A Folk History of Slavery.* Athens: University of Georgia Press.

Brown, W. W. 1969. *Narrative of the Life of William W. Brown, a Fugitive Slave.* Reading, Mass.: Addison-Wesley Publishing.

Bruner, J. 1990. *Acts of Meaning*. Cambridge, Mass.: Harvard University Press.

Cobb, Thomas R. R. 1858. *An Inquiry into the Law of Negro Slavery in the United States of America*. Philadelphia: T. & J. W. Johnson & Co.

Cooper Davis, P. 1997. *Neglected Stories: The Constitution and Family Values*. New York: Hill and Wang.

Devlin, P. 1965. *The Enforcement of Morals*. London: Oxford University Press.

Douglass, F. 1962. *The Life and Times of Frederick Douglass*. 1881. New York: Collier Books.

———. 1969. *My Bondage and My Freedom*. New York: Dover Publications.

Du Bois, W. E. B. 1976. *Black Reconstruction*. Millwood, N.Y.: Kraus-Thomson.

Finley, M. I. 1980. *Ancient Slavery and Modern Ideology*. London: Chatto and Windus.

Gates, H. L., ed. 1988. *Collected Black Women's Narratives*. New York: Oxford University Press.

Goodell, W. 1853. *The American Slave Code in Theory and Practice*. New York: American and Foreign Anti-Slavery Society.

Gutman, H. 1976. *The Black Family in Slavery and Freedom, 1750–1925*. New York: Pantheon Books.

Lerner, G., ed. 1972. *Black Women in White America: A Documentary History*. New York: Pantheon Books. Quoting M. Grandy, *Narrative of the Life of Moses Grandy, Late a Slave in the United States of America* (Boston: O. Johnson, 1844).

Morrison, T. 1992. *Playing in the Dark: Whiteness and the Literary Imagination*. Cambridge, Mass.: Harvard University Press.

Patterson, O. 1991. *Freedom*. New York: Basic Books.

S.F.D. 1827. People of Color. *New York's Freedom Journal* 1, no. 7 (April): 1

Stowe, H. B. 1853. *A Key to Uncle Tom's Cabin*. Boston: J. P. Jewett.

U.S. Congress. *Congressional Globe*. 1864. 38th Cong., 1st sess. Washington, D.C.

———. *Congressional Globe*. 1865. 38th Cong., 2nd sess. Washington, D.C.

———. *Congressional Globe*. 1866. 39th Cong., 1st sess. Washington, D.C.

Ward, S. R. 1968. *Autobiography of a Fugitive Negro*. 1855. New York: Arno Press.

Wells, W. 1837. Family Government. *Liberator* 1 (December): 192.

White, D. G. 1985. *Ar'nt I a Woman?* New York: Norton. Quoting J. W. Loguen, *The Reverend J. W. Loguen as a Slave and as a Freeman* (Syracuse, N.Y.: Truair & Co., Printers, 1859).

Chapter 6

The State of Marriage and the State in Marriage

What Must Be Done

Mary Lyndon Shanley

Few topics stir more passion than efforts to effect political and legal changes concerning marriage; for example, the reintroduction of fault grounds for divorce, legal recognition of same-sex marriage, and use of federal funds for programs aimed at persuading unwed parents to marry all have advocates and opponents. Much of the dispute over marriage has arisen from the fact that in the course of the second half of the twentieth century family life underwent remarkable change: effective birth control and changing mores made sexual relations outside of marriage, and family planning within marriage, common; women's labor force participation increased dramatically; rates of nonmarital cohabitation (including both heterosexual and same-sex couples), single motherhood, and blended families increased; and the "typical" family of two married parents and their children declined to 25 percent of American households. Despite these changes, conservatives have tended to hold on to traditional understandings of the public purposes marriage serves: it harnesses or channels sexual expression, particularly men's; it provides a stable environment in which to bear and raise children; and it identifies those who will be financially responsible for one another's support.

Many progressives hold that traditional marriage should not be the marker for the existence of a legitimate family, but they differ among themselves about the direction marriage law reform should take. Some suggest that what is needed is to open marriage to same-sex couples (and perhaps larger groups) by recognizing a right to marry or by holding that the exclusion of same-sex couples serves no legitimate government purpose. They believe that legal recognition of same-sex marriage would not only increase the number of people eligible to marry but also reshape marriage by unsettling the traditional gender roles of "husband" and "wife."[1] Others, rather than expanding the category of people eligible to marry, would abolish civil marriage. In the wake of such a reform, some people might choose to be together without any recognition or regulation by the state (as, indeed, many cohabiting couples do today). Those who suggest replacing marriage as a civil status with another form of legal regulation offer several models. Some would replace civil marriage with individual contracts in lieu of marriage.[2] Others would replace or supplement marriage with state-defined relationships like civil unions or domestic partnerships.[3] In addition to these three strategies to reform or replace civil marriage itself, some people suggest that in order to support a variety of relationships of emotional intimacy and economic interdependence (whether conjugal or not, same-sex or opposite sex), any law that refers to a relationship should be examined to identify its purpose, and all relationships relevant to achieving the statute's purpose should be brought within its purview.[4]

Each of these proposals carries with it significant dilemmas or trade-offs.[5] Legal recognition of same-sex marriage advances gay and lesbian rights, but gaining the right to marry leaves the legal understandings of marriage unquestioned. Abolishing marriage in favor of individual contracts enhances individual freedom and diversity of family forms but minimizes the public dimension to or interest in adult commitments whether or not partners share responsibility for a child. Establishing civil unions or domestic partnerships invites new thinking about the public purposes of committed adult relationships but risks marginalizing other relationships and substituting universal rules unreceptive to diversity.

In assessing the current debates about whether marriage law should be expanded to include same-sex couples, replaced by individual contracts, or supplemented or replaced by civil unions or other state-sanctioned relationships, it is helpful to understand the traditional law of marriage and criticisms of it. Law has not been a passive bystander in the process of shaping expectations about marriage. Indeed, two other waves of reform preceded the current struggles. One, beginning in the mid-nineteenth century, focused on equalizing the grounds of divorce for women and men and establishing married women's rights to hold property and enter into contracts. The other, beginning in the mid-twentieth century, focused on no-fault divorce and the continued subordination of married women in the home. Both of these waves of reform criticized marriage law for not living up to the demands of the two fundamental values of a liberal polity, liberty and equality. The current debate among those who would expand marriage to include gays and lesbians, make marriage a contract, or create other forms of civil recognition of committed relationships illuminates the tensions and trade-offs involved in state regulation of intimate, dependent, or interdependent relationships, whether emotional or economic (or both). I argue here that universal civil unions (which could be titled domestic partnerships or universal caregiving partnerships), rather than simply expanding marriage to include same-sex couples or moving to a regime of contracts in lieu of marriage, is the option best suited to the development of a just family law.[6] I retain the conviction that the state, that is, the civic community, must be instrumental in promoting the values of liberty and equality that are central to justice in both political and familial life.

A Brief History of U.S. Marriage Law

The traditional popular understandings and legal stipulations governing marriage in the United States have roots in Judeo-Christian religious views and church law. The English common law became the basis for the marriage laws of most U.S. states, and it reflected the tenets of marriage promulgated by the Anglican (and before it the Catholic) Church. When jurisdiction over marriage and children was transferred from church to common-law courts, for the most part "public law simply echoed what had been church doctrine."[7] Marriage was both an indissoluble and a hierarchical relationship. In the church's view, marriage was a covenant, like God's covenant with the Jews and later Christ's covenant with the church (the community of the faithful). Christian marriage was thus an unbreakable bond. Marriage was to be lifelong, and marital faithfulness was to include monogamy.

In addition to being indissoluble, marriage was regarded as a hierarchical relationship, and one in which husband and wife played complementary, not similar, roles. The man was given authority as the head of household. Blackstone, the eighteenth-century legal authority, explained that since Genesis declared husband and wife to be "one flesh" in the eyes of God, they were to be "one person" in the eyes of the law, and that person was represented by the husband. This suspension of the wife's legal personality was known as the doctrine of spousal unity, or "coverture." Under coverture, a married woman could not sue or be sued unless her husband was party to the suit, could not sign contracts unless her husband joined her, and could not make a valid will unless he consented to its provisions. As a correlate of these powers and his role as head of the family, a husband was obligated to support his wife and children. And since he would be held responsible for her actions, a husband had a right to correct his wife physically, and to determine how and where their children would be raised. As late as 1945 a New Jersey court wrote:

> The plaintiff [husband] is the master of his household. He is the managing head, with control and power to preserve the family relation, to protect its members and to guide their conduct. He has the obligation and responsibility of supporting, maintaining and protecting the family and the correlative right to exclude intruders and unwanted visitors from the home despite the whims of the wife.[8]

Marriage was to be a structure in which spousal roles were distinct and complementary, with the husband acting as wage earner, protector, and public actor, the wife as protected, private homemaker.

The husband was expected to govern his household without either interference or help from the state. By and large police turned a blind eye to violence between spouses; in most jurisdictions wives could not prosecute their husbands for marital rape because the law assumed that by marrying, spouses gave blanket consent to sexual relations; and judges enforced obligations of support only if spouses separated, not in an ongoing marriage.

The result of all these stipulations was that when people married, they consented to enter a relationship the terms of which are set by the state. This is what it means to call marriage a "status" relationship. Consent was necessary to enter the married state, but the agreement to marry brought with it rights and duties that were not set by the partners but were considered to be intrinsic to the state of being married.

The unequal and restrictive provisions of marriage law became the object of reform efforts in the mid-nineteenth century. Reformers attacked laws that granted divorce only for a wife's adultery, and not that of her husband, and added other wrongs, particularly physical cruelty and domestic violence, as grounds for dissolving the marital bond. Marriage, they said, must not make the home a "prison" for unhappy and wronged spouses, depriving them of essential personal liberty. Feminist reformers also invoked equality in their campaigns to pass married women's property laws that would allow wives to hold property, sue and be sued, and enter contracts in their own names. By the end of the nineteenth century, a number of states had passed married women's property statutes, freeing married women from many of the legal effects of coverture.

While this first wave of marriage law reform increased both the freedom to leave unsatisfactory marriages and equality between husbands and wives, many people were dissatisfied with the state of the law in the mid-twentieth century. The grounds for divorce were restrictive, and law still treated married men and women differently. Several states granted divorce only for adultery. Many states imposed alimony only on husbands, a stipulation that assumed, and perhaps helped to perpetuate, women's exclusion from the paid labor force. The age at which females could marry without their parents' consent was often younger than that for males, suggesting that boys needed to stay in school longer or learn a trade before marrying and that girls did not. Custody laws varied widely but often contained a preference for mother's custody, again assuming that the mother was and would in the future be the better caregiver.

In the mid-twentieth century, a variety of factors that I can mention only briefly here converged to spark a second wave of marriage law reform. Demographic changes since 1900 were dramatic: life expectancy for women was forty-eight years in 1900 and seventy-eight in 1980; increased life expectancy meant that most parents had years as "empty nesters" after their children left home, whereas in 1900 parents lived most of their lives with their children; and at midcentury women began childbearing at an older age and bore fewer children than had women in 1900. In the decades following World War II, economic changes led women, including married women and women with children, into the paid labor force in unprecedented numbers. This drew women out of the home for part of the day and gave them greater economic independence. The introduction of the birth control pill in the 1960s gave women more control over whether and when they would become pregnant. Greater ability to plan the timing of their children encouraged women to work outside the home and to think of "careers" rather than temporary jobs. All these changes predated the resurgence of feminism. Only beginning in the late 1960s and the 1970s did the ideology of equal rights developed by the black civil rights movement of the 1950s and 1960s help revitalize feminism, spurring the women's movement to insist on equality between men and women as spouses as

well as individuals. Also drawing on the legacy of civil rights and liberation struggles of the 1960s, in the 1970s gays and lesbians insisted on an
end to legal discrimination against homosexuals and an end to the ban on
same-sex marriage.

The dramatic transformation of divorce law that occurred between 1965
and 1974 took place independent of feminist influence. Herbert Jacob has
called the adoption of no-fault divorce the "silent revolution," a series of
"radical changes in legal expectations about family life" that came about
through "routine" (as contrasted with "conflictual") public policy processes that avoided becoming the focus of media and public attention.

In the mid-1960s, lawyers in California began the push for no-fault
divorce in large part to get rid of the subterfuge in many divorce proceedings that took place when couples tailored their stories to make them fit
the legal requirements for divorce. Although California courts were lenient
in granting divorce, to obtain a divorce a husband or wife had to prove
that the other had committed a marital offense like adultery, cruelty, or
desertion.[9] In most cases, the wife was the plaintiff and usually charged
her husband with "cruelty," which could range from disparaging remarks
to physical violence. "The testimony was often arranged and fake, disguis-
ing a mutual or negotiated decision to end the marriage. It was this element of dishonesty that provoked some of the proponents of change to
seek a no-fault statute."[10] No-fault divorce enabled a spouse to obtain a
divorce without proving wrongdoing by the other. The reformers' goal was
to eliminate the perjury that had become common and to decrease the
level of conflict between divorcing spouses. Neither greater equality for
women nor greater choice among alternative family forms was among the
aims of those working to enact no-fault divorce laws.

Proponents of no-fault divorce did not intend or anticipate what Elaine
Tyler May has called the "demographic watershed" in U.S. families that the
introduction of no-fault divorce brought about. In the wake of no-fault
legislation, the divorce rate rose dramatically. The changes in marriage
were reflected in the fact that in the last quarter of the twentieth century
only one-quarter of U.S. households fit the supposed "norm" of husband
wage earner and homemaker wife, living with their own biological or
adopted children.

Dramatic though these demographics are, for my purposes it is more
important to notice that no-fault divorce marked a sea change in the way
people began to *think about* and conceptualize marriage. The idea that the
marriage partners themselves, rather than the state, could decide to end

their marriage was revolutionary. It affected thinking about both the permanence of marriage and the nature of the marriage relationship itself. It seemed as if the observation of Henry Maine, the nineteenth-century legal historian, that "the movement of the law in the nineteenth century is a movement from status to contract" was finally coming to be true of marriage.

The egalitarian impulse that moved feminists to insist that unequal stipulations concerning wives and husbands be eliminated from the law combined with the dedication to individual liberty that underlay no-fault divorce to set the stage for various proposals to reshape marriage. Advocates of the legal recognition of same-sex marriage couched their demands in the language of the equal rights of every individual to marry the person of his or her choice. Advocates of single mothers invoked the notion of each individual's right to make reproductive decisions free from state interference (e.g., the requirement that any mother receiving welfare identify the child's father). Advocates of individual contracts in lieu of marriage worked to "extend [marriage's] founding principle of consent between the couple to all the terms of the relationship, allowing the contractual side of the hybrid institution to bloom."[11] By the early twenty-first century, the understanding of marriage as an indissoluble and hierarchical entity had by and large disappeared from both popular culture and legal doctrine, but there was considerable contestation over what understanding and regulations should take its place. In the following section I look at proposals to reform marriage by expanding marriage to include same-sex couples, to allow individuals to make their own marriage contracts, and to create civil unions for heterosexual and same-sex partners alike. Proponents of each of these proposals grapple with the question of how civil society can (and should) support a variety of caregiving relationships.

Proposals for Marriage Law Reform

Legal Recognition of Same-Sex Marriage

There have been two quite distinct debates about the desirability of legal recognition for same-sex marriages. In the first, those who maintain that in the U.S. tradition and law marriage is a union between one man and one woman have squared off against those who argue that this tradition discriminates against homosexual couples. Both sides in this debate regard marriage as desirable, and disagree about whether the state should allow same-sex couples to marry. In the other, which has taken place largely although not exclusively within gay and lesbian communities, those who seek legal recognition for same-sex marriage have been opposed by those who argue that marriage is not an institution homosexuals (or heterosexuals, for that matter) should seek to join. Marriage, these critics contend, is an exclusionary and hierarchical association, and same-sex marriage, rather than freeing gays and lesbians, will reinforce traditional social roles and further marginalize those who remain unmarried, whether couples or single persons (especially unmarried mothers). I do not examine the first debate here, but rather those among advocates of gay and lesbian rights who differ over the desirability of same-sex marriage.

Advocates of legal recognition of same-sex marriage have argued that marriage should be available to same-sex couples because it carries with it significant state benefits; acknowledges an emotional and psychological bond that, for some, is constitutive of the self; and provides the foundation for family life. The list of advantages that the state extends to married partners includes reduced tax liability if they file a joint return; survivor's benefits under the Social Security program; immunity from testifying against one's spouse in court; the right to inherit from a spouse in the absence of a will; and, if one is a foreigner married to a U.S. citizen, the right to residency in the United States.

Several advocates of same-sex marriage insist that denial of the right to marry is tantamount to depriving people of a full expression of their humanity. They point out that in *Loving v. Virginia,* the case in which the Supreme Court struck down Virginia's antimiscegenation law, the court said, "The freedom to marry has long been recognized as one of the vital personal rights essential to the orderly pursuit of happiness by free men. Marriage is one of the basic civil rights of man, fundamental to our very existence and survival."[12] Consonant with this theme, E. J. Graff argues that the title of her book, *What Is Marriage For?,* is "a question about what it means to be fully human,"[13] while Andrew Sullivan says that the denial of marriage, stemming from the social stigma attached to homosexuality, "attacks the very heart of what makes a human being human: the ability to love and be loved."[14] In Morris Kaplan's judgment, "Given the importance of interpersonal relationships in defining individual identities and in contributing to human happiness, full equality for lesbian and gay citizens requires access to the legal and social recognition of our intimate associations."[15] Not only decriminalization of homosexual sexual activity but also legal recognition of same-sex unions is essential to gay and lesbian dignity and well-being.

Although not all marriages involve children, and many households raising children do not contain a married couple, many people regard marriage as the foundation of family life.[16] Graff notes that while the form of "'the family' has never held still but has veered from one conception to the next," the family of some configuration "is where wave after wave of human beings are socialized and cared for, where children are raised to be useful members of society instead of dangerous cast-outs."[17] She endorses the view that "the family is not a thing but a network of human relations, which survive even when their forms change."[18] She makes two arguments that same-sex marriage would be good for children. First, it would protect children living with parents who are of the same sex; marriage would automatically create legal responsibilities for both parents. Second, it would teach children that "we get to choose our life course based on our inner gyroscopes, and must respect others' choices."[19]

Despite these considerations, some supporters of gay and lesbian rights oppose same-sex marriage. Paula Ettelbrick has argued since the 1980s that marriage, rather than being liberating, "will constrain us, make us more invisible, force our assimilation into the mainstream, and undermine the goals of gay liberation." Furthermore "attaining the right to marry will not transform our society from one that makes narrow, but dramatic, distinctions between those who are married and those who are not married to one that respects and encourages choice of relationships and family diversity," but will reinforce those distinctions. Legal recognition of same-sex marriage, in her view, would work against the validation of many forms of relationships.[20]

Nancy Polikoff and Judith Butler are among those who echo Ettelbrick's concerns. Polikoff predicts that "an effort to legalize lesbian and gay marriage would make a public critique of the institution of marriage impossible." The argument for inclusion is assimilationist, asserting that gays and lesbians will create no fundamental change in the institution of marriage. This, Polikoff contends, cannot possibly encourage the transformation of marriage that she seeks. The campaign for same-sex marriage will "require a rhetorical strategy that emphasizes similarities between our relationships and heterosexual marriages, values long-term monogamous coupling above all other relationships, and denies the potential of lesbian and gay marriage to transform the gendered nature of marriage for all people."[21] For a movement that takes as one of its aims greater acceptance of the diversity of sexual desire, "even one that may want to produce marriage as an option for nonheterosexuals," as Judith Butler puts it, "the proposition that marriage should become the only way to sanction or legitimate sexuality is unacceptably conservative."[22] Seeking state recognition of one's relationship is to seek "to vacate the lonely particularity of the nonratified relation." One cannot leave that particularity behind, however, and the effort to do so may become "the occasion to institute a new hierarchy of legitimate and illegitimate sexual arrangement."[23] One person's (or couple's) acceptance is won at the price of another's marginalization or subordination.

The predictions of Ettelbrick, Polikoff, Butler, and others that legal recognition of same-sex marriage could result in a reification of marriage as currently defined were borne out in the decisions in *Goodridge v. Department of Public Health,* the Massachusetts same-sex marriage case.[24] Winning access to marriage for same-sex couples was surely a victory for acceptance and equal rights, but even as it dealt that welcome blow to heterosexist barriers to full social and legal recognition, the majority decision reinscribed traditional understandings of marriage that are far from liberating.

The *Goodridge* majority accepts the current legal understandings but requires that these now be applied to same-sex couples. What we have done, says the court, is "refine the common law meaning of marriage," a remedy "entirely consonant with established principles of jurisprudence." By allowing same-sex couples to marry, we "redress[] the plaintiffs' constitutional injury and further the aim of marriage to promote stable, exclusive relationships."[25] All the court proposes is to admit an additional category of people to the existing institution.

The court identifies the public purposes of marriage as "providing a 'favorable setting for procreation'" and "ensuring the optimal setting for child rearing." It claims, "Marital children reap a measure of family stability and economic security . . . that is largely inaccessible, or not as readily accessible, to nonmarital children."[26] Such statements could be read as supporting proposals to facilitate and spread marriage, even by offering incentives to women on welfare to marry. They also could be read as support for the idea that is currently much debated among child psychologists, about whether marital status of those who take daily care of a child makes any difference to the child's well-being. Happy, stable families certainly benefit children, but many scholars contend that such families do not have to be marital families: "Economically secure families can provide children steady resources; but higher wages and better social supports for both single-mothers and two-parent families are the predicate for economic security, regardless whether parents are married."[27]

In addition, the Court asserted that civil marriage advanced the legitimate state interest in "conserving State resources."[28] This seems to suggest that marriage partners, not civil society, should bear the burden of supporting the vulnerable, although in extending the benefits of marriage to same-sex couples the Court made them eligible for a number of state-conferred financial benefits. Certainly the state has a responsibility to ensure that the vulnerable are clothed, fed, housed, and educated without regard to their membership in a marital family.

So even as legal recognition of gay and lesbian marriage must provoke a reconsideration of gender roles in marriage, it does not guarantee a reconceptualization of the terms of spousal relationships, pluralization of family forms beyond conjugal couples, or insistence on the public goods provided by the caregiving. The goals of autonomy, equality, reciprocity, and caregiving require looking beyond marriage to establish public support for crucially human relationships.

Contracts in Lieu of Marriage

While some suggest reforming marriage by allowing gays and lesbians to marry, others contend that legal recognition of same-sex marriage does not go far enough in recognizing what a commitment to pluralism and privacy in family law entails. For some, abolishing marriage as a civil status might make it psychologically and socially easier than it is today for adults to maximize their personal freedom and choice by living in committed relationships without seeking any recognition by the state. For those who *do* seek some kind of public recognition and regulation of their relationship, however, some reformers contend that the path that best recognizes a liberal society's commitment to freedom and pluralism is for the law to allow marriage partners to frame their own agreements. Such contracts in lieu of marriage not only would enable two persons of the same sex to marry but also would give partners the liberty to set other terms to their relationship.

There are two distinct sources for proposals to substitute contracts for marriage law, each drawing on different assumptions about individual and social responsibility. The first source is classical liberal theory's commitment to principles of individual liberty and equality. Some proposals to replace family law by private ordering reflect of a version of liberalism that understands freedom as the ability to determine and pursue one's goals without interference from government or other individuals. Marriage by contract replaces the gender stereotyping and protectionism of traditional marriage law with the recognition of the individuality and equal agency of the partners. Marriage partners should be treated as rational actors capable of knowing and articulating their interests. It is not surprising that feminist scholars like Lenore Weitzman and Marjorie Shultz put forward this kind of proposal in the 1970s and 1980s, when feminist legal theorists were struggling to remove the deeply embedded assumptions of sexual difference and inequality from many aspects of the law.[29] Their efforts revealed the ways in which both statutory law and court rulings dealing with the family rested on gender stereotypes and deprived women of the decision-making authority the law gave to men. In more recent years scholars like June Carbone and Margaret Brinig, Elizabeth and Robert Scott, and Jana Singer have continued to explore the ways in which contract law respects the decisions of free bargaining agents and so opens marriage to much greater diversity of roles and decisions about how to order intimate relationships.[30]

Another argument in support of contracts in lieu of marriage has arisen in the context of (and as a side effect of) another strand of feminist thought, one that in one early manifestation was called "maternalism" and that has been developed into a large body of work called "the ethic of care."[31] Care ethicists emphasize that all human beings are not only autonomous decision makers but also at one time or another dependent on others for their welfare or survival. Theorists working in the field of "the ethic of care" have demonstrated the inadequacy of classical liberal theory's focus on the autonomous adult to take account of the relationship of mother and child, and the consequent difference in the situation of men and women with respect to remunerative labor and traditional understandings of citizenship. Proponents of the second version of contractualism begin with the dependent relationship of child to parent, and insist that this relationship—not that between the adults—is the proper starting point for thinking about family law.

Martha Fineman (this volume) is a leading exponent of the view that family law must begin with the relationship between caregivers and those in need of care, including children, and many elderly, ill, and disabled persons.[32] Beginning with marriage, which focuses attention on the heterosexual couple, she argues, not only excludes same-sex couples but also diverts attention from people who are not linked by a sexual relationship but are caregiver and care receiver: "The pressing problems today do not revolve around the marriage connection, but the caretaker-dependent relationship. . . . Rather than marriage, we should view the parent-child relationship as the quintessential or core family connection, and focus on how policy can strengthen this tie."[33]

Fineman's proposal for abolishing marriage, then, is part of a strategy to gain state support and subsidies for relationships between parents and children, and between other caregivers and dependents. Because the United States privatizes the costs of caring and places primary responsibility for meeting the needs of dependents on family members, all those who have dependent children, particularly single mothers, shoulder enormous burdens. This is particularly true in an era in which employers are reducing both wages and benefits, and much of job growth is in the low-paying service sector. In placing the costs of care on the family, the United States departs from the practice of other industrial democracies, in which the state assures some floor of social goods to each citizen, as Fineman notes: "If our concern is with children, the question should [be] . . . how we can support all individuals who perform the important societal work of caretaking for those who because of their age or physical or mental conditions are dependent upon some form of family."[34]

The kinds of measures that would foster autonomy for adults and enable them to provide for children in their care include health insurance, affordable and quality child care, child allowances of the kind common in Europe, flexible workplace hours, and paid parental leave for both men and women. Without such measures, an adult who lacks a middle-class job will have great difficulty making sure that a child is provided with the safety and stimulation necessary for the development of her or his capabilities. "With [such measures], intimate relationships of any sort as well as the project of childrearing would be less entwined with the vicissitudes of economic life, and thus have better odds of thriving."[35] As things stand now, all wage earners fear the loss of income and health insurance if they cannot find work. Single women raising children are particularly vulnerable because women's wages tend to be lower than men's, fewer of them hold jobs that supply health insurance, and they experience a direct conflict between their child-rearing obligations and the demands of an eight-hour workday. It would be possible, however, for medical, basic income, and old age insurance to be guaranteed by the state directly rather than obtained through a spouse's employment.

Fineman contends that once the needs of children and their parents are given due attention by public policy, the relationships between individual adults can be arranged by contract: "[M]arriage is becoming more and more like other legal relationships in regard to the individual's ability to create or limit responsibilities and risks through contract."[36] She suggests transferring to the caretaker-dependent relationship all the social and material subsidies now associated with marriage; once that is done, "marriage should be replaced by contract in the first instance, allowing couples to structure their own relationships in the ways they want."[37]

An additional advantage of a regime of individual contract, in Fineman's view, is that it would enable people of the same sex, or more than two persons, to marry: "There is no reason for the state to be involved in the articulation and imposition of those terms any more than it would be involved in the enforcement of contracts in general."[38] Contracts would replace paternalism with autonomy and self-determination: "If people want their relationships to have consequences, they should bargain for them. . . . This would mean that sexual affiliates (formerly labeled husband and wife) would be regulated by the terms of their individualized agreements with no special rules governing fairness and no unique review or monitoring of the negotiation process." Because she believes that unregulated bargaining both reflects and enhances women's equal liberty, Fineman contends that abolishing marriage as a legal category is "a step necessary for gender equality."[39] The way to show respect for women's liberty and equality is to let women strike their own partnership agreements.

Abolishing marriage would also mean that heterosexual marriage would no longer define the normative family, and in Fineman's view this would be a help to many women, particularly single mothers. "Without marriage, motherhood would not be modified by the existence of a legal relationship between heterosexual partners. There would be no 'single' mothers—only the unmodified category of 'mothers.'"[40] This would also help children, because children of single parents are often portrayed as "'trapped' in a 'deviant' family situation, 'prisoners' or 'victims' of a family that is often 'broken' though divorce or 'pathological' in that it was never sanctioned by marriage."[41]

I am in favor of replacing marriage with universal civil unions and instituting a system of extensive public supports for family relations, but I do not think that individual contracts in lieu of marriage are the proper way to ground the principles of justice that should govern adult relationships within families. The responsibilities and the vulnerabilities that arise out of lives that are intertwined in the shared undertaking of building and sustaining family relationships exist independently of contract, and the state has a positive role to play in supporting committed relationships. The claims of the parties rest in the first instance upon principles of fairness or justice. Law may decide to let people agree to modify those obligations, but contract alone does not guarantee the liberty and equality that are proper in family as well as civic life.[42]

The British Columbia Law Institute's *Report on Recognition of Spousal and Family Status* includes both voluntariness and protection of the vulnerable in its guiding principles:

> People in a marriage or in a relationship that resembles marriage may suffer economic prejudice when the relationship ends. They are also in need of protection. Not recognizing these relationships and not offering the same legal protections that the community has agreed are necessary in more traditional family units may allow one party to take unfair advantage of another. It is in these cases that the principle of voluntariness must sometimes yield to the principle of protecting the vulnerable.[43]

The public is served by maintaining the principle that one person should not unjustly benefit at the expense of another; that principle is particularly important when people have relied on one another in a relationship of trust.

Interestingly, the battles over same-sex marriage suggest a vehicle by which to think anew about what terms should govern such relationships of mutual reliance and trust, and what the role of the state in defining and regulating those relationships should be. Eager to avoid legal recognition of same-sex marriages when gay and lesbian couples challenged the state's refusal to issue them marriage licenses, the legislatures of both Vermont and Massachusetts proposed creating "civil unions," a relationship that would create all the rights and responsibilities of marriage for gay and lesbian couples. The Vermont Supreme Court accepted this proposal; the Massachusetts Supreme Judicial Court rejected it as incompatible with equal protection of the laws; Connecticut later enacted civil unions without any pressure from its courts. These proposals for civil unions did nothing more (and nothing less) than duplicate the provisions of marriage laws. But in creating a new category of adult relationship, the Vermont legislature opened the door to thinking from a fresh perspective about the public purposes of committed adult relationships.

Civil Unions and Other Committed Relationships

On the day after the Supreme Judicial Court of Massachusetts handed down its decision declaring the withholding of marriage licenses to same-sex couples to be a violation of the Massachusetts constitution, President Bush said that he would work to see that the institutions of government supported "the sacred institution of marriage."[44] It is not the business of government to support "sacred institutions" in a society that endorses the separation of church and state. However, President Bush was not alone in failing to distinguish *civil* marriage from a *sacred* institution, and the practice in the United States of authorizing religious ministers to act as officials of the state in registering marriages contributes to such confusion. As if in an effort to avoid this confusion, the Supreme Judicial Court of Massachusetts has insisted in its decision that marriage is totally a creation of the state: "[T]he government creates civil marriage. In Massachusetts, civil marriage is, and since pre-Colonial days has been, precisely what its name implies: a wholly secular institution." But this is somewhat disingenuous. In a technical sense, of course, marriage law is the creation of the legislature. But marriage law in the United States is a modification of English common law, which in turn was based on the canon law of the Catholic Church. Marriage law in Massachusetts reflects Christian (not Jewish or Islamic or Hindu) understandings of marriage.

One of the benefits of replacing civil marriage by civil union is that it would make clear the distinction between the civil relationship and the religious one. In an increasingly diverse and religiously pluralistic society, the United States could bring public law into line with that of almost all other Western countries (including Catholic Mexico and France) by establishing civil unions as the state-created and supported relationship and leaving to the couple the decision whether to enter into a religiously sanctioned marriage as well. If the United States did this, then civil unions should be the state-sanctioned status for heterosexuals and homosexuals alike. Statutes in Vermont and, later, Connecticut, along with Massachusetts's proposed but unenacted law, all kept marriage for heterosexuals and created civil unions for gays and lesbians, creating a dual system by substituting "civil union" in place of "marriage" in relevant statutes. Such a dual system is unnecessary and is unacceptable on grounds of equality, as the

Supreme Judicial Court of Massachusetts recognized in its advisory opinion rejecting the proposed civil union statute.[45]

Creating a regime of civil unions requires identification of the *public* interest in adult relationships. Some traditional answers, like regulating sexuality and "legitimating" children, no longer conform to law and the trend in social practice: few jurisdictions prosecute fornication and adultery, and courts have ended the legal disabilities of nonmarital children. Other answers, like controlling the transfer of property, can be done just as well or better by other legal instruments like wills or contracts. Still others, like relieving the state of responsibility for financial support of the vulnerable, wrongly privatize what should be a social responsibility.

How does one begin to think anew about the public purposes of civil unions, or more generally of family laws? Tamara Metz suggests, "To decide what role the state should have in regulating marriage-like relationships, we should institute a more general status [than marriage] aimed explicitly at protecting and supporting intimate caregiving units of all types," which she calls a universal caregiving partnership (UCP) status.[46] Public recognition and support of civil union (or domestic partnerships or UCPs) assumes that there is a value both to individuals and to society in interpersonal commitment. Public status affirms the desire many individuals have to make lasting connection with others. As Morris Kaplan observes, "[T]he need for intimate human connection runs very deep and across differing modes of sexuality and . . . social recognition and legal support is needed to maintain the always precarious associations through which such needs are met."[47] Adults who commit themselves to one another even if they do not have any children for whom they are responsible may face vulnerabilities that arise from the relationship itself. All human beings can rightfully make claims for public support for shelter, sustenance, decent jobs, and health care. But it is not enough to give such benefits to individuals; rather, adults in a committed relationship may need public recognition of that relationship and its significance. Public recognition of civil unions would demonstrate society's commitment to helping people sustain their significant commitments. For example, being a partner in a civil union could be the basis for making claims that an employer grant time off from work to enable an employee to care for a sick partner. Relationships matter, and there is a legitimate role for the state in protecting and promoting relational interests.

The human connections that the state might recognize and regulate may take many forms, however. People can live together, love one another, and have (or not have) children, but which of these associations will receive the title "family" depends on political and legal decisions. What groupings or associations should receive recognition as civil unions? Asking the question exposes a deep tension for anyone thinking about the relationship between state and family. Legal recognition of same-sex marriage moves the line between those who are "in" and those who are "out" so that more families are legally recognized, but the line still remains between "legitimate" and "outlaw" families. Michael Warner has warned that the drive among gays and lesbians to become recognizable within the existing norms delegitimates sexual lives lived outside the dyadic and monogamous coupling that mimics marriage.[48] Judith Butler points out that gays and lesbians who cannot marry suffer a "disenfranchisement" that has "psychic, cultural, and material consequences." At the same time, however, "the demand to be recognized, which is a very powerful political demand, can lead to new and invidious forms of social hierarchy, to a precipitous closure of the sexual field, and to new ways of supporting and extending state power."[49] The same dilemma would exist under a regime of civil unions as under marriage; legitimation of any civil status that recognizes some but not all relationships cannot help but be double-edged in its effect.

One way to ease the fact that law will exclude some significant relationships whose members do not formalize their union, or relationships whose members rely on one another only in some aspects of their lives, would be to have government scrutinize all laws whose objectives involve taking relationships into account, and construct relational definitions in a way that does not rely on status alone. Brenda Cossman and Bruce Ryder point out that "conjugality or marriage-equivalence is a poor proxy for the relational attributes relevant to legislative objectives."[50] *Beyond Conjugality: Recognizing and Supporting Close Personal Adult Relationships,* a report of the Law Commission of Canada, concluded, "Recognizing and supporting personal adult relationships that involve caring and interdependence is an important state objective," and so the state "ought to support any and all relationships that have the capacity to further relevant social goals."[51] Such relationships might include those who may be compensated for relationship harm following negligently caused injury or death; those who may be entitled to bereavement leave; those who may be entitled to medical and family care leave; those who may be sponsored under immigration law; and those who may be entitled to Social Security old-age and survivor's benefits.[52]

Nancy Polikoff explains how recognition of relationships relevant to a particular statutory goal might work:

> Relationships characterized as primarily emotional, rather than economic, in nature might be registered to establish the individual entitled to make healthcare and burial decisions, take family and medical leave, and have testimonial privileges. Relationships that also include the care of one person by the other, through caregiving or financial support, might be registered to establish entitlement to government and private benefits, recovery for wrongful death, and treatment as a single economic unit for income tax provisions.[53]

In addition to using a legal status like marriage, civil union, or domestic partnership as a proxy to signify the existence of a relational right or responsibility, legislators, judges, and citizens should determine the rationale of specific statutes and what relationships and relational interests each is striving to support. The questions to ask are why and in what ways a variety of relationships matter to people, what rights and responsibilities should be attached to such relationships, and what state supports are warranted to help sustain them.[54]

Those questions apply to the relationships between adults and children, as well as to those between adults. Although the topic is beyond the scope of this chapter, adults' responsibilities toward children must be part of any consideration of relational rights and responsibilities—while not all adult relationships will encompass children, many will. Sociological trends, including increasing numbers of single mothers, cohabiting couples with children, and blended households; reliable DNA testing for paternity; and the increasing use of third-party genetic material and gestational services ("surrogacy") by heterosexual couples, lesbian and gay couples, and singles alike raise the question of what role the genetic tie on the one hand and actual caregiving activity on the other should play in establishing parental rights and responsibilities.

I offer just a few observations on adult-child relationships that touch on the themes of this chapter. While the traditional laws that held that all children born within marriage were the children of the husband (even if there was good reason to believe he was not the child's biological father) and that a child born outside marriage had no legal father (indeed, was *filius nulli*, the child of no one) are clearly outdated, contract is not an adequate replacement for status.[55] Adults who enter civil unions or domestic partnerships and have or adopt children together assume rights and responsibilities that arise from the child's needs, not from the adults' volition. For example, each parent has not only an individual responsibility to support and care for the child but also an obligation to help sustain the other partner's and any siblings' relationships with the child whenever possible. Some scholars propose in addition that some adults besides the custodial parents—possibly known and involved sperm or egg donors, or birth parents following adoption—could have visitation or other limited rights and responsibilities with respect to the child, and urge consideration of "nonexclusive" parenthood.[56] I have argued elsewhere that the interests of the potential child also set ethical boundaries to the means by which adults can obtain sperm, eggs, and gestational services.[57] As society moves to a pluralization of family forms, one of the most urgent tasks facing legal scholars and ethicists is to consider the relationship between adults' responsibilities to one another and to the children they raise.[58]

Conclusion

Advocates of expanding marriage to include same-sex marriage and those who propose abolishing marriage and replacing it with contracts in lieu of marriage or civil unions or other registered relationships share the perception that traditional marriage law does not adequately reflect principles of justice that should guide both familial and political life. I have suggested that while legal recognition of same-sex unions is desirable, adequate reform must go beyond either simply expanding the categories of those permitted to take out a marriage license or substituting individual contracts in lieu of marriage. The state has a role to play in setting some of the terms of committed adult relationships, recognizing the importance of nonconjugal as well as conjugal relationships in many areas governed by law, and creating the circumstances in which people can form and sustain caregiving relationships.

While I think adult partners should be able to set some of the terms of their relationship through individual agreements, I suggest that the individualism and emphasis on rational bargaining that are at the heart of contracts rest on misleading models of the person, of committed adult relationship, and of the proper role of the state. Committed partners are not only autonomous decision makers; they are fundamentally social beings. The model of the person on which contract doctrine rests gives too little space to temporality and need. In addition, regulation by contract removes the dimension of public deliberation and collective commitment in establishing the conditions of spousal (or partner) equality. The public has an interest not only in sustaining family relationships in the face of poverty or illness but also in securing the social bases of liberty and self-respect for all family members.[59] Civil unions reflect the facts that relationships of emotional and economic interdependency are not entirely reducible to their individual components and that the state has a role to play in recognizing and sustaining these committed relationships.

The next phase of the struggle to achieve familial and relational justice will have to entail a public commitment to liberty and equality, and must tackle not only family law and statutes involving relationships but also economic and workplace structures. One such reform is to ensure that people can find jobs that pay a living wage. Another is to structure work in such a way that it accommodates caregiving, for example, through family and medical leave, a shorter workweek, and more flexible scheduling.[60] Another is to make certain that parents have access to high-quality and affordable child care. These measures certainly do not exhaust what is needed. They make the point that in order to meet the principle of equality, men and women alike must be able to perform the tasks appropriate and necessary to the public and the private realm, to shoulder the responsibilities both of workers outside the home and of family caregivers.

With so much of our public discourse reducing individuals primarily to consumers in the market, it is especially important to insist on the social and relational sides of our lives. Civil unions and registered relationships would recognize the importance of relationships between individuals, of shared purposes that transcend the self and are important both to the partners and to the larger society. If such a commitment is a valuable aspiration and one that our political community wants to facilitate, then we need to examine and remove impediments to such relationships. Those impediments are legion, especially among the poor. Removing them thus confronts us with a formidable agenda—reforms of the workplace, of welfare, and of supports for caregiving. With the notions of public good and collective responsibility under constant assault, we need to insist that family law can and must be made to conform to the principles of justice. The debates over same-sex marriage are just one of many pressing issues that provide the opportunity for—indeed, that require—thinking about the purposes committed relationships serve and the role of civil society in supporting them.

NOTES

1. For example, see William Eskridge, *The Case for Same-Sex Marriage* (New York: Free Press, 1996); E. J. Graff, *What Is Marriage For?* (Boston: Beacon Press, 1999); Nan D. Hunter, "Marriage, Law and Gender: A Feminist Inquiry," *Law and Sexuality* 1 (1991): 9; Andrew Sullivan, *Virtually Normal* (New York: Vintage Books, 1996), chap. 5, "A Politics of Homosexuality."

2. As I discuss later in the text, proposals for expanding the use of contract in family law vary, but among advocates of contractualism are Lenore J. Weitzman, "Legal Regulation of Marriage: Tradition and Change: A Proposal for Individual Contracts and Contracts in Lieu of Marriage," *California Law Review* 62 (1974): 1169; Lenore J. Weitzman, *The Marriage Contract: Spouses, Lovers and the Law* (New York: Free Press, 1981); Marjorie Maguire Shultz, "Contractual Ordering of Marriage: A New Model for State Policy," *California Law Review* 70 (1982): 204–334; June Carbone and Margaret F. Brinig, "Rethinking Marriage: Feminist Ideology, Economic Change, and Divorce Reform," *Tulane Law Review* 65 (1991): 953; Jana Singer, "The Privatization of Family Law," *Wisconsin Law Review* 1992 (1992): 1443; Elizabeth S. Scott and Robert E. Scott, "Marriage as Relational Contract," *Virginia Law Review* 84 (1998): 1225. Martha Fineman advocates contractual ordering of adult relationships as a supplement and complement to government recognition and support of dependency and caregiving relationships; see, among others, *The Neutered Mother, the Sexual Family, and Other Twentieth Century Tragedies* (New York: Routledge, 1995); *The Autonomy Myth: A Theory of Dependency* (New York: New Press, 2004); and Fineman's chapter in this volume.

3. William Eskridge supports moving toward legal recognition of same-sex marriage through prior acceptance of civil unions in *Equality Practice: Civil Unions and the Future of Gay Rights* (New York: Routledge, 2001).

4. Brenda Cossman and Bruce Ryder, "What Is Marriage-Like Like? The Irrelevance of Conjugality," *Canadian Journal of Family Law* 18 (2001): 269; Nancy Polikoff, "Ending Marriage as We Know It," *Hofstra Law Review* 32 (Fall 2003): 201; Judith Stacey, "Toward Equal Regard for Marriages and Other Imperfect Intimate Affiliations," *Hofstra Law Review* 32 (2003): 331.

5. The proposals I discuss here all concern reform of marriage law, that is, *civil* marriage as distinct from religious marriage. The trade-offs concern state regulation of marriage; adopting any of the proposed changes in civil marriage would not affect religious understandings of marriage or religious laws governing marriage.

6. My position in this chapter differs from the one I expressed in "Just Marriage," which appeared first in the *Boston Review* (June–July 2003) and then, along with commentaries from thirteen scholars, in *Just Marriage*, ed. Joshua Cohen and Deborah Chasman (New York: Oxford University Press, 2004). In that essay I favored reforming marriage law and legalizing same-sex marriage, rather than

replacing marriage by universal civil union as a way of promoting careful thinking about the civil purposes of intimate associations. What has not changed is my conviction that legislation formulated and evaluated in accordance with criteria of liberty (or autonomy) and equality is preferable to a regime of individual contracts in lieu of marriage (although certain aspects of civil unions or other state-recognized status could be modifiable or replaced by contractual agreements).

Brian H. Bix, "State Interest and Marriage: The Theoretical Perspective," *Hofstra Law Review* 32 (2003): 93–110, contains an interesting discussion of the appropriate role of the state in regulating marriage; unfortunately, the article appeared after the thesis of this chapter was finished.

7. Herbert Jacob, *Silent Revolution: The Transformation of Divorce Law in the United States* (Chicago: University of Chicago Press, 1988), 5.

8. *Chapman v. Mitchell*, 44 A.2d 392, at 393 (N.J. 1945), quoted in Jacobs, *Silent Revolution*, 6.

9. Other grounds were willful neglect, habitual intemperance, conviction for a felony, or insanity. Herma Hill Kay, "Equality and Difference," *Cincinnati Law Review* 56 (1987): 28nn115–19, cited in Jacob, *Silent Revolution*, 184n11.

10. Jacob, *Silent Revolution*, 47.

11. Nancy F. Cott, *Public Vows: A History of Marriage and the Nation* (Cambridge, Mass.: Harvard University Press, 2000), 208.

12. *Loving v. Virginia*, 388 U.S. 1 (1967) 12.

13. Graff, *What Is Marriage For?* 250.

14. Sullivan, *Virtually Normal*, quoted by James Q. Wilson in *Same-Sex Marriage: Pro and Con*, ed. Andrew Sullivan (New York: Vintage Books, 1997), 166.

15. Morris B. Kaplan, "Intimacy and Equality: The Question of Lesbian and Gay Marriage," *Philosophical Forum* 25 (1994): 333.

Although critical of the gendered nature of the roles of "husband" and "wife" in marriage, Nan Hunter argues that same-sex marriage will undermine those traditional roles so central to many people's understandings of marriage. Marriage is a social construct, and "What is most unsettling to the status quo about the legalization of lesbian and gay marriage is its potential to expose and denaturalize the historical construction of gender at the heart of marriage." Nan D. Hunter, "Marriage, Law and Gender: A Feminist Inquiry," *Law and Sexuality* 1 (1991): 9.

16. James Q. Wilson, an opponent of gay marriage, writes, "[W]hat is distinctive about marriage is that it is an institution created to sustain child-rearing," and society has no reliable data to let us know how children raised by same-sex couples fare. Wilson, "Against Homosexual Marriage," *Commentary*, March 1996, reprinted in Sullivan, *Same-Sex Marriage*, 166.

17. Graff, *What Is Marriage For?* 92.

18. Ibid., 99, quoting Gaunt and Nystrom, in *A History of the Family*, ed. Andre Burguiere, Christianae Kapisch-Zuber, Martine Segalen, and Francoise Zonabend,

trans. Sarah Hanbury Tenison, Rosemary Morris, and Andrew Wilson (Cambridge, Mass.: Belknap Press of Harvard University Press, 1996), vol. 2, 486–87.

19. Graff, *What Is Marriage For?* 144.

20. Paula Ettelbrick, "Since When Is Marriage a Path to Liberation?" *Out/Look,* Fall 1989, 14.

21. Nancy D. Polikoff, "We Will Get What We Ask For: Why Legalizing Gay and Lesbian Marriage Will Not 'Dismantle the Legal Structure of Gender in Every Marriage,'" *Virginia Law Review* 79 (October 1993): 1549.

22. Judith Butler, "Is Kinship Always Already Heterosexual?" *differences: A Journal of Feminist Cultural Studies* 13 (2002): 21.

23. Ibid., 23.

24. *Goodridge v. Department of Public Health,* 440 Mass. 309 (Mass. 2003).

25. Ibid. at 343.

26. Ibid. at 325.

27. Gwendolyn Mink and Anna Marie Smith, "Gay or Straight, Marriage May Not Be Bliss," *Women's Enews,* March 31, 2004.

28. *Goodridge* (2003) at 342.

29. Weitzman, "Legal Regulation of Marriage"; Weitzman, *Marriage Contract;* Shultz, "Contractual Ordering of Marriage."

30. Carbone and Brinig, "Rethinking Marriage"; Singer, "Privatization of Family Law"; Scott and Scott, "Marriage as Relational Contract."

31. Sarah Ruddick, *Maternal Thinking,* 2nd ed. (Boston: Beacon Press, 1995); Nell Noddings, *Caring* (Berkeley: University of California Press, 1984); Eva Kittay, *Love's Labor: Essays on Equality, Dependency, and Care* (New York: Routledge, 1999); Mona Harrington, *Care and Equality* (New York: Routledge, 2000); Joan Tronto, *Moral Boundaries: A Political Argument for an Ethic of Care* (New York: Routledge, 1993); Joan Williams, *Unbending Gender: Why Family and Work Conflict and What to Do about It* (New York: Oxford University Press, 2001); Eva Kittay and Ellen K. Feder, eds., *The Subject of Care: Feminist Perspectives on Dependency* (Lanham: Rowman and Littlefield, 2003).

32. See Martha Fineman, *The Illusion of Equality: The Rhetoric and Reality of Divorce Reform* (Chicago: University of Chicago Press, 1991); "Why Marriage?" *Virginia Journal of Social Policy and the Law* 9 (2001): 239; and *The Autonomy Myth.*

33. Fineman, "Why Marriage?" *Virginia Journal of Social Policy and the Law.*

34. Martha Albertson Fineman, "Why Marriage?" in Mary Lyndon Shanley, *Just Marriage,* ed. Joshua Cohen and Deborah Chasman (New York: Oxford University Press, 2004), 50.

35. Wendy Brown, "After Marriage," in Shanley, *Just Marriage,* 88.

36. Fineman, "The Meaning of Marriage," this volume, 53.

37. Ibid., 29.

38. Ibid.

39. Ibid., 58.

40. Ibid., 60.

41. Fineman, "Why Marriage?" in Shanley, *Just Marriage*, 49–50.

42. Linda McClain, "Intimate Affiliation and Democracy: Beyond Marriage?" *Hofstra Law Review* 32 (2003): 379–413, contains an interesting discussion of Fineman's proposal to abolish marriage and replace it with contracts between sexual affiliates.

43. British Columbia Law Institute, *Report on Recognition of Spousal and Family Status*, quoted in Nancy D. Polikoff, "Making Marriage Matter Less: The ALI Domestic Partner Principles Are One Step in the Right Direction," *University of Chicago Legal Forum* (2004): 353. The report is available at http://www.bcli.org (visited June 28, 2004).

44. *New York Times*, November 19, 2004.

45. Supreme Judicial Court of Massachusetts, "Opinions of the Justices to the Senate" 2004 Mass. LEXIS 35 (Mass., February 3, 2004).

46. Tamara Metz, "Why We Should Disestablish Marriage," in Shanley, *Just Marriage*. Metz develops this idea in her dissertation, "Uneasy Union: Marriage and the Liberal State" (Harvard University, 2004).

47. Morris B. Kaplan, "Intimacy and Equality: The Question of Lesbian and Gay Marriage," *Philosophical Forum* 25 (1994): 333.

48. Michael Warner, *The Trouble with Normal: Sex, Politics, and the Ethics of Queer Life* (New York: Free Press, 1999), especially chap. 3, "Beyond Gay Marriage."

49. Butler, "Is Kinship Always Already Heterosexual?" 26–27.

50. Cossman and Ryder, "What Is Marriage-Like Like?" 274.

51. Law Commission of Canada, "Executive Summary," *Beyond Conjugality: Recognizing the Supporting Close Personal Adult Relationships* (2001), available at http://www.lcc.ca/en/themes/pr/cpra/report.asp (visited June 25, 2004). Brenda Cossman and Bruce Ryder (see preceding note) were advisers to the commission.

52. The Law Commission of Canada proposes looking at any existing law and asking a series of questions: (1) Does the law serve a legitimate policy objective? (2) If the law's objective is legitimate, are relationships relevant to that objective? (3) If relationships are relevant to the statute's purposes, could the law permit individuals to choose which of their own close personal relationships they want to be subject to the law? (4) If relationships do matter and the law must identify the relevant individuals who are in such a relationship, then can the law be revised to more accurately capture the relevant range of relationships?

53. Polikoff, "Ending Marriage as We Know It," 223–24.

54. Stacey, "Toward Equal Regard for Marriages and Other Imperfect Intimate Affiliations," argues that law and public policies should recognize diverse forms of intimate affiliation.

55. In the course of her argument for contracts in lieu of marriage, Fineman notes, "The state maintains a protective interest in the well-being of children

and parental obligations in regard to them cannot be individualized and reduced to contract," although she leaves open the question of whether contract would be an appropriate means for regulating reproductive services like gamete transfer and surrogacy. Fineman, "The Meaning of Marriage," this volume, 62. In my view, contracts alone are an inadequate and inappropriate way to regulate collaborative procreation.

56. Katherine Bartlett, "Rethinking Parenthood as an Exclusive Status: The Need for Legal Alternatives When the Premise of the Nuclear Family Has Failed," *Virginia Law Review* 70 (1984): 897; Matthew M. Kavanagh, "Re-writing the Legal Family: Beyond Exclusivity to a Care-Based Standard," *Yale Journal of Law and Feminism* 16 (2004): 83.

57. Mary Lyndon Shanley, *Making Babies, Making Families: What Matters Most in an Age of Adoption, Reproductive Technologies, Surrogacy, and Same-Sex and Unwed Parents* (Boston: Beacon Press, 2000).

58. I discuss various justifications for establishing parental rights in "Lesbian Families: Dilemmas in Grounding Legal Recognition of Parenthood," in *Mother Troubles: Rethinking Contemporary Maternal Dilemmas*, ed. Julia E. Hanigsberg and Sara Ruddick (Boston: Beacon Press, 1999), and in chapter 5 of my book *Making Babies, Making Families*.

59. For examples of such moral reasoning, see Martha C. Nussbaum, *Sex and Social Justice* (New York: Oxford University Press, 1999); Nussbaum, *Women and Human Development: The Capabilities Approach* (New York: Cambridge University Press, 2000); Susan Moller Okin, *Justice, Gender and the Family* (New York: Basic Books, 1989); Iris Marion Young, *Justice and the Politics of Difference* (Princeton, N.J.: Princeton University Press, 1990); and Carole Pateman, *The Sexual Contract* (Stanford, Calif.: Stanford University Press, 1988).

60. *Paid* parental leave for *both* men and women would create an incentive for men to participate in child care, particularly if a father could not transfer his leave time to someone else but had to use it himself or forgo the benefit.

REFERENCES

Bartlett, Katherine. 1984. "Rethinking Parenthood as an Exclusive Status: The Need for Legal Alternatives When the Premise of the Nuclear Family Has Failed." *Virginia Law Review,* 70:879.

Bix, Brian H. 2003. "State Interest and Marriage: The Theoretical Perspective." *Hofstra Law Review* 32:93–110.

British Columbia Law Institute. *Report on Recognition of Spousal ad Family Status.* http://www.bcli.org (visited June 28, 2004).

Brown, Wendy. 2004. "After Marriage." In *Just Marriage,* ed. Mary Lyndon Shanley, 87. New York: Oxford University Press.

Butler, Judith. 2002. "Is Kinship Always Already Heterosexual?" *differences: A Journal of Feminist Cultural Studies* 13.

Carbone, June, and Margaret F. Brinig. 1991. "Rethinking Marriage: Feminist Ideology, Economic Change, and Divorce Reform." *Tulane Law Review,* 65.

Chapman v. Mitchell. 44 A.2d 392 (N.J. Misc. 1945).

Cossman, Brenda, and Bruce Ryder. 2001. "What Is Marriage-Like Like? The Irrelevance of Conjugality." *Canadian Journal of Family Law* 18:269.

Cott, Nancy F. 2000. *Public Vows: A History of Marriage and the Nation,* 208. Cambridge, Mass.: Harvard University Press, 2000.

Eskridge, William. 1996. *The Case for Same-Sex Marriage.* New York: Free Press.

———. 2001. *Equality Practice: Civil Unions and the Future of Gay Rights.* New York: Routledge.

Ettelbrick, Paula. 1989. "Since When Is Marriage a Path to Liberation?" *Out/Look,* Fall, 14ff.

Fineman, Martha Albertson. 1991. *The Illusion of Equality: The Rhetoric and Reality of Divorce Reform.* Chicago: University of Chicago Press.

———. 1995. *The Neutered Mother, the Sexual Family, and Other Twentieth Century Tragedies.* New York: Routledge.

———. 2001. "Why Marriage?" *Virginia Journal of Social Policy and the Law* 9:239.

———. 2004a. *The Autonomy Myth: A Theory of Dependency.* New York: New Press.

———. 2004b. "Why Marriage?" In *Just Marriage,* ed. Mary Lyndon Shanley, 46. New York: Oxford University Press.

Goodridge v. Department of Public Health. 440 Mass. 309; 798 N.E. 2d 941 (Mass. 2003).

Graff, E. J. 1999. *What Is Marriage For?* Boston: Beacon Press.

Harrington, Mona. 2000. *Care and Equality.* New York: Routledge.

Hunter, Nan D. 1991. "Marriage, Law and Gender: A Feminist Inquiry." *Law and Sexuality* 1:9.

Jacob, Herbert. 1988. *Silent Revolution: The Transformation of Divorce Law in the United States.* Chicago: University of Chicago Press.

Kaplan, Morris B. 1994. "Intimacy and Equality: The Question of Lesbian and Gay Marriage." *Philosophical Forum* 25:333.

Kavanagh, Matthew M. 2004. "Re-writing the Legal Family: Beyond Exclusivity to a Care-Based Standard." *Yale Journal of Law and Feminism* 16:83.

Kay, Herma Hill. 1987. "Equality and Difference: A Perspective on No-fault Divorce and Its Aftermath." *University of Cincinnati Law Review* 56:1.

Kittay, Eva. 1999. *Love's Labor: Essays on Equality, Dependency, and Care.* New York: Routledge.

Kittay, Eva, and Ellen K. Feder, eds. 2003. *The Subject of Care: Feminist Perspectives on Dependency.* Lanham, Md.: Rowman and Littlefield.

Law Commission of Canada. 2001. "Executive Summary." In *Beyond Conjugality:*

Recognizing the Supporting Close Personal Adult Relationships. Available at http://www.lcc.ca/en/themes/pr/cpra/report.asp [visited June 25, 2004].

Loving v. Virginia. 388 U.S. 1 (1967).

McClain, Linda. 2003. "Intimate Affiliation and Democracy: Beyond Marriage?" *Hofstra Law Review* 32:379–413.

Metz, Tamara. 2004a. "Uneasy Union: Marriage and the Liberal State." Ph.D. diss., Harvard University.

———. 2004b. "Why We Should Disestablish Marriage." In *Just Marriage,* ed. Mary Lyndon Shanley. New York: Oxford University Press.

Mink, Gwendolyn, and Anna Marie Smith. 2004. "Gay or Straight, Marriage May Not Be Bliss." *Women's Enews,* March.

Noddings, Nell. 1984. *Caring.* Berkeley: University of California Press.

Nussbaum, Martha C. 1999. *Sex and Social Justice.* New York: Oxford University Press.

———. 2000. *Women and Human Development: The Capabilities Approach.* New York: Cambridge University Press.

Okin, Susan Moller. 1989. *Justice, Gender and the Family.* New York: Basic Books.

Pateman, Carole. 1988. *The Sexual Contract.* Stanford, Calif.: Stanford University Press.

Polikoff, Nancy. 1993. "We Will Get What We Ask For: Why Legalizing Gay and Lesbian Marriage Will Not 'Dismantle the Legal Structure of Gender in Every Marriage.'" *Virginia Law Review* 79.

———. 2003. "Ending Marriage as We Know It." *Hofstra Law Review* 32:223–24.

———. 2004. "Making Marriage Matter Less: The ALI Domestic Partner Principles Are One Step in the Right Direction." *University of Chicago Legal Forum* 2004:353.

Ruddick, Sarah. 1995. *Maternal Thinking.* 2d ed. Boston: Beacon Press.

Scott, Elizabeth S., and Robert E. Scott. 1998. "Marriage as Relational Contract." *Virginia Law Review* 84:1225.

Shanley, Mary Lyndon. 1999. "Lesbian Families: Dilemmas in Grounding Legal Recognition of Parenthood." In *Mother Troubles: Rethinking Contemporary Maternal Dilemmas,* ed. Julia E. Hanigsberg and Sara Ruddick, 178. Boston: Beacon Press.

———. 2000. *Making Babies, Making Families: What Matters Most in an Age of Adoption, Reproductive Technologies, Surrogacy, and Same-Sex and Unwed Parents.* Boston: Beacon Press.

———. 2004. *Just Marriage,* ed. Joshua Cohen and Deborah Chasman. New York: Oxford University Press.

Shultz, Marjorie Maguire. 1982. "Contractual Ordering of Marriage: A New Model for State Policy." *California Law Review* 70:204–334.

Singer, Jana. 1992. "The Privatization of Family Law." *Wisconsin Law Review* 1992: 1443.

Stacey, Judith. 2003. "Toward Equal Regard for Marriages and Other Imperfect Intimate Affiliations." *Hofstra Law Review* 32:331–48.

Sullivan, Andrew. 1996. *Virtually Normal.* New York: Vintage Books.

———, ed. 1997. *Same-Sex Marriage: Pro and Con.* New York: Vintage Books.

Supreme Judicial Court of Massachusetts. "Opinions of the Justices to the Senate" 2004 Mass. LEXIS 35 (Mass., February 3, 2004).

Tronto, Joan. 1993. *Moral Boundaries: A Political Argument for an Ethic of Care.* New York: Routledge.

Warner, Michael. 1999. *The Trouble with Normal: Sex, Politics, and the Ethics of Queer Life.* New York: Free Press.

Weitzman, Lenore J. 1974. "Legal Regulation of Marriage: Tradition and Change: A Proposal for Individual Contracts and Contracts in Lieu of Marriage." *California Law Review* 62.

———. 1981. *The Marriage Contract: Spouses, Lovers and the Law.* New York: Free Press.

Williams, Joan. 2001. *Unbending Gender: Why Family and Work Conflict and What to Do about It.* New York: Oxford University Press.

Wilson, James Q. 1997. "Against Homosexual Marriage." Commentary (March 1996). In *Same-Sex Marriage: Pro and Con,* ed. Andrew Sullivan, 159–68. New York: Vintage Books.

Young, Iris Marion. 1990. *Justice and the Politics of Difference.* Princeton, N.J.: Princeton University Press.

Afterword
Narrowing the Status of Marriage

Anita Bernstein

Building on the reflections on marriage as a status that this volume has offered, this afterword adds two approaches. Following up on Lawrence Rosen question about the legitimacy of coercion (Rosen, this volume), the first approach I broach here is jurisprudential: a look at marriage as an example of law-based compulsion. Next I move to two existing defenses of this status, both of them less comprehensive than the failed utilitarian "case" that sought to promote marriage as a source of social well-being (see Solot and Miller, this volume; Bernstein introduction, this volume). These two arguments—the first a "belonging" hypothesis, as advanced chiefly by Milton C. Regan Jr., and the second what contributors Martha Fineman and Linda McClain have called "the male problematic" (Fineman, this volume; McClain, this volume)—may not convince readers, but the claims are cogent and parsimonious. Inspired by what they have achieved in cogency and parsimony, I conclude that although a thick or robust defense of state-sponsored marriage cannot be sustained, a thinner one emerges.

What State-Sponsored Marriage Can Do:
A Statement about Boundaries

"State interference is an evil," wrote Oliver Wendell Holmes, "where it cannot be shown to be a good" (Holmes 1963). Although when recognizing and enforcing statuses American law at times applies coercion to individuals without an accompanying rationale about welfare, such instances are exceptions within a larger scheme rooted in public reason and ought to be challenged. Law constrains, but it should not do so without a good reason, one that is intelligible to interested and disinterested persons alike and that pursues welfare (Bentham 1970). This starting point about a good rationale, more conservative than the "harm principle" associated with John Stuart Mill and also more informative than such catchphrases as "substantive due process" and "fundamental rights," helps to explain why it might be a good idea for the state to sponsor marriage: marriage could increase welfare.

The sinking "case for marriage," however, applies welfare considerations wrongheadedly. As we have seen, the "case" uses data about outcomes to assert that individuals should choose marriage because of the institution's supposed payoffs (Bernstein introduction, this volume). Although the data do commend marrying rather than remaining unmarried (at least for most people), marriage partisans have not contemplated seriously a world without state-sponsored marriage. Their arguments in favor of marriage thus apply only, and at most, to the question of whether an individual should marry in a society where marriage exists and where this status bestows benefits on those who choose to wed. They do not refute the claim that marriage should be abolished.

Whereas the case-for-marriage argument fails because it is incomplete, other arguments fail because they are too particular. A public-reason justification for retaining marriage must lie within reach of all citizens to discover and debate as human beings, rather than as members of a subgroup. As Jonathan Rauch (1996) has argued, marriage policy in the contemporary United States requires a clear secular civic understanding. Accordingly, religious rationales for continuing marriage cannot shed light on what the state should do. Even putting aside First Amendment obstacles to these rationales, no single religion unites all Americans in the sense that they are united by shared reason. Family-values traditionalism and conservative references to the past—"it must be this way because it has always been this way"—fall short on the same ground of too much particularity. We are not all social conservatives. Not everybody embraces "family values."

If marriage is to survive as one of a dwindling number of comprehensive statuses that the law continues to respect, then it must pay attention to the dignity and autonomy of the individual, a concern that militates against status in general. Every status is inherently illiberal, but even illiberal categories or tendencies in the American legal system must recognize that the individual is fundamental. Getting married, then, must result in keeping some freedoms alive even if it must also extinguish others. Exit is the most fundamental of these freedoms: individuals not otherwise disabled must have the prerogative to go from unmarried to married and from married to unmarried. Beyond the prerogative of exit, a liberal version of marriage must tread cautiously on the expressed preferences and life plans of individuals.

At the same time it is also necessary—as many contributors to this volume, especially Linda McClain, remind us—to keep gender equity in mind when considering marriage as a status. Any move toward abolition or retention would affect individuals, who hold a range of views on whether American law should take a more egalitarian or liberationist approach to gender. Many people committed to liberality deplore the subordination of women in marriage and the unavailability of marriage to same-sex couples. I share these inclinations but do not press them strongly in a defense of marriage as a status that aspires to be thin. Like religious understandings of marriage and family-values beliefs, a commitment to diminishing the force of gender in marriage—that is, a stance that opposes constraints on women's freedom and the current opposite-sex criterion of access to this status—is still something of a particularistic stance. To many, the principles against subordination of women in marriage and in favor of access to marriage for same-sex couples are just as self-evident and as easy and as amenable to public reason as the stance against old miscegenation laws that prohibited individuals of different races from marrying each other (e.g., Koppelman 1994, 235–36). This perspective has not yet gained recognition in the law.[1]

It is possible, however, to advocate liberality with respect to gender in conservative terms—as an inclination rather than a source of yes-no rules. Because the constraint of public reason prohibits the state from coercing individuals unless there is a good reason to do so, the state should not craft its law of marriage to force individuals into a gender script—for instance, decreeing that a man may marry only a woman and a woman may marry only a man, or that a husband rather than a wife has the prerogative to choose the couple's place of residence—unless there is a good reason to impose this script on persons who will find it coercive. This position, unlike the stronger stance that views the law of marriage as illegitimate until it comes to comply with gender equity, has won influence in American law. While gender equity remains contested in public discussion in a way that race equity does not, it enjoys wide support and continues to make gains in public discourse.

Accordingly, the stance I advocate here emphasizes procedure rather than substance: the law of marriage should respect and bear in mind the claims that feminists and same-sex activists have made regarding marriage, without necessarily acceding to all of them.

Two Cogent Arguments in Favor of State-Sponsored Marriage

Scholars take state-sponsored marriage for granted. Almost none have set out to defend it against an abolitionist proposition. In the large body of writings that applaud "the family," an institution considered vulnerable to feminism and individualism as well as macroeconomic phenomena such as the decline of wage labor, however, one does find copious cheering for marriage. Among these cheers, two arguments warrant particular attention.

Belonging and Shelter in a Postmodern World

Bruce Hafen speaks of "belonging" as a necessary condition for human fulfillment. Although the idea of belonging to, or possessing, another person can connote enslavement or objectification, Hafen argues, "the bonds of kinship and marriage are valuable ties that bind." Hafen worries that liberal individualism has brought about a current "age of the waning of belonging," and defends marriage as integral to the struggle against loneliness (Hafen 1991, 31–34, 42).

Family law scholar Milton C. Regan Jr. has crafted a more detailed argument for the ongoing vitality of status-based family law within a liberal and feminist jurisprudence. Professor Regan aspires to a defense of status-based family law that, contrary to a long-standing tradition in the field, does not rest on children's vulnerability and dependence: he aspires to explain all of family law, including its childless aspects. As he must, Regan begins by acknowledging that status in family law is associated with oppression, especially oppression of women: "[T]he Victorians gave status a bad name" (Regan 1996, 165). Paradoxically, however, the constraint of status is necessary to generate the empowered self that individualism upholds.

Without status, Regan explains, a person bobbles from episode to episode without continuity of identity. The autonomous individual so prized in modernism and contractarian political thought is not a daughter, a husband, or somebody's child, hemmed in by the duties and commitments that these identities impose. These people are free. A transaction eagerly embraced today might become dull or distasteful tomorrow—the individual might feel less like a son then, or more like a mother. To Regan this figure does not embody "the Enlightenment dream of individual emancipation" (Regan 1996, 162) but rather is lonely and pitiful, worse off than he would have been without the ties of status. Buffeted by "the winds of each passing experience," unprotected from whatever stimuli come his way, this person cannot maintain the sense of being "a purposive agent" (164). And when one loses status, one loses identity and intimacy. Identity diminishes because only status can remind us that our past will shape and frame our present and future. Intimate commitment becomes harder to achieve because intimacy is dependent on identity. Without a self to unite last year's promises with tomorrow's array of options, there is no reason to feel bound to or even affected by an episode in the past that linked one person with another. So hampered in their pursuit of intimacy and identity, individuals suffer.

To assuage these harsh effects, individuals need the support of marriage. The fragmenting effects of postmodern life notwithstanding, most people seek a primary relationship as a base of romantic and sexual intimacy. The quest can lead to great pain: Regan notes the vulnerability that derives from looking for, and also from having found, a partner. Just as economic vulnerability justifies regulation to override freedom of contract, the emotional vulnerability that always accompanies the romantic dyad means that law should sponsor a status of marriage, Regan argues, in order to affirm responsibilities that derive from dependence and mutual vulnerability.

Could marriage, for Regan, exist without state sponsorship? Regan says little about the legal consequences of marital status in a harmonious or otherwise ongoing marriage. Regarding divorce, however, he finds doctrinal applications, suggesting to readers that his conception of status has state-sponsored marriage in mind, rather than an informal status relation like the boyfriend-girlfriend dyad in contemporary society or a pair united only by contract in the hypothetical future world, after state-sponsored marriage is abolished. At a minimum Regan appears to insist on retaining the legal category of "family," where individuals are constrained at least by social norms, if not legal rules, from doing whatever they please. He notes with disapproval the academic perception that "the family" is just one variant on "the close relationship situation" (Regan 1996, 171–74).

This vagueness on what "family" means mars an otherwise elegant argument and suggests that Regan's thesis does not complete the task of defending the existence of state-sponsored marriage. If all we need is any status label, however inconsequential to the law, in order to find refuge from postmodern clangor, then "partner" and "lover" would serve as well as "husband" and "wife." If, alternatively, Regan intends for marriage to be a status with significant law-based constraints, then he needs to explain how to balance individualism against respect for status in one's everyday life—that is to say, as a participant in one's own marriage—and family law. Regan purports to endorse two contrary values. He commends sensitivity to "the solitary and the social dimension of our being" but also urges "an equilibrium in which both status and contract play a role" (174). At this high level of generality, all answers to tough questions become possible, and the defense of state-sponsored marriage crumbles.

The Savage Hypothesis

From an array of disciplines and perspectives—feminism notably excluded—some scholars applaud marriage for its effects in socializing men: half the human race, they say, has brutish inclinations that society must moderate. In 1986, before the fathers' and marriage movements got under way, George Gilder offered a book-length exposition of this argument. His *Men and Marriage* begins with a claim that civilization is what human beings achieve when the long-term timetable and sense of futurity inherent in female sexuality overpower male sexual impulses:

> In creating civilization, women transform male lust into love; channel male wanderlust into jobs, homes, and families; link men to specific children; rear children into citizens; change hunters into fathers; divert male will to power into a drive to create. Women conceive the future that men tend to flee; they feed the children that men ignore. (Gilder 1986, 5)

As Gilder sees the sexes, women enjoy a unique serenity because of the capacities they find in their bodies. They are capable of diverse sexual acts and experiences, whereas men have only two meager ones, erection and ejaculation: "Nothing about the male body dictates any specific pattern beyond a repetitive release of sexual tension." Whether she bears children or not, each woman knows that she can "perform the only act that gives sex an unquestionable meaning, an incarnate result" (8–9). Contrast her tragic fellow human being:

> For men the desire for sex is not simply a quest for pleasure. It is an indispensable test of identity. And in itself it is always ultimately temporary and inadequate. Unless his maleness is confirmed by his culture, he must enact it repeatedly and perhaps destructively for himself or his society. . . . A man without a woman has a deep inner sense of dispensability, perhaps evolved during the millennia of service in the front lines of tribal defense. He is sexually optional. (11, 15)

The consequences to society are clear. Impulsive, trapped in the present, cut off physically from nurturing and consequently from caring about human beings—cut off even from valuing his own life—this person is not only uncivilized but an active menace to civilized people. Young single men, writes David Popenoe, "make up the majority of deviants, delinquents, criminals, killers, drug users, vice lords, and miscreants of every kind" (1998, 36). Compared with married men, single men drink almost twice as much; they are also more likely to have drinking problems, to drink and drive, and to get into fights (Waite 2002, 15–16). Although they constitute about 13 percent of the population over age fourteen, they commit nearly 90 percent of major and violent crimes. "Groups of sociologists venturing into urban streets after their seminars on violence in America do not rush to their taxis fearing attack by marauding bands of feminists, covens of single women, or angry packs of welfare mothers," writes Gilder. "[O]ne need have little fear of any group that so much as contains women —or, if the truth be known, of any group that contains men who are married to women" (1986, 65). Another writer claims that men, who "constitute the majority, and the most productive portion, of the workforce," would have less incentive to work hard if marriage were abolished—and none whatsoever if Martha Fineman were to succeed in having government pay women to care for their children at the same rate that marriage now compensates them (Cohen 1995, 2289). In this perspective, marriage rescues not only a man, who would be lonely and worth little otherwise, but the society around him.

Other writings have advanced the thesis that this bleakness is replicated in a second generation: they associate being deprived of a father in one's home with deviant or antisocial behavior. The sons of absconded scoundrels are the chief offenders, but writers worry also about daughters, more vulnerable to teen pregnancy and out-of-wedlock childbearing when their parents are separated or divorced. A correlation between fatherlessness and troubled children is widely accepted. In sum, here in the savage hypothesis men must marry and stay married—because if they don't, they will take us all down with them.

Toward a Third Way: Marriage Reenvisioned

Much of the utilitarian "case for marriage"—marriage is good because it makes people healthy, wealthy, and happy—reduces to tautology. Moreover, it collapses when its unstated beliefs, chief among them the notion that state-sponsored marriage can never be eliminated, fail to support its weight. The utilitarian "case for marriage" is not cogent.

The last two arguments, however, follow a sturdy inner logic. Having ably contended that an individual needs some kind of status role in order to achieve intimacy and identity, Milton Regan is able to portray marriage as tending to ease the existential sadness that comes from relating to other persons only through one's bargains and episodic encounters. The savage hypothesis is cogent, too. If one posits that men are inherently different from women, and that the ways in which they differ from women conduce to social instability and havoc, then the highly gendered institution of marriage becomes a way to cabin men, reducing the social harm they would otherwise cause. One need not agree with either argument in order to agree that both make sense on their own terms, in a way that the utilitarian "case for marriage" does not.

Mere cogency, however, cannot justify engraving an argument into public policy. Premises must be questioned, and then rejected if they prove wrong. The conclusion of wrongness can derive from varied commitments. For example, it would be wrong not to lower the speed limit on a highway just before a sharp curve, because principles related to automobile braking and deceleration make unreduced, pre-curve speeds dangerous. Such principles appear to be, and I would say really are, prepolitical and nonideological.

While the "belonging" argument of Regan, building on Hafen, contains no a priori affronts of this kind—we will get to its weakness later—the savage hypothesis is at best indeterminate as a matter of descriptive fact, the reality that lawmakers need to consider in such contexts as setting highway speed limits. One might say that descriptive fact, however politically incorrect or inconvenient, must always outweigh even the best-intentioned attempts to revise the truth. Perhaps. Yet the question of how inherently different men and women are from each other—before politics, before ideology, before even their birth as persons—cannot be measured in a setting so permeated with socially installed and enforced gender roles as the contemporary United States. Adequate laboratory conditions for such a study are not present; we do not have the data needed to support a hypothesis that men inherently demand extra measures of socialization. The farrago of proclamations from journalists and some social scientists that male and female human beings are fundamentally more different than alike—based on leaps of faith, tiny samples, tendentious inferences from ambiguous data, ideological readings of what anthropologists report, and the disregard of contrary evidence—proves only that strong versions of gender dimorphism have a big following in both the media and the academy, not that conjectures about that dimorphism are true or false. And so, forced to proceed without guidance from social science, policymakers must rely on American political and jurisprudential commitments.

True or false or something in between, the savage hypothesis affronts several distinct precepts of American law and lawmaking. Its claim that legal rules and institutions should regard men as brutes dishonors the equal protection clause of the U.S. Constitution, which limits the effect that government can give to gender-based stereotypes. Its sweeping denigration of millions of people offends procedural justice. If engraved into legal doctrine and public policy, it would, or should, hurt the "hearts and minds" of men and boys so insulted (*Brown v. Board of Education,* 494). Its dismissal of the passage of time and the accretion of culture—evolutionary psychology sees human nature as fixed in the savanna of the Stone Age —expresses a posture hostile to negotiation and political compromise, one that the Supreme Court has held to invalidate numerous laws. Its portrait of the male human being as destructive, sociopathic, and an enemy of order is at odds with such foundational documents as the Declaration of Independence and the Bill of Rights, which recognize the citizen's capacity for thought, speech, religious belief, association and assembly, giving and receiving counsel, and civic participation.

Although American lawmakers and policymakers are thus precluded from using the savage hypothesis as a condemnation, or even a reductive summary, of male humanity, they can share some of the values that happen to animate *Men and Marriage* and other expressions of the hypothesis

—those beliefs that do not affront equal protection, procedural justice, and civic governance. Classifying men as savages is categorically wrong. A concern for civil society and sociopolitical stability, however, is laudable.

From these two cogent arguments favoring state-sponsored marriage, then, we can see the outlines of a newer case for marriage, one that escapes both the vagueness of Regan's indeterminate endorsement of status, on the one hand, and the gender shackles of the savage hypothesis, on the other. The cogent arguments take a crucial step forward in defending marriage. Although marriage has let many people down, made them worse off, and caused harm to society, its ideals and practices offer genuine goods. In benefiting individuals it can benefit third parties and the larger society as well.

Marriage holds the potential of giving individuals more of a past and a future than they would otherwise have. When they marry, especially if they are relatively young at the time, couples convincingly report a feeling of connection to their ancestors, progenitor couples who entered unions of their own, while looking ahead (e.g., Blustain 2000). Past and future are partner concepts, not opposites. As Robert Nisbet and other scholars of progressivism have detailed, a sense of the past makes a sense of the future possible and coherent (Nisbet 1980; Pirie 1978). Neither human beings nor societies can flourish without a prevailing belief that the future holds some meanings and consequences for them. As a form of enforced commitment, state-sponsored marriage facilitates investment—that is, the sacrifice of short-term gain for the prospect of returns in the long term—just as other state-sponsored enforced commitments, like procedural rules and the protection of property holdings, facilitate economic investment.

To opponents of marriage, these values will sound ominous: a critic can hear the clink and rattle of chains. This critic might start by saying that even if marrying does give individuals a sense of connection to the past, other avenues toward this connection might work better. Perhaps marriage has obstructed their development. Moreover, Regan's elegant admonition that individual human fulfillment cannot emerge without the status roles that build a sense of self and permit intimate connection to another person notwithstanding, this idealized version of marriage—as shelter, continuity, investment base, buffer against impulses and seductive opportunities—overlooks much oppression inherent in the institution. The legal category of marriage has begotten a generation of pernicious newer categories: marital rape (and the Model Penal Code's "spousal exemption" to rape), family immunity from tort liability, tax rules that encourage husbands to make money and avoid their families while discouraging wives from earning wages, "bastardy" and "legitimacy" to describe the status of children, defense-of-marriage state laws that do nothing except denigrate same-sex unions, and numerous other hurtful concepts. I deny none of these harmful effects of state-sponsored marriage, and indeed have gone to some trouble to catalog and recite them (Bernstein 2003). But this reaccounting finds gain as well as loss: the "case" for state-sponsored marriage neglects a crucial point.

The point may be seen as the political and communal counterpart to Regan's postmodernist psychology, which focuses on marriage as a source of gain for individuals. To the extent he is persuasive, Regan redeems marriage from the perspective of a solitary person who seeks identity and intimacy, but he does not link this individual's opportunity with a societal interest in marriage. To demonstrate a distinct societal interest in marriage, one must show that letting human beings achieve identity and intimacy makes for a gain to the collective, such as better citizens or greater economic prosperity. It may be the case that because statuses always require societal recognition, Regan has necessarily made a political and social point as well as a psychological one. But the argument in favor of a status (a social construct) needs to show how societies gain when that status is in place.

If marriage and comparable statuses were to disappear, the individual would flutter from transaction to transaction, contract to contract, and encounter to encounter, Regan says, bouncing like images on MTV. What happens to society, to the body politic, as this person bounces? It, too, might be unmoored from a base of deep tradition and continuity. But unlike the individual, who in Regan's exposition dissolves and becomes lost, a society can hold itself together without state-sponsored marriage. Marriage as a law-based status arrived relatively recently in human existence. Humanity can live without it.

We arrive at the relevant question for legal policy: What would American society be like if the state were to withdraw from recognizing marriage, a status now derived from the romantic dyad? How would humanity live without it in the United States? Not by failing to cohere, like Regan's lost individual. Instead, some new source of power and governance would move into the space that marriage now holds. There are only two contenders for this role in governing private lives.[2] One is the state, regulating individuals directly rather than through its current indirect practice of making a status out of a pairing. The other is the market. As they do under contemporary liberal regimes around the world with respect to economics, the two would likely share power in a postmarriage legal regime. Moving toward the terrain that state-sponsored marriage now occupies, they would each gain the opportunity to grow stronger.

A liberal policymaker who is willing to consider abolishing state-sponsored marriage has good reason to proceed with caution before ceding new prerogatives to either the state or the market. To many who have contemplated the abolition of state-sponsored marriage, new state-sponsored initiatives—either well-framed default rules to be used when disputes arise within a relationship, or an array of official legal options that couples could choose when approaching state registries—would necessarily follow this particular law reform. Even if the state were to hold firm to its abolitionist agenda and refuse to recognize coupledom except in terms of what individuals choose to do, the result of abolition would be not one big new void in the legal realm, but a proliferation of new, smaller state-sponsored rules, covering the terrain that the old marriage regime once regulated more obliquely. The substantive content of these new state-sponsored controls would not necessarily move private life in a progressive or benevolent direction.

And if the state were to pull away from regulating the romantic dyad altogether, allowing contracts and transactions to control this kind of union, then social effects would follow. Although the abolitionist stance consistently disclaims any agenda to abolish the couple in any extralegal sense—two may merge into one in their own minds, say abolitionists, even as they remain two in the eyes of the law—reformers know from experience that when American law stops recognizing a particular status, that status goes into decline in day-to-day life, not just in legal form. As the concept of an *e pluribus unum* couple gets weaker in relation to the state's abandonment of marital status, intimate conjunction would move toward an exchange undertaken in the hope of individual gain, like the purchase and sale of goods in a market. We have seen that Regan thinks each player in this game is a loser, at least in relation to the alternative available through state-sponsored marriage. The societal perspective on this abolitionist picture is less bleak, but concerns emerge.

There is no reason to suppose that the human craving for paired connection would disappear with the abolition of state-sponsored marriage, and so abolition would throw most people into an uncharted competition for intimacy. The marital bond that now holds opposite-sex couples together (and by example encourages same-sex couples to think of themselves as conjoined) would loosen; pairing off might grow more provisional, requiring more effort to keep up. These struggles would take time away from other pursuits. It seems plausible to speculate that individuals who can never obtain respite from competing for intimacy would have less to offer (including, for instance, political engagement, the building of economic wealth, the care of children, or expanding the frontiers of human knowledge and accomplishment) than those not competing in this market. To the extent that individuals abjure the competitive market for romantic love and choose isolation instead, civic realms could benefit from the energies of full-time participants. But one might question the goodness of social settings and institutions in which solitary, intimacy-barren volunteers living in dissent from a common pursuit hold the reins. Moreover, markets are notoriously severe, tending to reward powerful persons at the expense of weaker ones. Wealth (in men) and reproductive-age youth (in women) are cold commodities now; they might be pursued and bought and sold and liquidated even more harshly in a world in which men and women could not take refuge in status.

If these concerns about direct state regulation and a triumphant market are valid—and their validity cannot be known, absent an abolitionist experiment—then state-sponsored marriage becomes a political force that, for all its numberless flaws, offers protections and benefits. Located at a kind of midpoint between the intrusions of direct regulation at one end and the laissez-faire prerogatives of the market at the other, state-sponsored marriage presents a unique blend of freedom and control. And just as the experience of getting married connects couples with their past and their future, marriage as a social institution manifests both continuity and change. Memories and archetypes of marriage occupy human consciousness: when same-sex marriage activists criticize *Baker v. State,* the Vermont decision that used a common-benefits clause of the state constitution to extend the legal privileges of marriage to same-sex couples, they mean to say, among other things, that one of the "common benefits" withheld under Vermont law is a connection to symbols and traditions derived from marriage in the past. State-sponsored marriage feels different from the state-sponsored granting of marital entitlements: the force of marriage lies in the fact that it combines legal privileges and duties with an extralegal, socially understood set of conventions.

Political philosophy and legal theory recognize the force of extralegal authority on individuals' lives. Although the words "norms" and "community" and "social meaning" and "anarchist philosophy" push separate buttons and engage (or affront) different advocates, these terms unite around their attention to intermediate institutions—buffers between law and no-law—that structure human relations. Numerous jurisprudential traditions acknowledge the existence of intermediate institutions as central to law in a complex society; there can be neither law nor society without them. For the moment at least, marriage is a crucial intermediate institution.

Readers thus far unconvinced that marriage is worth retaining might now consider the procedural obstacles to abolition. Even if marriage as a "third way," to reuse a hoary phrase, were discounted, and the market or direct state regulation preferred as a source of social control, the costs of abolishing state-sponsored marriage would be heavy, in several senses. No groundswell of popular feeling supports this change, and so marriage could be abolished only after considerable investment—either in fending off resistance or the slower-paced strategy of nurturing existing sentiments or tendencies against marriage.

The transition between state recognition of marriage and no state recognition of marriage yields numerous complications. Other legal statuses have disappeared or dwindled in a variety of patterns: the accretion of state-level reforms, judicial activism, presidential decree, public disapproval, and desuetude. While most legal statuses that have disappeared made their exit slowly, the abolition of slavery provides an example of status elimination that the government imposed on unwilling, bellicose Americans.

Advocates for the elimination of state-sponsored marriage can thus consider the frontal-assault pattern that characterized the Civil War and its aftermath, in addition to other precedents that got rid of statuses in ambiguous retreats. The most dramatic mechanism would be for Congress to declare every marriage null and void in the United States. Congress may not have the power to pass such a law, even if anyone would ever take such a violent prospect seriously as a plan of action. As an alternative, imagine years of investigation followed by enactment of a federal statute patterned on the Defense of Marriage Act: pick a day in the future and circle it on the calendar as the last date on which couples could enter into a marriage that the law would recognize. Would thousands rush to the altar? How could more than fifty jurisdictions, all of them with their own laws of marriage, coordinate the timing of abolition?

The abolish-marriage literature has been inclined to pass over problems of form and procedure, which include the division between federal and state regulatory authority to control marriage, the role of the judiciary in managing the abolition of state-sponsored marriage, the possibility of executive branch nonacquiescence, and the validity of legal judgments or entitlements that might arise based on a mistaken belief that parties were married in a way that the law recognizes. One must advert briefly to these difficulties here, however, to raise just a suggestion of how cumbersome it would be for the government to get out of the marriage business. Moreover, even if we assume an orderly shift from the current world into this future one, a large cohort would live in the in-between years, with some people entitled to call themselves "married" or needing to get "divorced" in order to "remarry," and others disabled altogether from the status. Strife and frustration within families, and among unrelated persons, would accompany the transition.

If, by contrast, state-sponsored marriage were to remain an option while also receiving some of the critical attention that this volume has cast on it, society would more likely maximize its gains. The benefits of marriage, whatever they really are, would continue. The detriments would be better understood, perhaps becoming more amenable to strategic minimization at the individual level (e.g., couples could anticipate future difficulties with antenuptial contracting) and law reform at the aggregate (we could rewrite Social Security rules, for instance). With marriage no longer fulsomely and tautologically praised as the source of everything good but rather treated as a mixed blessing, individuals would enter into this relation more soberly, and society would regain some of the losses now written off under tendentious bookkeeping. Kept alive and thus open to future gain, marriage could evolve into something better.

In 1997, when activists were beginning to achieve their first legislative successes in promoting marriage, one dissenting activist added a dash of rhetoric to the public mix:

> An enterprise has a fifty percent failure rate. The female participants are injured sixty-three percent of the time. Children in the system are physically and sexually abused from thirty to eighty percent of the time. If this were a business, its doors would soon be closed. If it were a workplace, OSHA would shut it down. If it were a school, the principal would be arrested. Instead politicians extol it, courts ruminate over its value to society, and business, religious, and cultural leaders pander to its mystique. (Post 1997, 283)

The passage is noteworthy not for its dubious statistics—the "failure rate" of marriage is hard to measure; the 30 to 80 percent range is so wide as to be meaningless; and the percentage of women "injured" by marriage is probably not precisely 63—but as a specimen of the fervent discourse that altered American law at a particular time, and has not yet finished its work.

With the exception of specialists in family law and policy, few commentators dwelled much on state-sponsored marriage until the late 1990s, when the discussion grew too noisy to ignore. Contributors to this volume (especially Fineman, McClain) have described these changes. Federal welfare reform enacted in 1996 attacked as pathological those families made up of low-income, unmarried mothers and their children. The federal Defense of Marriage Act and its isomorphs in the states ventured for the first time into legal definitions of marriage. These proclamations underscored marriage as Status, an institution that rests on fixed and immutable ascribed characteristics. "Covenant marriage" and related reforms began to make divorce harder to get. "Fatherhood initiatives" and other small-scale programs, first supported by federal grant money out of Temporary Assistance to Needy Families (the program that replaced Aid to Families with Dependent Children) and then by new appropriations, meddled overtly in private lives. Antidivorce state-government spending flourished in bastions of marital breakdown like Oklahoma and Arkansas. For their part, as most of the contributors to this volume have recalled here, gay activists took up same-sex marriage to the exclusion of older causes, such as funding for the AIDS crisis and the expression of radical social critique. A well-funded movement soldiered in behalf of marriage, using surveys and other quasi-scientific means; one book, *The Case for Marriage* (Waite and Gallagher, 2000), told readers that if they get with the program they will be healthy, wealthy, and wise.

In short, observers of contemporary American law and policy reform have now been provoked. The more activists "pander to its mystique," as Dianne Post wrote, the more state-sponsored marriage invites a citizen to consider a challenge: Why marriage? Who needs it? Not children and their parents, with whom the state can deal separately. Not believers in the sanctity of marital union: such persons remain free to perform rituals celebrating the pair bond. Why shouldn't American law abandon the status of marriage—just as it has abandoned other notorious comprehensive personal statuses related to race, gender, and mental condition—and allow the ordinary law of torts, property, crimes, and (especially) contracts to govern relations between adults?

As this volume has shown, the answer cannot be found in the familiar "case for marriage." The marriage movement has installed marriage promotion as state and federal policy and may have led some couples or individuals toward the license-and-ceremony route rather than a more casual affiliation like cohabitation. But it has failed to justify the existence of state-sponsored marriage. Taking as fixed and unquestioned the gross favoritism that the government lavishes on marriage (in its current opposite-sex, antipolygamous, officially sanctioned form), activists cite the prosperity of married persons to justify this law-based favoritism and argue for its extension. The project is propaganda, not reason or social science. It is specious to applaud marriage as better than its absence on the ground that married people are happier or healthier or richer or more fecund than unmarried people; these disparities in welfare may derive from arbitrary laws that could be rewritten or repealed. And even if marriage makes an individual better off, the societal stake in marriage requires a separate rationale, and on this point marriage-movement partisans have not gone beyond vague platitudes. To entrust the entire case for marriage to the marriage movement risks missing better points, a deeper case.

Accordingly, contributors to this volume have gone deeper, and in this afterword I have put state-sponsored marriage to a straightforward jurisprudential test. Recalling the writings of Jeremy Bentham and Oliver Wendell Holmes on government power, I would start with the premise that any artifact of the law deserves to be abolished if it does not promote human well-being. This starting point fits the case for marriage into a study resembling cost-benefit analysis. While the benefits and detriments of marriage cannot be measured precisely, some counting is possible.

Satisfactory arguments, it turns out, might support state-sponsored marriage as a comprehensive, capital-S personal Status, the legal artifice that Henry Maine pronounced dead or dying in 1861. At an individual level, marriage gives persons something valuable, enhancing the gains they achieve when they venture toward intimacy with another person. At a communal level, the space where law reform works, marriage is a valuable locus of political and social power, a counterweight: without marriage, the force that would expand to control citizens private lives is either the state or capital, an unrelenting press of the market. No blithe, freeing, choice-affirming alternative to this extraordinary institution is available.

Yet honest bookkeeping demands vigilance in aid of repair. The endeavor to mend marriage—that is, to fulfill its promises for the benefit of individuals and society, and to ameliorate its lingering ills and injustices—can begin only with recognition of the good that it achieves.[3]

NOTES

1. In a prescient 1986 opinion, however, which Justice Kennedy cited in his later opinion for the Court holding that states could not criminalize consensual same-sex sexual acts, Justice John Paul Stevens invoked the miscegenation analogy. *Bowers v. Hardwick,* 478 U.S. 176, 216 (1986) (Stevens, J., dissenting).

2. Marriage scholar Steven Nock elaborates on where this power can lie, finding five possible locations:

> As a sociologist, I see norms as the primary source of social order and conformity. Norms, that is, are the building blocks of social institutions. My perspective begins by viewing any society as a cluster of integrated social institutions. While there may be many such institutions in any one society, all societies have at least five. There is always an organized system of securing and distributing goods and services, or an economy. There is always some organized method for transmitting knowledge from one generation to the next, or an educational institution. There is always an organized pattern of protection and formal social control, or a state. There is always an organized system of dealing with the ultimately unknowable, or a religion. And there is always a patterned system to distribute the obligations for dependent individuals (children and the elderly), or a family. (Nock 2000, 1972)

Educational systems are not contenders for power over intimate lives, and the First Amendment disqualifies religion from overt governance within American law (although it would undoubtedly gain power if state-sponsored marriage were abolished). The three other institutions remain available to govern family life.

3. Thanks to Steven Tipton for his contributions to this afterword.

REFERENCES

Bentham, J. 1970. *An Introduction to the Principles of Morals and Legislation.* London: Athlone Press.

Bernstein, A. 2003. "For and Against Marriage: A Revision." *Michigan Law Review* 102:129.

Blustain, S. 2000. "Counterproposal." *Lilith,* Spring. Available at http://www.pop politics.com/articles/2000-06-19-counterproposal.shtml.

Bowers v. Hardwick. 478 U.S. 176 (1986).

Brown v. Board of Education. 347 U.S. 483 (1954).

Cohen, L. R. 1995. "Rhetoric, the Unnatural Family, and Women Work." *Virginia Law Review* 81:2275.

Gilder, G. F. 1986. *Men and Marriage.* Gretna, La.: Pelican.

Hafen, B. 1991. "Individualism and Autonomy in Family Law: The Waning of Belonging." *Brigham Young University Law Review* 1991:1.

Holmes, O. W. 1963. *The Common Law.* Ed. M. A. D. Howe. Cambridge, Mass.: Belknap Press of Harvard University Press.

Koppelman, A. 1994. "Why Discrimination against Lesbians and Gay Men Is Sex Discrimination." *New York University Law Review* 69:197.

Nisbet, R. A. 1980. *History of the Idea of Progress.* New York: Basic Books.

Nock, S. L. 2000. "Time and Gender in Marriage." *Virginia Law Review* 86:1972.

Pirie, M. 1978. "Trial and Error and the Idea of Progress." La Salle, Ill.: Open Court.

Popenoe, D. 1998. "Life without Father." In *Lost Fathers: The Politics of Fatherhood in America,* ed. C. Daniels. New York: St. Martin Press.

Post, D. 1997. "Why Marriage Should Be Abolished." *Women Rights Law Reporter* 18:283.

Rauch, J. 1996. "For Better or Worse?" *New Republic,* May 6, 8.

Rauch, J. 2004. *Gay Marriage: Why It Is Good for Gays, Good for Straights, and Good for America.* New York: Times Books/Henry Holt.

Regan, M. C. 1996. "Postmodern Family Law: Toward a New Model of Status." In *Promises to Keep: Decline and Renewal of Marriage in America,* ed. D. Popenoe, J. B. Elshtain, and D. Blankenhorn, 157. Lanham, Md.: Rowman and Littlefield.

Romer v. Evans. 517 U.S. 620 (1996).

Waite, L. J. 2002. "The Health Benefits of Marriage." In *Marriage, Health, and the Professions: If Marriage Is Good for You, What Does This Mean for Law, Medicine, Ministry, Therapy, and Business?* ed. J. Wall, 17. Grand Rapids, Mich.: Eerdmans.

Waite, L. J., and M. Gallagher. 2000. *The Case for Marriage: Why Married People Are Happier, Healthier, and Better Off Financially.* New York: Doubleday.

About the Contributors

Anita Bernstein is the Sam Nunn Professor of Law at Emory University and the Wallace Stevens Professor of Law at New York Law School. At both schools she has taught a course of her own creation called "Marriage," a survey of how the law regulates engagements, intact marriages, broken and terminated marriages, and unmarried couples. She writes also on the relation between society and law, with particular attention to civil liability, and has published two books on accident law, *A Products Liability Anthology* (ed. 1995) and *Torts: Questions and Answers* (2004, with David P. Leonard). She received a B.A. from Queens College and a J.D. from Yale Law School.

Peggy Cooper Davis is the John S. R. Shad Professor of Lawyering and Ethics at New York University and director of the university's Lawyering Program, a curricular innovation designed to promote responsibility and intellectual versatility in professional practice. Much of her scholarly work draws on her experiences as a family court judge and as a civil rights litigator. Her published work includes an influential body of writing on the legal and social position of the family, and also on legal process and pedagogy. Her book *Neglected Stories: The Constitution and Family Values* (1997) revives the ideologies of antislavery as guides to interpretation of the Reconstruction amendments' guarantees of liberty and democratic citizenship. She received a B.A. from Western College for Women and a J.D. from Harvard Law School.

Martha Albertson Fineman received a B.A. from Temple University and a J.D. from the University of Chicago. She is Robert W. Woodruff Professor of Law at Emory University. Fineman is the founder and director of the Feminism and Legal Theory Project, which holds workshops and "uncomfortable conversations" on issues of law and policy of particular interest to women. As a corollary to her work in the Feminism and Legal Theory Project, she has edited and contributed to several books on feminist legal theory. *At the Boundaries of Law: Feminism and Legal Theory* (1991) was the first anthology on the topic of legal feminism. Her latest collection is entitled *Feminism Confronts Homo Economicus (Economic Man)* (2005). She is sole author of *The Illusion of Equality: The Rhetoric and Reality of Divorce Reform* (1991); *The Neutered Mother, the Sexual Family and Other Twentieth Century Tragedies* (1995); and *The Autonomy Myth: A Theory of Dependency* (2004).

Linda C. McClain is Rivkin Radler Distinguished Professor of Law at Hofstra University School of Law, where she teaches in the areas of family law, feminist legal theory, jurisprudence, and welfare law. She is the author of *The Place of Families: Fostering Capacity, Equality, and Responsibility* (forthcoming 2005), which offers a liberal feminist approach to the link between families and the political order and to a number of contested issues of family law and policy. She is a former Faculty Fellow in Ethics at the Harvard University Center for Ethics and the Professions. She holds an A.B. from Oberlin College, a J.D. from Georgetown University Law Center, and an LL.M. from New York University.

Lawrence Rosen received a Ph.D. in anthropology and J.D. at the University of Chicago. He is the Cromwell Professor of Anthropology at Princeton University and adjunct professor of law at Columbia Law School. He has taught family law at Duke and Northwestern law schools and has been a member of the Institute for Advanced Studies at Princeton and a fellow at Corpus Christi College, Cambridge, and Wolfson College, Oxford. He was among the first group of recipients of a John D. and Catherine T. MacArthur award. His most recent books are *The Justice of Islam* (1999) and *The Culture of Islam* (2002).

Mary Lyndon (Molly) Shanley is a professor of political science at Vassar College, where she holds the Margaret Stiles Halleck Chair. She is the author of *Feminism, Marriage and the Law in Victorian England* (1989); *Making Babies, Making Families: What Matters Most in an Age of Reproductive Technologies, Surrogacy, Adoption, and Same-Sex and Unwed Parents* (2001); and *Just Marriage,* ed. Deborah Chasman and Joshua Cohen (2004). She is editor, with Carole Pateman, of *Feminist Interpretations and Political Theory* (1990), and, with Uma Narayan, of *Reconstructing Political Theory: Feminist Essays* (1997). Her articles and reviews have appeared in a wide range of scholarly journals. Her current work is on feminist perspectives on ethical issues in family law and

on bioethics and human reproduction. She received a B.A. from Welles-
ley College and a Ph.D. from Harvard University.

Dorian Solot and *Marshall Miller* founded the national Alternatives to
Marriage Project (www.unmarried.org), a nonprofit organization for
people who choose not to marry, cannot marry, or live together before
marriage. They are the authors of *Unmarried to Each Other: The Essential Guide to Living Together as an Unmarried Couple* (2002) and *Let
Them Eat Wedding Rings: The Role of Marriage Promotion in Welfare
Reform* (2002). In their work advocating for fairness on the basis of
marital status, they have made hundreds of media appearances, including NPR's *Morning Edition,* CNN, the *Wall Street Journal, Time* magazine, the *O'Reilly Factor,* and the *New Yorker.* They are graduates of
Brown University.

Index